PRESIDENTIAL
COURAGE

PRESIDENTIAL COURAGE

JOHN B. MOSES, M.D.

and

WILBUR CROSS

W · W · Norton & Company

New York · London

Library of Congress Cataloging in Publication Data

Moses, John B.
Presidential courage.

Bibliography: p.
Includes index.
1. Presidents—United States—Health.
I. Cross, Wilbur, joint author. II. Title.
E176.1.M924 1980   973   79–28737
ISBN 0–393–01314–6

1 2 3 4 5 6 7 8 9 0

Ulsm 11.95/8.01 - 3/81

973
Moses

Contents

Introduction

When I was a young student in medical school, an eminent physician lectured one day on the trend toward specialization, urging all of us to look at medicine and health in very broad terms before we committed ourselves to the confines of a particular field. To make this point, he emphasized that the state of the body, whether healthy or disordered, inevitably affects the functions of the mind, if not the spirit. As a consequence, many of the most far-reaching decisions and events in history have been influenced by famous persons suffering from intense pain or distress that might have been prevented by relatively modest medical advice or common prescriptions.

"The accidents of health," he said, "have more to do with the march of history than even the historians themselves may realize."

It occurred to me at the time, and again as I began to practice my profession, that there must be some provocative and meaningful object lessons for all of us in the lives of one specific group of leaders: American presidents. The more I thought about the ways in which illness and pain must have shaped their administrations and revealed truths about their characters and capabilities, the more attention I paid to the medical/historical research that has long since become my consuming hobby.

My interest was heightened and my curiosity piqued when I discovered a curious fact: there seemed to be a conspiracy among historians to suppress all but the vaguest information about the health and disabilities of the men in the nation's highest office. To read the history books and biographies, one would have thought that the office of president was open only to a superrace of humans to whom even the common head cold or stomach ache were unknown. If a president was out of action for a few days, a week, several months, it was simply because he was—in the language of the historian—"indisposed." If he died in office it was usually because he was assassinated or done in by exposure to extremes of weather during the course of carrying out his duties. Only on rare occasions—such as the case of Woodrow Wilson or during the heart attacks of Dwight D. Eisenhower, when there was no way of diverting public attention from medical crises in the White House—have biographies recounted the details of presidential disorders.

After I had been in the practice of medicine for some 15 years and had seen at close quarters many of the diseases that victimize mankind, I started on a systematic search of medical journals from the year 1800 to the present. These publications were far more enlightening than the history books, not only focusing on the physical ills, but in many cases revealing astonishing facts about the mental and emotional upsets that most certainly influenced the course of American history. Unique as a class, presidents often have been afflicted with unique diseases, some brought about directly by the stresses and demands of office. James K. Polk entered the White House in the best of health. He left four years later an old man, and died within a month. His term of office aged him, then killed him. The lavish entertainment of visiting dignitaries was almost too much for Chester A. Arthur's delicate stomach. Symptoms of a peptic ulcer called a halt to his twelve-course banquets. The presidents were also prey to the same illnesses that bring patients to doctors' offices in villages and towns and cities across America. It has been fascinating to note that the sore throat or gastrointestinal upset that put most of us off our feet for a few days might have gone totally ignored in the White House—or on the other hand, might have had a major impact on war or peace.

What struck me as most peculiar as I poked and probed was the fact that American presidents and their families rarely turned to the outstanding medical men of their day for treatment and counsel. Perhaps because so many of our chief executives, especially during the nineteenth century, had been generals before entering politics, they frequently appointed army and navy surgeons as their personal medical advisors. Before World War II, the armed forces attracted only mediocre medical talent, doctors who were little experienced in general health care and quite out of place in civilian hospitals.

Even in those few instances when presidents were fortunate enough to have selected top practitioners, the unusual pressures of the White House and the very special nature of the patients seemed often to rob these physicians of their objectivity and throw their professional judgements badly off balance. During major political crises, when presidents were in serious or critical condition, the situation was further complicated and disturbed by the fact that whole teams of medical specialists made their way to the presidential sickbeds—teams composed of individuals who often held conflicting opinions about treatment and medication. The physician who scrambled above the others to take charge was often the one with the greatest ego rather than the finest talent.

In the course of my investigations, I have met some unusual people and enjoyed some bizarre experiences. I have examined some unusual artifacts, including seventeen glass slides, specimens of the malignant tumor on the tongue of Ulysses S. Grant; dried chips from Lincoln's shattered skull, along with the metal probe used to remove them; five vertebrae, wired together and carefully shellacked, from the spine of Garfield; and slices of tissue, preserved in alcohol, from the cancerous jaw of Grover Cleveland. My intention is not to dwell on these grim reminders that American presidents have indeed had some pressing medical problems, but simply to point out that this is one phase of history long overlooked by both professional archivists and amateur collectors.

I lay no claim to being an historian. I am a physician fascinated by the practice of medicine, past and present. My explorations and observations have only served to strengthen what that medical professor hoped to get across to our class so many years ago: that the accidents of health and the accidents of history have a great deal in common.

John Bromley Moses, M.D.
Scarsdale, New York
March 1980

Acknowledgments

The authors have been assisted in their research by institutions, individuals, and sources almost too numerous to mention. They are particularly indebted to the following:

Medical librarians at the White Plains, New York, Hospital Medical Center; Lawrence Hospital, Bronxville, New York; and the Yale University School of Medicine.

Research librarians at the Library of Congress in Washington; the Scarsdale, New York, Library; the National Medical Library, Bethesda, Maryland; the Armed Forces Institute of Pathology, Bethesda, Maryland; Colby-Sawyer College Library, New London, New Hampshire; the Mutter Museum, Philadelphia, Pennsylvania; Dartmouth College Library, Hanover, New Hampshire; the New York City Public Library; the Stamford, Connecticut, Public Library; and Sterling Memorial Library at Yale University.

Librarians and staff members at the Rutherford B. Hayes Memorial Library, Fremont, Ohio; The Hermitage and Jackson Museum, Nashville, Tennessee; Lincoln Home National Historic Site, Springfield, Illinois; Lawnfield, home of James A. Garfield, Mentor, Ohio; Woodrow Wilson House, Washington, D.C.; home of Franklin D. Roosevelt, Hyde Park, New York; and Mount Vernon, Mount Vernon, Virginia.

Special appreciation goes to Mrs. Eliot B. Weathers of Scarsdale, New York, and Mr. and Mrs. Roswell Farnham of Lexington, Massachusetts, who were instrumental in bringing the authors together and without whom there would be no book; and to the following individuals who arranged for some of the lectures given by Dr. Moses on the subject over many years and who often invited guests who provided new information on American presidents and their illnesses: Mr. and Mrs. David I. Mead, Waccabuc, New York; Mr. and Mrs. Norman W. Cook, Old Greenwich, Connecticut; Dr. and Mrs. Robert E. Johnson, Framingham, Massachusetts; Dr. W. P. Laird Myers, New York City; Mrs. Frank Gordon, New London, New Hamsphire, and Scarsdale, New York; Mr. and Mrs. Alan Ferrin, Pawling, New York, and Scarsdale, New York; Mrs. David Hitchcock, New London, New Hamsphire, and Hamden, Connecticut; Dr. Raymond E. Phillips, Tarrytown, New York; Dr. Joseph M. Ford, New York City; Dr. Herman Tarnower, Scarsdale, New York; Mr. and Mrs. Philip C. Reville and Ms. Cynthia Reville, Scarsdale, New York; Mrs. Kenneth R. Berol, Greenwich, Connecticut; Mrs. Charle N. Peabody and Mr. Charles N. Peabody, Jr., Framingham, Massachusetts; and Mr. Leon Weisel, Lakehurst, New Jersey.

Friends and relatives who studied some of the preliminary manuscripts and made constructive suggestions were many, but in particular: Mrs. G. Estabrook Kindred, Mrs. James M. Naughton, Mr. John Neill, Dr. John D. Fernald, Dr. R. W. Buddington, Mr. and Mrs. Clement Sawtell, Mr. Henry C. Moses, Mr. Henry C. Moses III, Mr. Edmund R. Beckwith, Jr., and his late wife Jean Orr Beckwith, Mr. and Mrs. John B. Moses, Jr., and Mr. William A. Moses.

Over the years, a number of fellow internists have provided information for co-author John Moses as well as covering his practice while he was engaged in editorial research or lecturing on the subject of presidents and their disabilities. Of special help were Drs. Robert B. Fath, Robert E. Lee, Charles J. Morosini, and Roy C. Swingle. He also received continuing support and encouragement from his office staff: Mrs. Warner W. Kent, Jr., Mrs. Robert S. Herbert, Mrs. Bette Jean Lothrop Merwin, Mrs. Rodman J. Zilenziger, and Mrs. Daniel Rogers.

Although she shares no byline, Elisabeth (Mrs. John B.) Moses deserves a major share of credit for the concept and development of the book, particularly during its formative stages. A graduate of Smith College with a major in American studies, she has made an avocation of collecting presidential memorabilia for many years and is an outstanding authority on presidential campaigns and related events. She collaborated in much of the research for the book, as well as providing invaluable assistance in the writing and editing of numerous chapters.

PRESIDENTIAL
COURAGE

1

When the President Vanished

A little before seven on the hot, humid morning of Saturday, May 27, 1893, President Grover Cleveland shuffled drowsily into his White House bathroom and began brushing his teeth. That commonplace act touched off a series of events that are recounted in very few history books or biographies—events that were ingeniously camouflaged to prevent a public panic that would have jolted the entire American economy.

Running his tongue across the roof of his mouth, the fifty-six-year-old President felt a rough spot that disturbed him. Later in the morning, after dressing and eating breakfast, he asked one of his aides to summon Dr. Robert M. O'Reilly, a physician assigned to the care of government officials. There was no White House doctor during that era. Nor was there any practitioner in the Washington region who was familiar with Mr. Cleveland and his medical history, which included, among other infirmities, hypertension, obesity, and susceptibility to frequent biliousness.

Not liking what he saw when he examined his heavy-jowled, bull-necked patient, Dr. O'Reilly, a major in the Army Medical Corps, asked the White House dentist to look at the President's gums and teeth. When O'Reilly was solemnly informed that this was no mere dental problem, he immediately contacted Dr. Joseph D. Bryant, a friend of the President and a prominent New York City surgeon whose specialty was the head and neck. Dr. Bryant lost no time in visiting the White House and within the next ten days he had examined the lesion several times, had taken small samples of tissue for biopsy review, and had proposed his plans for an operation.

The fears of the President's medical attendants were confirmed by Dr. William H. Welch, a noted pathologist at Johns Hopkins Medical School. After examining the tissues under the most powerful microscope available, he declared positively that the President had a cancer of the mouth and that it appeared to have spread to at least one side of his jaw. To be certain of this diagnosis, O'Reilly and Bryant sent the slides containing the specimens to the Army Medical Museum for examination by its staff of pathologists. The patient was not identified, but O'Reilly made it clear to his military colleagues that the matter was urgent, as well as confidential. The army specialists confirmed the findings of Dr. Welch.

From the start, all outsiders who examined slides or otherwise worked on the case were told to use the utmost diligence and skill, that the specimens were "the most important ever submitted for examination," and that the name of the patient could not be divulged for reasons of national security. All efforts—sometimes devious or misleading—were made to keep the secret not only from the press but from White House staff members, friends, and even relatives.

When Grover Cleveland was finally informed that he had cancer, he showed less personal concern about the outcome than did the doctors who had to report the grim news. The President's greatest and most immediate fear was that the public might find out. "We cannot risk any leak that would touch off a panic," he confided to Bryant, "If a rumor gets around that I'm 'dying,' then the country is dead, too."

Cleveland had good reason to be apprehensive during the spring and early summer of 1893. Although he had displayed great optimism and confidence when he pressed a button opening the World Columbian Exposition in Chicago on May 1, he knew that the country was already in the grip of a spreading depression. The Philadelphia and Reading Railroad had recently gone bankrupt. The Atcheson, Topeka, and Santa Fe was shaky, following the revelation that its officers had defrauded the public of $7 million. And Wall Street was increasingly unstable, as experts tried to evaluate the impact of escalating unemployment and the failure of some 500 banks and 15,000 businesses. The country's financial footings had been left in a rickety state when Benjamin Harrison turned his office over to the new President, with the Treasury depleted by more than $100 million.

Faced with such adversities (later to be described by historian Charles Francis Adams as "the most deep-seated financial storm in the history of the country"), Cleveland was actually at his best —a positive-thinking, active leader. He had already taken a firm stand in his adherence to the gold standard, despite continuing pressures from western legislators who insisted on the free coinage of silver and the circulation of more money. Though winning that battle, he was fully aware that his control would be severed if his opponents sensed that he had a serious physical disability. He was concerned about his Vice-President, Adlai E. Stevenson of Illinois, assuming power. Stevenson was a free-silver man. To put it in the blunt phrases of the influential *Commercial and Financial Chronicle*, whose editors did not realize the import of their words, "Mr. Cleveland is about all that stands between this country and absolute disaster, and his death would be a great calamity."

Thus it was that Cleveland, rather than being unnerved by the diagnosis, looked upon the situation as a fateful challenge. After asking questions about the nature and extent of the facilities that would be needed to perform the operation, he appointed Dr. Bryant to take charge. At the outset, he made two points clear: first, he said, "I cannot leave here before the end of June under any circumstances. So I will say to you that I will be ready on the first day of July." Second, he ruled out hospitals as too risky from the standpoint of secrecy, even if he could be disguised and smuggled in after dark. The press would become suspicious about any unexplained absence from the White House, and there was always the chance that a nurse or orderly would leak the news, whether unintentionally or for personal gain.

They would all have to give the problem enough thought to come up with a foolproof alternative.

From that day on, all letters, memos, telegrams, and other communications referred to the President as "your friend" or "my patient" or "our guest." So jittery were the doctors that they might make a fatal slip that they took some measures which, in retrospect, seem too melodramatic to have taken place. Bryant, for example, decided that he would need the assistance of Dr. William Williams Keen, professor of surgery at Jefferson Medical College in Philadelphia, an outstanding surgeon and pioneer in neurosurgery. He wrote Keen a letter, requesting consultation "in a very important matter," and insisted on meeting one afternoon at 3:15 on the deserted deck of the Fall River Line boat on which Keen was to leave for Boston three hours later. Here, surrounded by empty deck chairs, gently slapping ropes, and clanking rail chains, they plotted a course of action.

O'Reilly, who had not intended to be present at the operation, became so involved in the conspiracy of silence that he feared his very nervousness and preoccupation would be a giveaway if he were to remain apart from the scene. So he elected to be present, but only after instructing his colleagues that henceforth he was to be referred to as "Major Mills," and in no way associated with his office of attending surgeon.

Now the big question was, *where?*

Gray Gables, Cleveland's summer home on Buzzard's Bay in Marion, Massachusetts, was considered—and quickly rejected. Although the excuse of a "brief vacation" sounded credible, there were too many reporters prowling about, certain to be curious about the arrival of unusual visitors or equipment, no matter how well disguised. The house would be a natural for the later period of recuperation. But the operation and the immediate postoperative care required a location that was beyond suspicion or access by outsiders.

Ultimately, Cleveland himself came up with a solution. He would make arrangements with his good friend, the noted Commodore Elias C. Benedict, to spend a few days aboard the latter's seventy-five-ton yacht, *Oneida*, on which he had already cruised upward of 40,000 miles enjoying respites from the demands of office during his first term, from 1885 to 1889. With the yacht floating at anchor in New York City's East River, members of the medical team could arrive by small boats, leaving inconspicuously from any number of piers that lined the east side of Manhattan. Or the yacht could anchor in the Hudson River, with easy access from the New Jersey shore as well as from New York.

Each could bring a share of the instruments and supplies in suitcases and handbags. Once under way, this floating operating room would be unassailable by either the press or the curious public.

Bryant was in full accord. A vessel of this size, cruising in protected waters, would pose no problems for experienced surgeons, providing they had adequate lighting and suitable support for the overweight patient. The doctor's greatest concern was that the President, under even the best of conditions, might not be able to withstand the radical surgery proposed without serious complications. Although generally in good health, the man suffered from the side effects of his obesity, was afflicted with gout, and had punished himself physically in earlier years with excessive eating, drinking, and partying. Moreover, no one knew how fatigued Cleveland really was after four arduous months in office wrestling with the growing financial crisis.

To cap it all off, no matter how successful the operation turned out to be, would the patient's condition be such that he could be seen by the public within a week or ten days without causing instant alarm? It is no wonder that Dr. Bryant later commented to Commodore Benedict, "If anything happens to the President, get your navigator to run us on the rocks and sink us all!"

There seemed to be no other alternative. As a final safeguard, Bryant called in yet another noted specialist, Dr. Edward Gamaliel Janeway, professor of medicine at Bellevue Hospital in New York City and a member of an esteemed medical family associated with the profession for many generations. Janeway knew as much about anaesthesia as any doctor then in practice. He also knew that he could make no mistakes, for the mortality rate from anaesthesia alone was 14 percent during simple operations and a great deal higher for more radical surgery, especially if complications set in or if the patient had to be anaesthetized for longer than anticipated.

Now Janeway's ingenuity was put to the test. He would have to arrange for the secret transfer of tanks of compressed gas and other seldom-moved equipment from hospital to ship without arousing suspicion or curiosity. He laid his plans with the adroit-ness of an undercover agent. At the same time, he also took one step that widened the circle of those who were in on the secret and thus increased the chances of exposure. To lessen the risk of an accident with anaesthetics, which were in those days somewhat unstable and unpredictable, as well as inadequately researched, he enlisted the aid of Ferdinand Hasbrouck, a young dentist with experience in the use of the recently discovered nitrous oxide. Janeway felt that nitrous oxide (later to be popularly known as "laughing gas") would hold the President for the duration of the operation.

Hasbrouck, who would also start the operation by removing several teeth before the surgeon took over, did not share Janeway's optimism. In his opinion, laughing gas could only hold the patient for the first part of the ordeal—the removal of the teeth and possibly the cutting away of soft tissue in the gums. But ether would then be required to knock out the corpulent Cleveland for the removal of those parts of the jaw bone and hard palate tissues that were thought to be cancerous. Ether was tricky, difficult to administer under the most well-controlled conditions, and sometimes ineffective when metered out in doses that were considered safe. Ether frequently brought on pneumonia and almost always triggered side effects. A further risk, as yet unknown to Janeway, was that a urinary exam would indicate the beginnings of chronic nephritis, a condition that Dr. Keen recognized as being dangerously aggravated by the administration of ether.

The President, informed of the risks and the lack of emergency equipment and facilities on shipboard, was unwavering in his decision to use the *Oneida*. Thus it was that at 4:20 on the afternoon of June 30, he left Washington on a private Pennsylvania Railroad car (belonging to Frank Thompson, one of the company's vice-presidents), attached to the New York Express. Few people knew of his departure and even fewer of his arrival in Newark, where he was hustled into a waiting carriage and hidden from public sight. The carriage then crossed by ferry to the lower tip of Manhattan, where it proceeded almost unobserved along Cortland Street and part of Broadway to Pier A. There a launch transported Cleveland to the *Oneida*, lying at anchor some distance from shore. The President was accom-

panied by only a handful of people, including Secretary of War
Daniel S. Lamont, who functioned as a personal aide and press
secretary. The *Oneida* then proceeded slowly down the bay and
anchored in the Narrows off Bay Ridge for the night.

June 30 was a Friday, a perfectly logical time for a brief
sojourn away from the heat and pressures of Washington. That
morning, in a bright show of confidence, Cleveland had issued a
call for a special session of Congress to meet on August 7 for the
purpose of repealing the Sherman Silver Purchase Act. To all
outward appearances, he was in robust health and so soundly in
control of executive affairs that he could absent himself from the
White House long enough to relax and enjoy life, and such a
statement was released to the press.

Why was he not accompanied by Mrs. Cleveland, the pretty
young Frances Folsom who was just half his age and the most
attractive First Lady yet to grace the White House? To any who
might inquire, there was good reason: she was in her seventh
month of pregnancy and naturally had to avoid the risks of travel.
There was little likelihood that Frances would slip up and reveal
her husband's dark secret—she did not even know that he was
sick.

That night, the President was in excellent spirits and able to
sleep without sedatives. A medical examination the following
morning found him fit enough to proceed with the plans. At 8:30
he drank a single cup of coffee, ate a slice of toast, and was
reported to have "moved his bladder and bowels in a natural
manner." In the meantime, the *Oneida* was proceeding slowly up
the East River, headed for Long Island Sound. A major crisis
seemed imminent when Dr. Bryant noted that the vessel was
almost as far upriver as 26th Street, the location of Bellevue
Hospital. Hastily, he ordered all doctors and members of the
President's party to leave the deck and go into a cabin where they
could not be seen and inadvertently recognized. (It was later
reported that some interns had set up a telescope on the roof and
were observing the yacht. Whether true or not, nothing ever
came of the incident.)

Besides the captain of the yacht and Commodore Benedict,
the only member of the ship's crew who was aware of the pro-

ceedings was a steward (described as "extremely loyal and faithful") who had been assigned the arduous task of fetching hot water, towels, and other supplies on demand. The steward, together with members of the crew, had been informed that the President was to have two badly ulcerated teeth extracted and that extra precautions were being taken to prevent any blood poisoning, which naturally would be disastrous because of his high position. The explanation sounded logical enough to stir up little or no curiosity.

At noon on Saturday, July 1, the President steeled himself for the ordeal. At 12:25, he undressed in his cabin and by 12:31 was seating himself in a large chair that had been lashed to the interior footing of the ship's mast so that it would not slide in case the vessel rolled or pitched unexpectedly. He was wedged in a sitting position for the expected two-hour ordeal, head slightly tilted back and held securely in position by pillows that had been tied in place. In attendance were Doctors Bryant, O'Reilly, Keen, and Janeway; Hasbrouck, the dentist; Bryant's young assistant, Dr. John F. Erdmann; and Secretary of War Daniel S. Lamont.

At 12:32, Hasbrouck began administering the nitrous oxide gas, which took effect so quickly that he was able to swab the President's mouth thoroughly with Thiersch's solution, a disenfectant, and begin the removal of teeth by 12:40. A few minutes later, with the bleeding under control, Dr. Bryant stepped in to perform the critical part of the operation. He carefully injected cocaine along the lines of his intended incisions, then called upon Hasbrouck to administer the ether under the direction of Janeway, who was keeping a close watch on the patient's breathing, pulse, and general condition.

Together, Bryant, Keen, and Erdmann dissected part of the inner cheek, arresting the bleeding by applications of hot water and pressure. Among the unusual instruments of the day that were called into play were a "cheek retractor," an ingenious instrument Keen had brought back from Paris, and a "white-hot electric knife." The former made it possible for the doctors to hold back the heavy jowls so often caricatured in cartoons of Cleveland, without having to leave any external scars. The latter device, deriving energy from two large storage batteries, instantly cauterized tissues that were beginning to bleed. The front of the jaw was then chiselled loose and part of the palate removed. Examination revealed that the disease had begun at the roots of the left molars and spread into the antrum, the hollow cavity of the upper jaw, in the form of a gelatinous mass which Keen described as a sarcoma, or malignant tumor.

Faced with this evidence, there was nothing the surgeons could do but remove all but a small portion of the President's left upper jaw. Bryant, as surgeon in charge, made the critical decision to cut back as far as the orbital cavity (which contains the eye socket), beyond which he could not go without endangering the President's sight. Fortunately, there was no evidence that the lower jaw had been affected yet, or that the malignancy had spread to other areas.

By 1:55 that afternoon, the operation was finished. Erdmann disinfected the cavity with further applications of Thiersch's solution and packed it firmly with gauze. Janeway observed that the patient's pulse was 80, that the President was perspiring moderately, and that his color was good. He estimated that, despite their preoperative fears of hemorrhaging, they had been able to limit the loss of blood to well under a pint. Within two hours from the time the President was brought into the makeshift operating room, he was back in his own stateroom in bed, further drugged by an injection of morphine to kill the pain. At that time, no ill effects from the ether were noted.

A key decision on the part of the doctors, one largely motivated by Cleveland's insistence on secrecy, had been the agreement to perform the operation entirely through the mouth so there would be no external evidence that the Chief Executive had undergone anything but substantial dental work. It is doubtful that this could have been accomplished without Dr. Keen's "retractor," the newly invented cauterizing device, or the skill of the surgeons.

The President was described as "up and about" on July 3, following the removal of abscessed teeth. But the crisis was by no means over. As the doctors were well aware beforehand, the removal of such a large section of the jaw and palate would have a severe effect on the speech. However, when Bryant visited his patient, heard his pitiful attempts to communicate, and saw the anguish on his face, he was struck by a feeling of helplessness and dread. Had he cut away too much tissue? Would the President *ever* be able to talk again coherently? Everything would now depend upon the experience and skill of a New York dental surgeon, Dr. Kasson C. Gibson, who was at that very moment on his way to Cleveland's summer home, "Gray Gables," on the Massachusetts shore. Gibson had been selected as the expert best suited to molding and fitting an artificial jaw.

By this time, the *Oneida* had cruised leisurely through Long Island Sound, eastward toward its destination, Buzzard's Bay. As it approached Plum Island, off the inner tip of Long Island, it veered suddenly northward toward New London, Connecticut. When Bryant inquired of the captain if anything were wrong, he was informed that Ferdinand Hasbrouck was being landed. Bryant knew that the President would be alarmed because of possible exposure to the prying eyes of the press. But Hasbrouck insisted so strongly that there seemed to be no alternative. He had already promised to be at New London a day earlier to administer nitrous oxide for a surgical operation at the hospital there. His unexplained delay and continued absence would arouse far more suspicion than any change in the vessel's course.

On the evening of Wednesday, July 5, the *Oneida* docked in Marion, Massachusetts, and the President walked briskly from the shore to Gray Gables, unassisted and virtually unobserved. Thus far he had avoided public notice.

Colonel Lamont was experienced enough in communications to know that he could not press his luck too far. Therefore, he scheduled a "routine" press conference in a barn, some distance from Gray Gables on Friday of that week. How was the President? Well, he was feeling slightly better, following the extraction of a couple of teeth, but he was not going to try to get around for awhile because he had a lame knee and slight swelling of the foot. Nothing serious, but certainly more difficult for a man of Mr. Cleveland's size and weight than for the average citizen. In any case, he had spent the greater part of the previous day playing checkers with Mrs. Cleveland, who had arrived from Washington at the beginning of the week.

What about the rumor that the President had a malignant growth? A distorted account, engineered by his opponents who were trying to weaken his position on gold. One of the President's medical advisors was there and could confirm his health and general well-being. As a result of the press conference, the *New York Times* reassured the nation. "Dr. Bryant said the President is absolutely free from cancer or malignant growth of any description," reported the *Times* on July 8. "No operation has been performed except that a bad tooth was extracted."

Lamont, Bryant, and the others were able to put up a good front only because of the skill of Dr. Gibson, who had established a small dental laboratory in a back room at the cottage. He had fashioned an artificial jaw from vulcanized rubber and had already positioned it temporarily in place in the President's mouth. The effect was astonishing. Without this device, Cleveland's speech was described by Dr. Keen as being "wholly unintelligible, resembling the worst imaginable case of cleft palate." With it, however, Cleveland could speak in a manner that was easily understood, though his words sounded heavy and slow. Gibson confidently explained that it was now simply a matter of refining and refitting the prothesis and training his patient in its most effective use.

In mid-July, as Lamont was beginning to breathe more easily about the President's recuperation, he received a shock. Bryant had detected a suspicious-looking growth along the inner margin of the surgical wound. It would have to be removed immediately. Plans were quickly laid and announced for a short pleasure cruise around Martha's Vineyard and into Nantucket Sound. The President was gone for only two days, during which time the growth was surgically removed with no complications.

By August 7, the scars of both operations had healed successfully enough, and the artificial jaw fitted snugly enough, so that the President was able to entrain for Washington and address the special session of Congress which he had called for on June 30. His speech, though brief, was forceful enough to motivate the House to repeal the Sherman Act by a vote of more than two to one. Tired by the stress and tension of playing his role in public for the first time after his ordeal, Cleveland returned once more to his summer home.

The battle for secrecy was over. Or was it?

On August 29, suddenly and unexpectedly, the *Philadelphia Press* published a disturbing letter from its investigative reporter in New York City, E. J. Edwards, who used the byline "Holland." The implications were sensational and alarming. Did Congress and the public know that the head of the nation was critically ill with a malignancy that was possibly terminal? The death of the President would split the country in two and make it vulnerable to the "absolute disaster" that had been prophecied by the *Commercial and Financial Chronicle* should such a misfortune occur. According to Edwards, an operation of the most critical kind had been performed on the President, raising the question of whether he was fit for office and capable of leading the country. Edwards named the doctors in attendance and supplied details that seemed too factual to be discounted.

The press was divided. Some newspapers termed the story an irresponsible hoax. The editor of a rival paper, the *Philadelphia Public Ledger,* denied that it had been scooped, since the story was obviously just another "cancer fake." Cabinet members—notably Daniel S. Lamont, who was the foremost spokesman for the White House—indignantly denied everything. They conceded only that Mr. Cleveland had been subjected to painful tooth extractions that were slow in healing. As for the doctors, they avoided the press for the most part, or when cornered asserted that it was unethical for any practitioner to break the confidentiality of the doctor/patient relationship. As Dr. Erdmann later confessed, "I did more lying during this period than in all the rest of my life put together."

One fact is certain: every other member of the medical team who had been present on the *Oneida* was disgusted with Ferdinand Hasbrouck. The finger was clearly pointed at the young dentist as the source of the leak. It was said that he had blabbed the full story to a Dr. Leander Jones of Greenwich, Connecticut, after being chided for arriving late for his anaesthesia appointment in New London. Jones later told the story to reporter Edwards, who then confronted Hasbrouck and somehow pressured him into talking. Dr. Bryant was so upset by the dentist's breach of his confidence that he never again spoke or wrote to him. In fact, when he finally paid Hasbrouck the sum of $250 for his services, he sent the check by messenger, with no note or other comment.

President Cleveland faced the challenge head on and with remarkable fortitude. He was his own best press agent, simply by undertaking his normal duties at the end of the summer as though nothing unusual had taken place. He neither shied away from public appearances nor sought refuge in seclusion. Those who heard him speak publicly could not help being convinced that the story in the *Philadelphia Press* was fictitious, for the President's voice was stronger and clearer than ever, providing little comfort to his enemies that he might be in weakening health.

On September 5, he welcomed Congress with a voice that was described as "even clearer and more resonant" than when he had given his inaugural address six months earlier. According to the *Times*, his speech "removed every lingering doubt of his entire soundness of body." Cleveland's position was further enhanced when, on September 9, his pretty young wife, Frances, gave birth to a second daughter—the first child of a president to be born in the White House.

The strange secret of Grover Cleveland was kept for more than two decades. Finally, in 1917, long after Cleveland's death, the full story was told in *The Saturday Evening Post*. The author was William Williams Keen, M.D., who, in addition to having participated in that historic operation, was a prolific writer during his later years. Keen was able to state, with justifiable pride, that the cancer operation had been a complete success for the patient and doctors alike. Cleveland not only survived his second term of office but continued a fairly active life, living with his family in Princeton, New Jersey. In his last years, he continued to be plagued by gout and suffered a number of heart and kidney diseases. On June 24, 1908, at the age of seventy-one, he died of a heart condition, undoubtedly complicated by his obesity but in no way related to his historic cancer operation.

For many years, the case of President Cleveland was shrouded in mystery, a controversial issue that provoked some doctors to assert that he had never had a cancer after all and that the whole story had been embellished. The tumor that was removed was described variously as an epithelioma, a sarcoma, and a malignant growth by the doctors present. Although the remains of the tumor were sealed in a bottle of alcohol in the possession of the Mutter Museum of the College of Physicians in Philadelphia, which also has John Marshall's kidney stones and Florence Nightingale's sewing kit, the curator steadfastly refused to permit any analysis of the sample. Only recently was the question resolved when pathologists were finally given the sample for examination. They pronounced it to be a "verrucoid carcinoma," common in smokers and *very malignant.*

The medical dilemma of President Cleveland, while perhaps more dramatic than some presidential illnesses, was by no means unique. The public—and even people close to the White House —would be astonished, if not horrified, to learn about the infirmities, accidents, and mental disorders that have been hushed up from the time of George Washington down to the present. It is ironic to think that Cleveland, despite his medical history of obesity, hypertension, stomach trouble, and cancer, can be numbered among our *healthier* chief executives. It is doubtful that many of our leaders would have survived the ordeal that Cleveland experienced, under the circumstances that prevailed in 1893. It is certainly safe to assert that few of them would have emerged robust enough to convince a jittery public that they had never had any operation at all.

2

The Heritage of Disability

The adroit vanishing act performed by Grover Cleveland and his cooperative colleagues may be unique in the annals of American presidents. Yet it was just one of a multitude of feats of legerdemain, juggling, double-talk, and tricks of magic that have been performed by occupants of the White House for almost two centuries to avoid public panic when the president is gravely ill. How well they succeeded in camouflaging these infirmities can be demonstrated by a simple experiment: look through the indices and contents pages of all the volumes you can quickly locate in your public library relating to American history or the biographies of the presidents, individually or collectively. You will discover a curious omission: except for those shocking instances in which presidents have been assassinated, there is only sparse reference to illnesses, accidents, mental breakdowns, or other infirmities that have plagued America's heads of state.

One immediate assumption seems credible: that these men were an unusually healthy lot because they had to be in order to aspire to such a demanding office and be prepared for the enormous and constant pressures. True? Not in the slightest. Paradoxically, this congregation of human beings who have been voted into the nation's highest post has a history of disease, dementia, and disability—not to mention violence—higher in proportion than that of almost any other professional body on record.

Someone wrote that history is made by men, that men have bodies, that bodies are sometimes healthy, sometimes infirm, and that the condition of the body inevitably affects the responses and actions of the mind. Thus, the study of the human body would seem a logical occupational function of the historian. Accidents of health often have more to do with the march of great events than have the most astute plans and preparations. Yet the investigation of presidential disabilities has revealed a disturbing facet of American government, let alone the recording of history: everyone—legislators, statesmen, jurists, the press, the public—shies away from acceptance of the fact that men in high public office are susceptible not only to the usual human illnesses, but to some special maladies and risks as well.

For generations, there were no realistic provisions for presidential succession in the event of medical crises or incapacity. Not until 1886 did Congress even authorize a procedure to be followed in case of a president's total removal by death, accident, or disease. Another sixty years passed before Congress determined the line of succession from president to vice-president to Speaker of the House. In 1956, a Constitutional amendment supposedly defined the procedures for installing the vice-president as acting president in the event that his chief should be rendered *hors de combat.*

Yet the procedure is so befogged as to be all but unworkable. What is "disabled"? Who is to determine the president's true "condition," especially if the problem is mental? What kind of pressure can, and cannot, be brought to bear if the chief executive *insists* that he is competent? Should the ultimate burden of proof lie with administrators or physicians?

From a purely statistical viewpoint, the chances are overwhelming that in the ranks of the next ten presidents two will suffer heart attacks; one will be hit by a disabling cerebrovascular accident; one will require surgery, radiation, or chemotherapy for cancer; one will suffer a critical accident; one will develop serious emotional problems that will be partially or totally disabling; and several will require radical general surgery. This sobering medical profile does not take into account the statistic that one out of every ten presidents is assassinated.

In any discussion of presidents, historically, administratively, or biographically, the focus has to start with George Washington. The office was almost tailor-made for him, since he had been president of the Constitutional Convention convened in Philadelphia in 1787. When the first Electoral College met in New York City two years later, he was unanimously elected president, an honor that has never been repeated. In the matter of presidential health, George Washington set something of a precedent, just as he did when he established the first veto, defined the relationships between the three main branches of the federal government, and formed the first cabinet. Washington assumed office as a national hero, a kind of demigod in bearing and strength of leadership. Americans, who knew him mainly through myth and hearsay, found it almost impossible to think of him as a human being subject to the same ills and anguish that they themselves had to cope with.

Consequently, the history books that describe his towering physique, bravery under fire, and unflagging determination never reveal that he achieved greatness in the face of constant illness, burning fevers, organic weaknesses, and sometimes excruciating pain. A modern physician would immediately have noticed the telltale signs of some ten major illnesses that ravaged his body during his span of sixty-seven years: the chest that was broad, yet hollowed in the center from tuberculosis; the skin that was tough and leathery from years of exposure to the outdoors, yet pockmarked from his bout with smallpox; the thighs that were solid and powerful from many years of riding the finest horses in Virginia, yet brutally scarred where a bone-deep tumor had been hacked out by crude surgery; the prominent nose that seemed ample for the greatest exertions, yet even when he was at rest was barely able to supply enough oxygen to lungs that had been frequently attacked by pneumonia and other respiratory illnesses; and even the chin made famous in the Gilbert Stuart portrait, yet highlighting the incessantly painful distortions in the jaw that had been caused by tooth decay, extractions, and the insertion of clicking, ill-fitting wooden dentures.

In short, that eminent hero who was "first in war, first in peace and first in the hearts of his countrymen," was also first in experiencing the unfortunate truth that the presidency brings with it an inordinate amount of pain and anguish.

Washington has been described as a hypochondriac—and perhaps he was, in the true meaning of the word. He had an enormous preoccupation with disease and, during his frequent periods of despondency and depression, with death. Still, he had a right to this obsession (more prevalent than that of any other president), since he fought ill health as frequently and as stubbornly at home or in the field as he fought more visible enemies. Through his personal encounters with disease, he evolved a number of theories. He was, for one, a great believer in bloodletting and had perfected the art of bleeding himself so that he could drain off suspected "humors" and poisons without having to await the arrival of a practicing surgeon. He was convinced, too, that certain foods were either preventive or aggravative and that diet, therefore, held the real key to health. This led, in part, to occasional consultation with quacks who dispensed hexes and herbs, often for imaginary illnesses that were created out of thin air and hence could be "cured" before they struck.

Washington headed for the presidency with a long history of illnesses behind him. In 1787, two years before taking office, he suffered great pain for six months from a rheumatic condition so severe that he could barely raise his hands above his head or turn himself in bed. Six weeks after taking the oath of office at Federal Hall in New York City (then the seat of government), he was gripped by violent cramps in his thigh, accompanied by fluctuations of chills and fever. The culprit turned out to be a huge carbuncle, or tumor, which had to be carved out—with no anaesthetic—by a father-son team of doctors, the Samuel Bards, Senior and Junior. The extracted mass was described as "malignant," which in those days meant that it was highly inflamed, sensitive to the slightest touch, and erupting with pus. Two months after the operation, as he was just beginning to sit up and ride in a specially built carriage, complications set in. He developed conjunctivitis in eyes which were already giving him visual problems, a severe cold, and finally pneumonia.

In all, he was disabled for 109 days, during which time he conducted very little official business. Within less than a year, he contracted pneumonia again. From that time on, although he spent some time at Newport, Rhode Island, which was a leading health resort, he never regained his health. He was described by one senator as having a complexion that was "pale, almost cadaverous," and a voice that was "hollow and indistinct."

Despite afflictions that would have immobilized the average man and kept him in a cocoon of convalescence, Washington was known for great achievements during his two terms of office. These included the complete organization of a fledgling government, standardizing and balancing financial matters, alleviating the tensions between the United States and Great Britain, and negotiating treaties with the Indians along the country's ever-stretching frontiers.

Washington had planned to retire at the end of his first term, and remained in office only at the urging of several of his compatriots, notably Thomas Jefferson. He was sixty-one at the time of his second inauguration on March 4, 1793, this time in Philadelphia, which had before that date become the national capital. His age and his growing infirmities presented something of a risk. But the presidency was so new and the affairs of state so evolutionary that it is doubtful that the founding fathers were greatly concerned about a successor, should the President suffer a fatal illness.

As it was, he survived for two and a half years after leaving office. As in the case of a later president, Friday the Thirteenth proved to be the beginning of the end. He felt the first symptoms of the illness that would be terminal—a severe sore throat, hoarseness, an aching neck, difficulty in breathing, and an increasing fever. He was given a mixture of molasses, vinegar, and butter, which almost choked and suffocated him. At his own request, he was bled of a pint of blood. Some flannel dipped in an ammonia solution was wrapped around his neck, and his feet were bathed in warm water. None of these remedies improved his condition, nor did a mixture of vinegar and sage tea with which he was supposed to gargle. By the time he had received his fourth bleeding in twelve hours, he was beyond hope.

On Saturday, December 14, 1799, his physician, Dr. James Craik, realized that his eminent patient was dying of pneumonia and called in two consultants. In addition to the bleeding, they experimented with various other applications of solutions and powders, but without providing the suffering man with any relief. One of the consultants, Dr. Elisha Dick, recommended as a

last resort the use of a surgical method that had been successful
in England: tracheotomy, the cutting of an opening in the wind-
pipe. Although Washington was having immense difficulties
with his breathing late in the afternoon of that day, the other
doctors refused to take the chance.

At about half past four, the former president made a great
effort to sit up in bed and gave last directions concerning his will
and the disposition of his estate. A few hours later, he indicated
that he was fully prepared for death. With the greatest difficulty,
he said, "I die hard, but I am not afraid to go. I feel myself going.
. . . Let me go quietly. I cannot last long."

It was characteristic of Washington that he dismissed his
doctors, thanking them for their efforts, and then showed an
almost clinical interest in the inner forces that were carrying him
out of this world. He died shortly before eleven that night—with
a finger carefully pressed against his left wrist, taking his ebbing
pulse.

The question arose in a recent medical discussion: "Would
George Washington have been an even greater president had he
not had to contend with so many infirmities and so much physical and mental distress?"

The answer is probably No, based on the records of all the
presidents who followed and their individual and collective
achievements in sickness and in health. John Adams served two
terms as vice-president under Washington and one term as president, with hardly a day spent on a sickbed. He was destined for
a long, healthful life, living to the age of ninety. Yet he did not
even begin to match the achievements of his predecessor or approach him in stature and leadership.

The third President, Thomas Jefferson, was a man of a completely different mold. He was undoubtedly the most brilliant of
American presidents, unmatched for sheer brain power, ingenuity, and intellect. Since he had opinions on just about every major
topic of the day, it is not surprising that he evolved medical
theories of his own, resulting from discussions and lengthy corre-
spondence with the outstanding medical practitioners of his era.
His general opinion of the medical profession was so low that he

refused to use the services of a doctor. On one of the few occasions when he ever admitted to an disability—in this case, a broken arm—he treated himself. Unfortunately, he was not very adept at setting it and ended up with a crooked right wrist that interfered with his writing for the rest of his life.

Madison, Monroe, and John Quincy Adams survived the presidency—what Jefferson referred to as "a splendid misery"—with varying records of success, failure, and achievement during their administrations. Though they were far healthier than Washington, they, too, were far below him in stature. The progression inevitably leads to Andrew Jackson, the man who really molded the presidency into the office it is today and whose achievements have been given only part of the recognition they deserve. He was a doer, an expeditor, a fighter, and an innovator.

He was also the most disabled president in American history.

3

The President Who Walked
in the Shadow of Death

For Grover Cleveland, the crisis was over in a matter of only two months. Because he and his close associates had managed to keep his disability secret, the subject of the President's health never became a serious public issue during his remaining time in office.

But what happens to the nation and the course of history when the chief executive has serious health problems, and when not only his immediate associates but also the American public are aware of this threat to the national well being? In many instances, the consequences have been severe, the published news reports unnerving and demoralizing. Such was the case during the administration of Andrew Jackson, seventh President of the United States, who had to face up to the most arduous demands of office during a number of periods of crisis, both administrative and economic.

Jackson stands as a classic example of the human capacity to function on sheer nerve, guts, and will power while trying to nurse a body riddled with illness and seared by pain. His health was so miserable and his endurance so questionable that, had he lived in the twentieth century, he would not have qualified for the most liberal life insurance policy. He was thin as a cadaver, yet he carried himself erect as a ramrod in the military fashion, standing not quite six feet in height while weighing only 129 pounds. Physical pain, which so often causes patients to retreat and become absorbed in themselves, with little consideration for others, had the opposite effect on the man who was to become known as Old Hickory. It intensified and heightened his interest in people and what they had to say, however trivial. Suffering did not smother his gaze, but instead seemed to kindle sparks in his deep blue eyes, as though the pain itself was a kind of fuel making them burn more brightly.

The illnesses that drained the blood from his veins and the fluids from his system left him with a rawboned appearance that was more tough than sickly. And they may have accounted for the fact that his hair—at first sandy, and later snow white—was extremely dry and bristling, elongating his silhouette, but also adding a formidable sign of warning that he was not a man to trifle with!

As a schoolboy, Jackson was as "fragile as a pipestem." Yet he was pugnacious, always itching for a fight with anyone he felt was slighting or maligning him. Though he seldom won these adolescent battles, he constantly came back for more, taking on any boy, regardless of size or ability, with the kind of temper typically ascribed to a red-headed Irishman. Furthermore, young Andrew was a "drooler." He salivated excessively, especially when his emotions were aroused or he was under stress. He was constantly spitting and dribbling, which of course simply made him a target of teasing and touched off more fights.

He was always a slight eater, existing on a bit of bread, a few vegetables, and endless draughts of milk, which he felt soothed his stomach as well as furnishing most of the nourishment he needed.

The first record of any enduring illness was a report that he suffered from an odd malady then called "the Big Itch," chronic urticaria, which caused him to itch ceaselessly from head to toe. While not serious, it was irritating in the extreme.

A more serious blow to his health occurred when, on April 10, 1781, at the age of fourteen, he was captured, with his brother, by the British during the Revolutionary War. With characteristic obstinacy and a show of independence, he refused to black the boots of a British officer when ordered to do so. For his boldness, he was rewarded with saber cuts on his wrist and temple, the scars of which were in evidence to his dying day.

While still wearing crude, dirty bandages after this assault,

Jackson caught smallpox in the filthy bunkroom where prisoners
were housed. He and his brother, who also caught the dread
disease, might have died there had not their mother prevailed
upon the British to release the two boys. Then she undertook a
forty-mile trek back to the family cabin in Waxhaw, North Carolina, with Andrew on foot and his brother, Robert, on a broken-
down nag, the only transportation available. Robert did not survive the trip, made mostly in driving rain. Somehow, Andrew
made it, though he was afflicted with raging fever and delirium
for many weeks. As a result of this, fevers and agues continued
intermittently throughout his life.

Through his late teens and early twenties, Jackson's health
was maintained fairly well. His father had died at the time of
Andrew's birth, both brothers died when he was fourteen and his
mother when he was fifteen. Andrew stayed with relatives, and
when an Irish grandfather died and left him a small inheritance,
he took off for the big cities—Charleston and Baltimore—and the
wild life, and ran through his inheritance within two years. Returning to the frontier, he settled down, "read the law," and
began to practice.

But by the time Jackson had finished his education and had
become the government's prosecutor for the territory, his health
was tottering badly. His dysentery, which had started slowly,
was becoming a problem. He was aggravating this by lack of care,
or worse yet, by his insistence on taking remedies that did more
harm than good. He was a virtual one-man advertising campaign
for a concoction known as "Matchless Sanitive," a tonic whose
origins and composition have faded into the obscurity they deserve. It was a fruit-flavored potion, with enough alcohol—as
much as 30 percent—to provide the patient with a rosy glow,
camouflaging some of his miseries. There were also numerous
formulations of his favorite sugar of lead. It could be taken by
mouth as a syrup, but also ingested by way of the rectum as an
enema. In a diluted concentration it doubled as an eye wash
(increasingly applied by Jackson as he grew older and his sight
dimmed). It could also be obtained or prepared as a thick salve
for rubbing on affected portions of the skin.

It was about this time—the early 1800s—that Andrew Jackson met and fell in love with Rachel Donelson Robards. Rachel was the daughter of an innkeeper and was married to Lieutenant Robards, who was off on military duty much of the time. The Robards' marriage had been less than perfect for several years, and Jackson's appearance on the scene brought things to a head. Lieutenant Robards finally agreed to petition the legislature for a divorce, naming Jackson as adulterer and Rachel adulteress, so that Rachel and Andrew could marry. Two years after the marriage it was discovered that the divorce decree had never become official, so that they had been living in sin all this time. There was a good deal of chuckling over this along the frontier—the prosecutor should know the law—and Jackson's temper did not take kindly to the kidding he received. A second marriage ceremony made everything legal.

Jackson and Charles Dickenson fought a duel over this. The two already had had words over the result of a horse race they had wagered on—Jackson's horse having won by default—so that when Jackson heard Dickenson snickering with friends in a tavern over the necessity of a second marriage ceremony, he lost his temper and challenged Dickenson to a duel. Charles Dickenson was a twenty-seven-year-old dandy and he was noted as "the best shot in Tennessee," thoroughly experienced in the art of duelling, to the regret of numerous opponents who had suffered wounds and six who had died from his deadly accuracy with the duelling pistol.

The event took place in May of 1806, early one morning. Dickenson arrived promptly, dressed in the traditional outfit, a tight-fitting shirt with lace, tight pants and a jacket which he carefully removed and hung on a branch. Jackson arrived late— intentionally. He felt that this bit of trickery gave him a slight psychological advantage, which he further enforced by his choice of costume.

He wore an ill-fitting black cape, which covered his skinny frame from shoulders to ankles, flaring out several feet at the ground. This effectively hid the body landmarks that a successful duelist must see.

The traditional eight paces (about twenty-four feet) were measured off and the two opponents stood facing each other, pistol arms upraised.

"Are you ready?" asked the second, John Overton.

"I am ready," replied Dickenson.

"Ready" echoed Jackson.

At the command to fire, Dickenson took instant aim at the spot where Jackson's heart seemed to be located and pulled the trigger. The ball struck directly in the chest, causing threads of fabric to explode like a puff of smoke. Andrew Jackson staggered and seemed about to fall to the ground. For a moment he pressed his left arm against his wound. Then he regained his balance, pointed the barrel of his pistol and fired back at Dickenson who was forced, by the dueler's code of honor, to remain in position.

The bullet lodged in the abdomen, where it caused a fatal wound that brought about Dickenson's death a day later, after the greatest agony.

As for Jackson, the bullet he took missed his heart by little more than an inch, breaking two ribs, tearing chest muscles, and coming to rest in the left lung, where it eventually caused a putrid abscess from which Jackson coughed up pus and blood for the rest of his life. He was forced to convalesce for more than a month before he could be back on his feet, but never fully recovered. Recurring chest pains, fevers, and difficulties with his breathing plagued him. Later in life, Jackson consulted surgeons about the possibility of removing the bullet, but not one would ever agree to take the risk of killing the patient in the process. Thus, Jackson was committed to one more cycle of illness. He would go through a period of well-being, during which the abscess remained stable and drained well. Then a period of coughing would inflame or irritate the area, causing hemorrhaging, infection, and fever. Often he would be shaken by chills and drenched in sweat. When the coughing and bleeding finally reduced the pressure in the abscess, he would return to a period of stability again, though greatly weakened, faint, and exhausted.

Not infrequently, too, the irritations and discharges would erode blood vessels in the chest cavity, causing further bleeding, sap Jackson's vitality and endanger his mental capacity for endur-

ing the greatest discomforts. During these periods he experienced continuous exhaustion with every move.

In 1825, the General suffered a severe fall, which tore apart the
poorly healed ligaments in his left shoulder and caused profuse
hemorrhaging in the already battered left lung. This caused the
eruption of what he referred to as "great quantities of slime," a
variation of the pus that had been draining for many years from
his abscess. By now, however, the discharge had infected the
entire bronchial system, leading to a chronic condition known as
bronchiectasis, an abnormal enlargement of the bronchial tubes,
with accumulations of mucous and the puddling of secretions in
the lungs.

It seems almost trivial to mention that Jackson's teeth were
in such an advanced state of decay that he could hardly eat any
solid foods. This condition led not only to severe tooth- and
jawaches, but also seems to have been at least a partial cause of
the pounding headaches he began to experience in the late 1820s.
Often they were so excruciating that they temporarily affected
his vision, and may have played a part in his partial blindness a
decade later.

There is no doubt that physical problems, pain, and distress
affected his outlook, his moods, and his entire nature. Impatient
and aggressive by nature, he was thus easily provoked by almost
any kind of frustration, and certainly to flare up in anger, sometimes violence, when he felt slighted or insulted. His "terrible
rages" are referred to often, in one way or another, by his peers
and colleagues. With all due respect to the man, though, it should
be understood that many of his rages and apparent lack of self-
control were indulged in as one way of letting off steam, and
frequently simply to scare the hell out of the opposition.

It was during this period, when he was resolutely ignoring
his personal afflictions and agonies and heading toward nomination for the presidency, that he received a tragic setback which
he could not alleviate by sheer will power or by diverting himself
into other channels of activity. In December 1828, his wife, Rachel, suffered a massive heart attack, a coronary artery thrombosis. The immediate treatment in those days was bloodletting, a
practice that was often fatal but which, in this case, apparently

relieved some of the pressure that was building up and temporarily helped to improve her condition. Six days later, she was sitting by the fire, seemingly on the road to recovery, when she cried out, "I am fainting," and pitched forward to the floor.

In near-panic, Jackson called in the nearest physician and had Rachel bled, first at the wrist, then at the temple. But no blood flowed—the lady was dead. Unable to accept the fact that she had died without a struggle, the General futilely wrapped her in blankets and sat with her throughout the night, certain that her pulse and breathing would return.

At the time of the inauguration in Washington in March 1829, the new president was still in a state of shock, more than showing his sixty-two years in his stark white hair, pasty complexion, and well-lined face. Yet it is said that he walked in the cold, bareheaded and gaunt, most of the way from the Capitol to the White House. Perhaps Rachel's death was for the best; she had dreaded the very idea of living in the White House and, only a few days before her death, had proclaimed, "I had rather be a doorkeeper in the house of God than to live in that palace!"

Jackson's campaign for election in 1828 had been supported by the snowballing power of the common man. State after state had eliminated property requirements for voting and the land owners were in shock. Andrew Jackson had felt that Adams and Clay had conspired to cheat him of the presidency in 1824 (Jackson had gotten a plurality of the electoral votes, but not a majority), and was therefore more than happy to enlist the aid of the average voter to oust the establishment. The campaign had sunk to a new low, Clay's supporters going so far as to resurrect the old stories of Andrew's and Rachel's courtship and marriage. "Ought a convicted adultress and her paramour husband be placed in the highest office of this free and Christian land?" But Jackson, casting President John Q. Adams and his cabinet in the role of tyrannical oppressors, was able to win with ease. At the inauguration, the grounds and interior of the White House were the setting for a mob scene. People from the very lowest level of society identified with this tough, choleric old man who had risen from poverty to embody the great American dream. And thousands of these common folk had been jamming the lodging places of Washington for days, sleeping four and five to a bed, or on the floors, just to witness the inauguration and if possible to attend the festivities in the East Room. None was excluded who could possibly squeeze through the doors.

In the midst of what one eyewitness described as "a regular Saturnalia," Jackson escaped through a back door, too exhausted to endure more, and spent the night at nearby Gadsby's Tavern, where he had been staying.

On several occasions during his election campaign, Jackson had appeared so ill that rumors flew about that he was dying. In one case, he was approached by a hulking laborer, who looked at him somewhat doubtfully and said, "General Jackson—I guess."

The General nodded in acknowledgment.

"Why they told me you was dead."

"No," replied Jackson, "Providence has hitherto preserved my life."

"And is your wife alive, too?"

"No," said the General, shaking his head mournfully.

"Aye," responded the laborer with a burst of understanding shining through his dull eyes, "I thought it was one or t'other of ye."

An article in the *Boston Medical School Journal,* recalling "The Gentleman from Tennessee," described Andrew Jackson as "a tottering scarecrow in deadly agony." Referring to his condition at the time he was about to take office in 1829, the article said, "What an astonishing physical specimen he was to sit in the Presidential chair. Sixty-two years old, racked with pain, fainting from weakness, his constituents brought him to Washington at an unpublicized hour to spare him the overenthusiasm of the crowd . . . he was hidden away and handled like fine china so that he might be well enough to take office on inauguration day."

Only a few months later, reported this same account, "the President's whole system seemed out of sorts. His feet and legs began to swell. . . . He complained bitterly of pain in the chest and his shortness of breath was noticeable to anyone who was in the room with him. His headaches grew excruciating and left him for only a few hours at a time. His vision was very trouble-some." In addition to these complications, he had a continuing fever, his stomach was described as "unmanageable," and "he had a true nephritis with those nephritic headaches that only a kidney sufferer can understand." The *Journal* pointed out, too, that an ensuing rise in blood pressure probably was one of the symptoms of "an early cardiac decompensation," and that "meanwhile, of course, the pulmonary focus of infection, the malaria, the dysentery, the osteomyelitis, and the bronchiectasis were going on, and on, and on."

It is little wonder that William L. Marcy, one of a group of men giving consideration to candidates for the vice-presidency, wrote in a letter to Martin Van Buren on the health of Andrew Jackson, "I must say, however I wish otherwise, that I think the chances are against his lasting five years longer."

Men of far greater wisdom and foresight than the common folk who were concerned about their hero had already counted his days as being numbered. His intimate friends all predicted that he would never live to complete his term of office. And even Jackson went so far as to anticipate what would happen if he were removed from the scene by death or total disability. He composed a "resignation" plan, which he fully expected to put into effect before his term was over. In 1830, he presented his proposal directly to the somewhat astonished Martin Van Buren, at that time his secretary of state. Jackson's plan was that he would groom Van Buren to replace the Vice-President (who would become president) and then, when affairs of state were running smoothly, Jackson would announce his resignation and retire to the Hermitage, his lovely mansion in Nashville. Van Buren would not listen to this scheme, despite the President's protestations that he would eventually die in office, and possibly at a time when it might seriously disrupt the nation. Later, the situation became even more worrisome when John C. Calhoun resigned as vice-president (the only man ever to do so until Spiro T. Agnew was forced out of office in 1973), leaving Jackson with more than his share of the burdens.

Jackson's concern about his health and his ability to continue holding office was not unlike the constant medical declarations of his predecessor, George Washington, who was a confirmed hypochondriac. In effect, though, Andrew Jackson took over the nation's highest office as an undeniable invalid. As one biographer of presidents described him, "The emaciated Andrew Jackson looked like a broken-down refugee from an old-soldier's hospital . . . virtually a one-man clinic. . . . The wonder is that he preserved as creditably as he did the dignity of his high office."

One of the great contradictions of Andrew Jackson's first term is found in the formation of his cabinet. He deliberately selected members who were essentially weak, rather than those who might be able to shoulder the burdens whenever he was incapacited. Why? Because despite his infirmities and the dire prognostications of physicians and colleagues alike, he fully intended to *dominate* these men and control his administration with a strong will and iron hand. The only person of consequence in the cabinet was Secretary of State Martin Van Buren, who would later succeed Jackson as president.

Shortly after taking office, Jackson actually suspended regular meetings of his appointed cabinet and came to rely almost entirely on a small group of men who had played a prominent part in his election and who became known as his "Kitchen Cabinet." Among them were John Eaton and William B. Lewis, old pals from Tennessee, and his nephew, Andrew Jackson Donelson, who served as his private secretary.

"Complaining never eased pain," Jackson used to quip, but he did discuss his health problems with his Kitchen Cabinet and others close to him, largely in regard to the problem of succession should he die or be unable to perform his official duties in the manner he desired. In the summer of 1829, he became so alarmed at his deteriorating condition that he wrote in a letter, "My time cannot be long upon earth," expressing the assurance that he was putting his "earthly house in order."

During this critical period, when the presidency itself seemed in jeopardy, and shortly after the delivery of his first message to Congress, Jackson became greatly concerned about his would-be successor. He was afraid that John C. Calhoun, rather than Van Buren, might usurp the crown. William B. Lewis, alarmed at the increasing amount of swelling in the President's legs, and frankly afraid that he was dying of dropsy (an uncontrollable accumulation of fluids in the tissues), urged a drastic measure: the President should draft a "political will."

Jackson readily agreed. The document that he then composed and signed praised Van Buren as "frank, open, candid, and manly," deserving of the confidence of the nation, an able and prudent counselor, and well qualified to fill the highest office. By contrast, he dismissed Calhoun as having failed to retain his confidence to such an extent that he did not even want to speak about it.

Historians have marvelled over the fact that Jackson, the "one-man clinic," was the first, and certainly one of the greatest, exponents of the real power of the presidency. "It was settled by the Constitution, the laws, and the whole practice of the government," he himself wrote, "that the entire executive power is vested in the President of the United States." Not all of his contemporaries agreed with this viewpoint, especially those opponents who scornfully referred to him as "King Andrew the First."

One of his earliest biographers, attempting to define his contradictory nature, wrote that Jackson was ". . . one of the greatest of generals, and wholly ignorant of the art of war. A writer brilliant, elegant, eloquent, without being able to compose a correct sentence, or spell words of four syllables. The first of statesmen, he never devised, he never framed a measure. He was the most candid of men, and was capable of the profoundest dissimulation. A most law-defying, law-abiding citizen. A stickler for discipline, he never hesitated to disobey his superior. A democratic autocrat. An urbane savage. An atrocious saint."

To these comments he might have added that Jackson was also the sickest and most miserable of patients and yet the strongest and most forceful of leaders. He faced up to innumerable challenges and not a few national and international crises during his two terms in the White House. One of the most notorious was the "Eaton Affair," in which Secretary of War John Henry Eaton was forced to resign in the spring of 1831 in the face of a national scandal. A social feud had developed when the wives of cabinet members refused to accept Eaton's wife, Peggy, on the grounds that she had been a "barmaid" at one time and that he had married her under questionable circumstances. Jackson staunchly stood up for the Eatons, but in the end was forced to admit to one of the few strategic defeats in his life and let Eaton go.

Another crisis, this one, however, demonstrating Jackson's leadership and initiative in civilian life as well as in battle, was his handling of a long-standing diplomatic problem with France. American citizens had bombarded the government with claims against France for the destruction of property and seizure of ships during the Napoleonic Wars, from 1803 to 1815. France had stubbornly refused to make reparations and had added insult to injury by honoring the claims of Europeans while at the same time brushing aside the pleas of mere "colonists."

Jackson displayed uncharacteristic patience during some two years of negotiations and was rewarded—or so he thought—with victory when, on July 4, 1831, the French signed an agreement to pay 25 million francs in six annual installments. Months went by, then a year, with no appropriations forthcoming from the French Chamber of Deputies.

Since Jackson was so well known, personally, to a number of high officials in France, it is possible that they were counting on his failing health to divert him and prevent him from taking a firm stand in the matter. It was widely known, for example, that he had been seriously wounded in duels and other violent acts and left with permanent scars and physical handicaps. During his later youth and early manhood, the frequent boyhood boxing contests were replaced by more serious personal encounters. One historian claims that Jackson engaged in no fewer than one hundred duels during his lifetime, from which he received his share of injuries.

It is no wonder that, by 1831, the French were convinced they had exhausted him into submission and legislators in Washington were conceding that the President had finally been outflanked. Paris had made absolutely no further response. Furthermore, the President was so riddled with ailments that it seemed impossible for him to devote his energies to anything but the most pressing domestic business, certainly not a frustrating overseas campaign, via letters and emissaries. The dropsy he suffered was becoming more advanced, affecting not only the feet and legs but the lower part of his body as well. Evidence indicates that this condition was caused by a degenerative illness called amyloidosis, the formation of undesirable proteins stimulated by chronic infections in various organs, which is aggravated and multiplied by the presence of other diseases in the body. The edema that resulted left the President weak and anemic and was visibly evident to those around him in the form of doughlike swellings on his otherwise emaciated frame.

The pessimists who predicted that Jackson would relinquish his demands on the French forgot that he had not acquired the name Old Hickory for nothing. The man's miserable health played a strong part in his actions and decisions—but in an unexpected manner. The physical anguish he was going through only served to make him more irascible and short-tempered than ever. He gave the French to understand that he had a short fuse and would take punitive action, including the cessation of trade, if the claims were not honored. The French finally got the message, but attempted one more delaying tactic by proclaiming that the funds would not be paid until Jackson explained some of the threats he had made in his message to Congress on the subject—in other words, an apology.

"I am of the opinion," thundered Jackson, "that France will pay the money without apology or explanation—*from me, she will get neither!*" As expected, France *did* pay and he did *not* apologize.

Jackson's ill health was productive in another, completely different way, unsuspected by any except his most intimate associates in the White House. Many legislators and officials had the erroneous opinion that he gave scant attention to details, since he seemed to be either fuming and whipping up battle smoke or else flat on his back trying to recuperate from the most recent attack of one disease or another. What they did not observe was the man himself, the quiet, methodical Jackson who worked late at night, often into the small hours of the morning, doing his homework and studying the infinite details of issues with which he was faced. He worked long and late for a very simple reason: he was plagued with insomnia and even when he was exhausted was often in too much pain to sleep, except for a few hours at a time. If he awoke in the middle of the night, he would immediately slip into the chair behind his desk and continue where he had left off—reading documents, studying legislation, and writing letters or reports.

Again and again, this kind of concentration and attention to details paid off in his continuing battles with Congress and other forces that opposed him. Nowhere, during his entire administration, did this work habit get results better than in the case of "the Bank War," the most important and far-reaching issue during his eight years in office.

4

The President Who Walked
in the Shadow of Death (Continued)

When the Philadelphia National Bank recharter bill was presented to Jackson to sign early in July 1832, the President was on
his back on a sofa in the White House. The summer heat of
Washington was insufferable and he lay there with his white hair
disheveled and his thin, gaunt face as pasty as clay. The President, who believed that the bank favored the wealthy and offered
few services to the common man, called it "the Monster" and said
he would crush it. He had weak legislative and executive support.

Jackson had suffered from some acute recurrent effects of
wounds inflicted in another of his early brawls, in this case with
two brothers, Jesse and Thomas Hart Benton. During the course
of the confrontation, Jackson had caught a pistol ball square in
his left shoulder and another that had shattered his left arm and
buried itself against the bone and heavy muscle. He had almost
bled to death. The bullet in the arm had been eventually
removed, some nineteen years later, without any form of anaesthetic and with Jackson gripping the back of a chair to avoid
flinching and interrupting the surgery in progress.

By 1832, the differences with the Bentons had long since been
forgotten. In fact, Thomas Hart Benton was now a greatly respected senator and a supporter of the President. According to
one story, the bullet removed from Jackson's arm was offered to
Tom Benton as a keepsake that rightfully was owned by the
Benton family. The senator politely declined the gift, observing
that the President "acquired clear title to it in common law by

20 years' peaceable possession."

That summer, when Martin Van Buren returned to Washington unexpectedly after a sojourn in the country, he could see that the old maladies caused by the Benton brawl and other encounters were contributing to the President's involuntary withdrawal from the battle with the bank. Yet, fortunately, his reappearance caused Jackson's lethargy to vanish and his face to brighten.

When asked what was the matter that kept him on his back, Jackson replied to his old friend, "The bank, Mr. Van Buren, is trying to kill me, but I will kill it first." His voice sounded firm and resolute, his manner more determined than bitter.

The only course of action, asserted Old Hickory, was to veto the bill. Van Buren began to protest. He pointed out the risks of jeopardizing not only his own chances for reelection but those of the other Democrats running for office. Jackson was adamant. Two days later, with the President back on his feet and apparently fully recovered again, his cabinet tried in vain to persuade him to take a more tactful course. He could easily disapprove the bill in such a way that it was not an outright veto and would leave the issue open for legislative discussion at a later date—long after the election.

The veto outline prepared by the President required three days for fleshing out into draft form. When it was finished, with final touches of style and rhetoric by the gifted Van Buren, it was described by one later historian as "a work of art." It focused heavily on Andrew Jackson's rapport with "the common man" and his genius for anticipating the desires and emotions of the citizens at large. In effect, it leaped right over the heads of disgruntled politicians and angry congressmen and touched the man on the street with its message of action on his behalf.

The presentation of the veto, dated July 10, was described as "bursting like rolling thunder" across the nation, as its impact spread outward from the nation's capital. One account has referred to it as "the most important Presidential veto in American history, a powerful and dramatic polemic that can still reach across a century and more of time and excite controversy among those who study it." In the veto, the President declared that the

Second Bank of the United States was a monopoly, with exclusive privileges in both foreign and domestic exchange. He stressed the fact, not generally known to the average citizen, that foreigners were exerting an economic control in the United States, since they held some eight million shares of the bank's stock.

"If our Government," wrote Jackson, "must sell monopolies . . . it is but justice and good policy . . . to confine our favors to our own fellow citizens." Furthermore, he added, "It is to be regretted that the rich and powerful too often bend the acts of government to their selfish purposes. Distinctions in society will always exist under every just government. Equality of talents, of education, or of wealth can not be produced by human institutions. In the full enjoyment of the gifts of Heaven and the fruits of superior industry, economy, and virtue, every man is equally entitled to protection by law."

The acceptance of the veto and Jackson's election in spite of it were real victories for him and a tribute to his leadership. Yet the Bank War had only entered another stage in a battle that was to continue for several more years. The next major step was to plan the removal of the government's money in an orderly fashion and its transfer to the system of state banks through a selection procedure that was soon to earn them the name of "pet banks" from the opposition.

The President was unable to take the necessary action during the fall of 1832 and the winter of 1832–33. For one thing, he was embroiled in a bitter clash with South Carolina, which had reacted to the passage of a federal tarriff by calling a convention to declare the tariff null and void in that state. This was no isolated case of putting a rebellious state back on track. Rather, it was a critical test of presidential strength in dealing with states, and it was something of a test of the man's own courage, since he might well have left the issue to Congress and avoided the tensions, strains, and censure that resulted.

Another force that made it difficult to take immediate action in the Bank War was—as usual—the President's health. One of his most persistent disabilities was dysentery, which at best made life miserable and at worst could knock him out of action for many days at a time. This health problem had started in late September 1813, when as a major general he volunteered to lead his troops against the Creek Indians who had risen up in revolt and massacred some 250 settlers in the Mississippi Territory (now Alabama), under the leadership of Chief Red Eagle.

Jackson was already in a weakened condition, and far from recuperated from his bloody encounter with the Benton brothers, but he struggled up from his sick bed. With a characteristic display of wrath, he insisted that he would wreak vengeance on Red Eagle, who was seven-eighths white and had renounced his Christian name, William Weatherford, and was in Jackson's eyes a no-good renegade. There is no doubt that this frail, forty-six-year-old invalid displayed enormous fortitude when he offered to go into the field again, barely able to mount his horse without assistance. His left arm was useless. His shoulder was wracked with constant pain. His body vacillated between attacks of deep fever and chilling sweat.

The only concession the general would make was to permit the accompaniment of a physician, Dr. William May, whose most immediate and pressing duty was to make his patient dismount frequently and wash him from head to foot with sugar of lead. This solution was supposed to reduce the inflammation and control the fever. In actuality, the procedure did little more than irritate the general and keep him in a continuous bad humor, a situation that may have contributed to his determination to annihilate the enemy. Jackson was obsessed with the belief that sugar of lead, which had a mild astringent effect, was a cure-all. He not only relied on it for external applications, but drank quantities of it to alleviate internal problems.

His most serious problem during the Creek campaign was dysentery, which forced him to dismount as frequently as fifteen or twenty times a day and squat by the side of the trail to relieve his bowels. One of his periods of greatest suffering came at the height of the battle of Talladega, on November 9, a critical encounter in which his men killed more than three hundred of the opposing warriors. The General was in such pain that he was unable to lie down or sit. During the worst seizures, he had to prop himself in a bizarre and awkward manner over a contrivance made of two poles and a cross bar, from which he would hang for an hour or two at a time. Somehow, this seemed to relieve the pressure on his internal organs.

To compound his woes, he and his men were almost without food supplies, forced to exist on raw acorns and at one time the discarded entrails of a hog that had been recently slaughtered and carted off by other soldiers. The remedy for dysentery was thought to be calomel, a white powder which he consumed in copious quantities. Since calomel is essentially a purgative, it undoubtedly aggravated his entire intestinal tract rather than providing any relief or medicinal benefit. In addition, since the formula contained elements of mercury, there is good reason to believe that Jackson's continuing use of it from that time on may have caused mercury poisoning throughout his system. One of the side effects of the constant irritation was what was known as "bloody flux," or intestinal bleeding during bowel movements. This bloody diarrhea was a common occurrence for Jackson by the time he entered the White House, and almost "normal" for him.

Jackson seldom complained about his ailments, preferring to subjugate them to his steel will. When he mentioned his personal health problems, he usually did so in a methodical, factual manner, as though they were all part of what most people had to endure. "I have been oppressed with a violent cough," he wrote in one letter, "and have been vissited (sic) with my old bowell complaint, which has weakened me very much, having . . . in the last twelve hours upward of Twenty passages. . . ."

The conditions under which Jackson had to function during that nonmilitary campaign, the Bank War, were as distressing as the dangers and discomforts he had experienced as a soldier. The most obvious difference was that, as president, he could retire briefly out of sight when in the throes of diarrhea, stomach cramps, and hemoptysis (the coughing up of blood)—attacks that he could not easily hide as a general in the field.

The President's chief adversary in the Bank War was the debonair and brilliant Nicholas Biddle, president of the Bank of the United States, a man whom Jackson regarded as something of an "extinct volcano." Biddle himself was at times so feeble that he had to be supported by a servant on each arm. Biddle launched a campaign to open new branches of the bank, add to his staff, and make long-term loans, particularly to influential people like Daniel Webster, Henry Clay, and William T. Barry. As he reasoned, no bank was going to go out of business when to do so would undermine the whole American economy and cause men in high places to be financially embarrassed.

Old Hickory saw these signals for what they were in the spring of 1833. He tended to be melodramatic about the situation, partly because that was his nature, but also because his language appealed to the layman. "I long for retirement and repose on the Hermitage," he wrote characteristically, effectively painting an image of the rosy retirement he spurned in order to champion the cause of the common man, "But until I can strangle this hydra of corruption, the Bank, I will not shrink from my duty or my part."

He had good reason to portray this dark image of the bank as the personification of an individual assailant who was attacking him and thus had to be dealt with summarily. Biddle resorted to questionable tactics, including at one time the intentional creation of a panic, in order to pressure the government into rechartering the bank.

Jackson reacted to a case of *physical* assault almost as though he were dealing with his perennial assaulter, the bank. As a "man of the people," who often insisted on seeing citizens who had come to Washington with the most petty problems and complaints, Jackson left himself wide open to personal attacks. One of the most noted assaults occurred on May 6, 1833, when he was aboard a steamboat which had departed from Washington with the presidential party aboard and had just docked at Alexandria, Virginia.

The President was seated in his cabin reading a newspaper when a stranger entered unannounced and without once having been stopped or questioned by an aide. As it turned out, he was one Robert Randolph, a former naval lieutenant who had been dismissed from the service for an alleged theft of funds and therefore had a grudge against the government.

"Excuse my not rising, sir," said the President, looking up, though not in great surprise, since he was frequently accosted by people who wanted a word with him, "but I have a pain in my side which makes it difficult for me to rise."

Randolph started to remove his glove, at which move the President extended his hand in greeting and said, "Never mind your glove, sir." At this moment, the former naval officer punched Jackson with full force in the face, almost knocking him backward, chair and all, to the floor. Fortunately, at this moment the captain of the ship entered the cabin, saw with alarm what was happening and wrestled the assailant away from Jackson. Several members of the presidential party, hearing the scuffle, arrived on the scene and together hustled Randolph off the ship before any of the passengers realized that the President had been assaulted.

Jackson was furious as he wiped the blood away from his face, not so much because he had been attacked but because he had not realized Randolph's purpose in time to rise up and take the offensive himself. "No villain has ever escaped me before," he fumed, "and he would not, had it not been for my confined situation."

Characteristically, Andrew Jackson did not permit any charges to be pressed against Randolph. He considered it to be his own fault that he had not been more alert and counterattacked before he became the victim rather than the victor.

Jackson was anxious to take strong and positive steps to settle the bank question in early June of 1833. But he badly needed a rest, an escape from the explosive pressures of Washington, and a tour of New England to cement his relationships with his Yankee constituency. Accordingly, he set out for Connecticut in the company of several close friends, including young Josiah Quincy, Jr., the son of the president of Harvard, who was to act as host during their intended stay at the university.

By the time Jackson's entourage had passed through Connecticut, amidst continuous ovations and never-ending speeches, young Quincy confessed that he was already worn out and hopeful that his boss would sooner or later shorten the trip. But

Jackson was refreshed by the acclaim, even when receptions and dinners overlapped. Typical of the enthusiasm of the citizens was the instance when Old Hickory stood on a bridge at Pawtucket in the early dawn, on his way to Massachusetts. A unit of the Rhode Island militia touched off an artillery farewell salute of such proportions, it was reported, that half the windows in town were shattered.

The trip to Boston was marked by other events, such as ceremonial breakfasts, factory inspection tours, more salvos of artillery, and endless military reviews. The triumphant arrival was likened to the display of honor for Lafayette at the end of the Revolution. Yet these occasions were also marked by a somber warning: on the fourth day of his visit to Boston, Jackson began to suffer from a severe cold, accompanied by ominous bleeding from the lungs. He was immediately ordered to bed, and the physicians who had been called in for consultation proceeded with the common practice of bleeding the patient. Looking at the spindly figure of the chief executive, observers might well have wondered whether there was any blood left in that mummy-like torso.

Somehow Jackson not only survived, but was soon sitting up drafting letters to Secretary of the Treasury William J. Duane, instructing him about the transfer of funds from the Bank of the United States to the state banks. These were no mere notes—one communication is said to have been as long as twenty pages of print in a book.

A few days later, the President was out of bed and insisting on continuing his planned tour. On the morning of June 26, he was beginning a round of feverish activities in the vicinity of Boston. First on the schedule was a visit to Harvard, where he was presented with an honorary degree by the university's president, Josiah Quincy. To the distress of his friends, Jackson insisted on shaking hands with professors and students, who immediately after the ceremony formed a lengthening line in anticipation of the honor. It was only after the President's face grew so pale he seemed in danger of fainting that an aide persuaded him to bow out. Yet no rest was in sight, for that was merely the start of an eventful day that was to include five dinners and receptions, tours of Boston, Charleston, Lynn, and Marblehead, climbing the uncompleted Bunker Hill monument, addressing numerous throngs, and listening attentively to the speeches of others.

The younger Quincy begged the President to cut out some of his planned activities, but Jackson remained as stubborn as ever. "These people have made their arrangements to welcome me," he bellowed, "and so long as I am not on my back I will gratify them." By the time the party had driven through Lynn and Marblehead and was on its way to Salem, Quincy was boldly ignoring the old gentleman and ordering the carriage to proceed directly to an inn, where he immediately hustled the patient to bed, under the care of a local physician. That night Jackson suffered acute hemorrhaging of the lungs.

Quincy arose the next morning, went down to the breakfast table and began making his plans for canceling the rest of the tour. All at once, there was a sound of footsteps behind him. The seated members of the staff turned and looked up, to see the President arriving for breakfast. His step was hardly a stride, yet, as the aide-de-camp later described the phenomenon, "an immaterial something flashed in his eye, and it was evident that the faltering body was again held in subjection."

After one final tour, this time of the Boston Navy Yard, where a figurehead of Andrew Jackson was being carved for placing on the venerable old U.S.S. *Constitution,* the President headed northward, bound for Portland, Maine. He journeyed no farther than Concord, New Hampshire, where he greeted some aged veterans of the American Revolution and proudly showed them his own "certificate of service," the saber scar that he had carried, at the age of fourteen, from the British prison camp.

A few hours later, he collapsed completely.

Now there was no doubt in the minds of his friends. The President was dying. They commandeered a small river steamer, as the most comfortable form of transportation available, and headed south on the Merrimac River to Newburyport, Massachusetts and thence on a larger vessel to Washington.

For two days and nights following his arrival back at the White House, Jackson appeared to be beyond hope. Then he rallied and immediately began calling for Secretary of the Treasury Duane so they could get on with the business of the banks. As an old soldier, he was incensed that banker Nicholas Biddle had stolen a march on him and created some economic confusion while he was attending to other matters of state. The doctors, backed by members of the cabinet and his family, ordered him to take a four-week rest at Rip Raps, an island at the mouth of the Chesapeake, where he sometimes went for short periods of vacation. There, he fretted and fumed, spending most of his time working on a memorandum and plan for transferring government funds from the Second Bank to the state banks. By August, when he was back in the White House, the national situation was grave, and depositors near panic. The state banks that had been approached with his proposals seemed for the most part reluctant to acquire government deposits, certainly not under the operating safeguards that Old Hickory wanted to impose.

Looking beyond the restraints, private banking officials were found to be in the grip of a real, and growing fear: that Nicholas Biddle held so much power that he could take devastating retaliatory action against smaller banks and eventually force Congress to renew the charter of the Second Bank of the United States. In the course of doing this, he would cripple any banks that attempted to go along with Jackson's plan. An example of the kind of pressure Biddle could bring to bear to make his point occurred in the summer of 1833, as Jackson was trying to build his strength and rally his forces. Merchants in Massachusetts needed about $1 million to pay import duties on goods arriving at Boston wharves. When the importers applied to local state banks for loans to carry them through until their goods were sold, they were shocked to find that the banks were unable to make sufficient cash available. Biddle's bank had suddenly discontinued discounts and demanded the immediate return of the funds it carried on balance in the state banks.

The nation was being relentlessly divided into two factions: those who supported Jackson, and were fearful of what might happen if Biddle were not put in his place, and those who really hoped that these tactics would force Congress (and the President) to agree to renewing the charter. The latter group played heavily on the President's ailments, urging him to take a rest, and certainly to remove himself from Washington during the month of September, when the air was hot and humid and filled with "miasmas" and "vapors" injurious to the health. They succeeded in scaring Jackson's friends and relatives enough so that he was often shielded from knowing about some of the critical problems.

There was no doubt that the nation faced an historic crisis. On September 25, 1833, Jackson had finally badgered his cabinet into issuing an order to the effect that, commencing October 1, all future government deposits would be placed in state banks. Since the government would be continually withdrawing funds from its deposits in the Bank of the United States, the process would eventually result in the total transfer. Biddle countered by ordering that the branches of the Bank of the United States should immediately curtail loans. This action was so sudden and unexpected that the East was thrown into an economic panic, a panic that steadily spread westward across the country. The Democrats urged their leader to back away from his decision to force the issue, fearing a nationwide financial collapse.

"The monster must perish!" bellowed Old Hickory, with a fierce display of Jacksonian temper, assuring his critics that he had the bank "in chains" and under control.

The situation changed little throughout the rest of 1833, and carried right over into the early spring of 1834. The President was beleaguered by delegations of businessmen from major cities who begged for a change in policy, to prevent them from going bankrupt. When one such group informed Jackson that they were insolvent, he raged right back at them, *"Insolvent,* do you say? What do you come to me for, then? Go to Nicholas Biddle. We have no money here, gentlemen. Biddle has all the money . . . and yet you come to me to save you from breaking. I tell you, gentlemen, it's all politics."

The constant tension was beginning to tell on Jackson. Although he refused to give in to his infirmities, he was beset by unceasing, debilitating headaches and threatening pains in the chest. He admitted to physical distress, but also added that the excitement kept him on his feet and in action. His most melodramatic description of the enemy as a "monster" was certainly not a figment of his imagination. As Marquis James wrote in his biography, *Andrew Jackson, Portrait of a President*, Biddle was positive that he could crush the old man in the end, since he could outlast him and would eventually see him overwhelmed by his numerous maladies. "The banker's deliberate purpose," wrote James, "was to make people suffer, to bring upon the Administration a storm of protest by the threat of panic and, if that did not suffice, by panic in fact. The blame, he felt, would fall on Jackson and ruin him."

There was no doubt that his strategy was having its effect. The prices of securities were in a slump; workers were being laid off; gold and silver was being hoarded in anticipation of worthless paper; the pace of commerce and industry slowed noticeably; wages were reduced without warning; and interest rates tripled. Much of the blame for this economic slowdown began to shift to Jackson, aggravated by editorials in opposition newspapers and by legislators eager to sing the old "I told you so" refrain.

As the panic worsened and alarmed merchants and customers began stashing away all metal coins, communities tried to make up the difference by issuing temporary scrip, which the President's detractors referred to as "Jackson money." On the surface, Old Hickory seemingly remained strong, confident, and unperturbed. Yet he found it almost impossible to hide the fact that his headaches were becoming more acute and the pains in his chest more frequent and sharp.

When Congress convened in December 1833, Henry Clay, Daniel Webster, and John C. Calhoun loomed as a triple threat to Jackson as they argued in favor of the Second Bank, urged that the charter be renewed, and went so far as to challenge the President on the validity of his orders to transfer government funds to the state banks. Clay, known for his talents as an orator, made a speech in Congress that took three days to deliver, charging that Jackson had violated the laws and the Constitution. This led, in March 1834, to the adoption by the Senate of a resolution of censure. Jackson, understandably furious, held his temper in check for two weeks before entering a formal protest against the censure, declaring that he had been charged with an offense so outrageous that it really insinuated impeachment, but he was not given an opportunity to defend himself.

He received what was, for a man of his temperament, the most devastating response of all: the Senate refused to make his protest part of its official record.

Nicholas Biddle was able to fuel the fire in Washington and make things hot for the President by using one of the oldest and most persuasive forces of all: money. He made large advances to Webster in the guise of "loans," and paid smaller sums to Clay, or to others suggested by anti-Jackson legislators as being in financial need. In Webster's case, unusually large amounts were dispensed as "retainers." The debilitating effect of *stress* on Jackson's health was well understood by his opponents. They had learned that a few hours of real pressure, enough to penetrate the President's armor and arouse his excitement, could cause physical prostration. It was reported that this sometimes led to a form of paralytic rheumatism that was disabling enough to prevent him from writing letters, memoranda, and reports.

The Senate was inundated with "memorials," written communications from many of the nation's cities "complaining of great embarrassment and pecuniary distress because of the removal of deposits from the Bank of the United States. A few of these memorials, largely from citizens' groups, supported the President, but when the count was tabulated, the bank held a wide margin: more than 150,000 names in protest, as compared with only about 17,000 speaking out for Jackson.

It was Biddle who had first made the mistake of believing that Andrew Jackson's frail and disease-riddled body would collapse under the strain. He did not know the gentleman from Tennessee well enough. But what excuse did his opponents in Congress have—men who had seen him stand up repeatedly under the most devastating fire—for assuming that he would weaken? Fundamentally, they were convinced that they could simply wear him to exhaustion. Each time he was forced into temporary retreat, spitting blood or nursing a deep fever, or trying to bring his tortured intestinal system back into balance, they believed that he was moving one more step down the ladder. But surprisingly, after some four years of open controversy, the President now seemed to be gaining the upper hand. His repetitious suggestion, "Go to Nicholas Biddle!" was no longer being laughed at. In fact, more and more citizens and groups were doing just that. The suave Philadelphian was cautioned that the bank's pressure tactics were now being regarded as evidence that the institution was—just as Jackson had warned—too powerful.

By the spring of 1834, Andrew Jackson had the bank in full retreat; largely by the force of public opinion. The *Baltimore Register,* an influential publication which had previously supported Biddle's cause, ran an editorial criticizing the Bank of the United States for having amassed too much power over the common welfare. When Biddle asked an old friend, Governor George Wolf of Pennsylvania, to prepare a message to the legislature in support of the bank, he was in for a shock. Wolf denounced the bank for having carried the campaign of panic so far that even Biddle's home state had been unwittingly forced into an embarrassing financial situation when its request for a standard loan was turned down. The Pennsylvania legislature, instead of encouraging support of the bank, adopted a resolution that *"the present bank of the United States ought not to be rechartered by Congress."*

Calhoun, Webster, and Clay all attempted some last-ditch measures to halt the growing sentiment against Mr. Biddle and his bank, but it was too late. In April, James K. Polk, then chairman of the Committee on Ways and Means, reported four resolutions by the House, all against the bank and in support of Jackson: (1) that the charter should not be renewed; (2) that the public deposits in the Bank of the United States would not be restored; (3) that the state banks would take over the deposits; and (4) that a House committee would investigate the bank's affairs and the actions that had led to a nationwide crisis.

The directors of the bank were now the ones who were furious, so dismayed that one expressed the desire that "The history of this day should be blotted from the annals of the Republic."

Jackson's own comment was brief, "I have obtained a glorious triumph," he wrote in a letter at the time. Then he dosed himself with two spoonfuls of Matchless Sanative, a little sugar of lead, and a cup of gin and water and rode back to the Hermitage for a badly needed rest.

Jackson's final months in office were times of great personal misery and often excruciating pain. His feet had swelled so much that he could hardly walk; his headaches were so severe and constant that he found concentration difficult; he was plagued by the old complaints—diarrhea, indigestion, shortness of breath, hemorrhaging, and deep pains in his chest. He seldom set foot out of the White House and often had to postpone or cut short cabinet meetings that he had scheduled in his own office. Adding to his woes was the blindness in one eye, a blurring of vision in the other, and an ear infection that affected his hearing.

The old man had planned on delivering a farewell address to Congress during his final days in office, but was totally incapacitated by fits of coughing, during which he spat up copious amounts of blood from his lungs. Despite his condition, he refused to stop puffing on his pipe, chewing tobacco, and dosing himself with calomel or strong gin and water. He still bled himself on occasion, whenever he felt that he should release a bit of poison from his system. It probably was not surprising to his contemporaries that he eventually got the better of his physical disabilities and *did* make the farewell speech. He also managed to hobble, with the help of friends, to a seat of honor to listen to Martin Van Buren's inaugural address, as the latter assumed the presidency in 1837.

Yet he was far from a pathetic figure, fading from the scene. A visiting Englishman described the man's incredible vigor, saying that he displayed a "natural and most peculiar warlikeness," and commenting on his "gamecock look."

Three days after the inauguration of Van Buren, Andrew Jackson left Washington for retirement at the Hermitage. He was so ill that he was accompanied by several physicians, yet insisted on taking several weeks for the trip, so that he could visit with friends along the way and frequently stop to acknowledge the accolades of cheering crowds that formed wherever he happened to appear. Now 70 (69 years and 354 days, to be exact), he appeared to be failing so steadily that the accompanying doctors were not at all certain he would survive the trip home.

Jackson himself seemed to have no doubts whatsoever that he would reach the Hermitage. And he did. In fact, he lasted for eight more years and as many additional illnesses, including erysipelas, which discolored his skin to a beet red, delirium spells, and an enormous swelling of his elongated head that gave him the appearance of a macabre caricature of himself. Such maladies did not prevent the old soldier from setting out for New Orleans in January 1840, for a celebration in his honor on the twenty-fifth anniversary of his historic victory over the British. As might be expected, he suffered debilitating hemorrhaging en route, but succeeded in making what was his last real public appearance, before a cheering crowd.

By 1843, he was an almost total invalid and forced to admit that he could no longer make his habitual hobble along the path to Rachel's grave. By 1844, having lost all power of voluntary motion, the pathetic old man suffered the ignominy of having to be lifted in and out of his bed and his favorite chair. Largely, his mind was still clear, his will as strong as ever, and he was able to write short letters. "I am swollen from my toes to the crown of my head," he wrote in one to his foster son, "and in bandages to my hips."

Inexplicably, a painter from France arrived on the scene with the glorious thought in mind that he would paint a portrait of Old Hickory in retirement. What he found was, as one biographer described him, "a tall man propped up in a chair, fighting for breath, his face a mask of swollen flesh crossed by the lines of pain; one eye was covered by a white scar, the other a glowering slit between puffed eyelids. Jackson was a gruesome sight."

Mercifully, death came on June 8, 1845, at the age of seventy-eight. He was irascible and feisty to the very end. Just before his death, he wrote the last of many letters to Washington, advising the administration on issues of the day. This one was to President James Polk, with advice about the country's economy and a warning to the new Secretary of the Treasury about redeeming worthless Texas script. Later, when he collapsed back in his bed in exhaustion, his adopted son, Andrew Jackson, Jr., took his hand and whispered in his ear, "Father, how do you feel? Do you know me?"

Jackson opened one eye, with a show of indignation, "Know

you?" he echoed tartly, "Yes I know you. I would know you *all* if I could see. Bring me my specs."

When he heard some of the people assembled by his bed moaning with grief, he said his final words, "What is the matter with my dear children? Have I alarmed you? Do not cry. Be good children and we will all meet in heaven."

What did Jackson finally die of? Just about everything. His debilitating illnesses can be traced back through his life—some to his childhood. Certainly he suffered from acute recurrent and chronic infections. His respiratory tract was infected from top to bottom. Most noteworthy were his bronchiectasis and his putrid lung abscess, the latter left over from his duel with Charles Dickenson. His gastrointestinal tract was a constant source of irritation, with spastic colitis or ulcerative colitis producing continual flare-ups of diarrhea, pain, cramps, and bleeding. These symptoms also were often aggravated by his treatments, such as lead, an irritant for the intestinal tract, and calomel, a mercury compound which in itself can produce a raging colitis. The bullet wound in his shoulder was the site of a draining osteomyelitis, spitting bits of pus, clothing and bone for years after the original injury. Rotten teeth, draining sinuses and constant blepharitis and conjunctivitis added to his miseries.

With the 20/20 vision of hindsight, it seems most likely that his final illness, described as dropsy and heart failure, was really due to nephrotic changes in the kidneys caused by amyloidosis. Intermittent fluid retention over a period of fifteen years finally culminating in massive edema of the whole body, including the face, is not the usual picture of congestive heart failure. The odds are much more in favor of secondary amyloidosis with fluid retention due to a nephrotic kidney. This type of amyloid disease always follows many years of infection—colitis, lung abscess, osteomyelitis—all conditions that Andrew Jackson harbored from his twenties till his death at age seventy-eight—a period of about fifty years!

One of our strongest presidents was one of our sickest.

5

The Inner Assassination
of Abraham Lincoln

Martin Van Buren was, from the standpoint of health, at the opposite pole from the man he succeeded, Andrew Jackson. Van Buren may well have been our healthiest president, a man who never had a serious illness until he was more than seventy years old.

The nation was not so fortunate with William Henry Harrison, who was sixty-eight when he took over the White House from Van Buren. Although he was in comparatively good health for his age, he had never had a very strong constitution and suffered from recurring digestive upsets and occasional bouts of malaria. The day of his inauguration, March 4, 1841, was one of the coldest inaugural days in history. Yet Harrison, trying to live up to his image as a fearless field general and Indian fighter, insisted on standing on the exposed platform without overcoat, hat, or gloves. Moreover, he delivered the longest inaugural address on record, lasting for an hour and forty-five minutes, in the teeth of a biting north wind.

It is little wonder that he contracted a severe chest cold and started his presidency confined to bed in the White House. By mid-March the cold, which had seemingly started to clear up, returned with greater severity. On Saturday, March 27, he suffered a severe chill while holding a cabinet meeting and was immediately ordered back to bed by his personal physician, Dr. Thomas Miller. The next day he was flushed with fever and beset by an almost insatiable thirst. The diagnosis was pneumonia,

complicated by a severe intestinal inflammation and a liver condition that unquestionably was jaundice. Other physicians were
called in as his condition became alarming. Unfortunately, the
battery of doctors began a series of "cures" that aggravated Harrison's condition. They used suction cups and stinging ointments
on his side, in a treatment popularly known as "blistering." They
administered drastic doses of cathartics—castor oil and calomel,
and ipecac, a powerful emetic. No one seemed to remember that
the patient had a history of colitis and that even mild laxatives
brought about strong reactions.

When the consequent purging and vomiting left the President totally debilitated, the physicians did an about-face and
began to administer opium, camphor, and shots of brandy. When
the patient grew weaker instead of responding, the desperate
doctors resorted to the most primitive Indian remedies, including "Virginia snakeweed" and crude petroleum. Hepatitis set in,
along with constant, watery diarrhea. On April 4—one month
after the inauguration—William Henry Harrison lapsed into delirium and coma and died of lobar pneumonia with pleurisy and
overwhelming septicemia.

With this, the first death of a president in office, the nation
faced an historic crisis: the matter of presidential succession. The
cabinet, Congress, and top legal authorities held numerous conflicting views regarding the situation and the interpretation of
the Constitution itself. The office might not have been filled for
months had not two decisive actions been taken. The first was on
the part of the esteemed Daniel Webster, who knew exactly what
had to be done. He sent his son, Fletcher, riding into Virginia
posthaste to alert John Tyler and bring him back to Washington.
Tyler, for his part, as vice-president, knew that he was now in
full command. He cited constitutional language, "In case of the
Removal of the President from Office, or his Death, Resignation,
or Inability to discharge the Powers and Duties of the said Office,
the same shall devolve on the Vice President."

The test came quickly. When Tyler was handed an official
document to sign, he noted that the words "Acting President"
were written below the space for his name. Taking the second
decisive action, he signed the paper, but only after obliterating

"Acting" with a bold stroke of his pen. He thus resolved the question of the moment, although it was to surface on other occasions, not always with such decisive results.

Tyler *almost* became the only president ever to die in office as the result of an accident. On February 28, 1844, he and some 350 other dignitaries boarded the Navy's showpiece, the steam frigate *U.S.S. Princeton,* to view the latest in armament. At the height of the proceedings a new bow gun, named the *Peacemaker,* exploded. Eight men, including the Secretary of State, the Secretary of the Navy, and Tyler's future father-in-law, were killed. The President was spared only because he had just gone below-decks for a few minutes.

Tyler not only survived his only term in office, but was married while still in the White House to Julia Gardner. He is the most notable president in one respect: the father of the most children. He had seven by Julia, to add to nine that he fathered by his first wife, Letitia, who had died five months after he took office.

The nation had another close call during the administration that followed, that of James Knox Polk. Polk entered the White House in excellent health, a man described as temperate, industrious, punctual, calm, and unemotional—a nonsmoker and an abstainer. Yet he had a frail physique and was apparently not hardy enough to discharge the heavy demands of office without great personal sacrifice. His own diary registered a steady decline, with entries describing heat exhaustion, chills, malaria, gastrointestinal upsets, dysentery, and increasing fatigue. Unlike Jackson and several other presidents who were so engrossed in the challenges and the stature of the office that they were able to ignore serious disabilities, Polk was motivated by a compulsive sense of duty. He established long-range plans which he pursued relentlessly, never taking time off for relaxation and unable to enjoy occasional programs of entertainment that were presented at the White House. "The Presidency is not a bed of roses," he once wrote in his diary, painstakingly describing the pressures, labors, and anxieties that made the job one of the most gruelling and unrewarding on earth.

By the time Polk left the Capitol on March 5, 1849, he had

aged so much in four years that his friends were shocked. He was badly enervated. He was in great pain from chronic diarrhea. He had a fever and was finding it difficult to breathe. On June 15, less than fifteen weeks after leaving the presidency, he died. He was only fifty-three.

If James Polk had barely managed to elude the allegations that election to the presidency was equivalent to signing one's death warrant, Zachary Taylor was not so fortunate. Taylor was sixty-four when elected, but his age was more a positive than a negative factor in an era when maturity and wisdom were important criteria in Washington. Furthermore, Taylor was one of the hardiest of men, a tough general who was known for having exposed himself to enemy fire countless times during campaigns along the frontiers and in Mexico. Short and stockily built, he was a determined and resolute leader, whose only physical defect seemed to be an imbalance of his eye muscles, called divergent strabimus, which often produced double vision. He had no difficulties in seeing when he was standing on the battlefield looking into the distance, but was bothered only when trying to focus on something, or some one, up close. He compensated for the imbalance by closing one eye tight, which gave him a droll, confidential look, as though he were about to make a joke. On more than one occasion, ladies became flustered because they thought that the President was winking at them.

On the Fourth of July, 1850, the President stood bareheaded in the sun for several hours during lengthy ceremonies commemorating the erection of the Washington Monument as well as America's independence. Against the advice of his physician, he later consumed large quantities of water, iced milk, and cherries. As a result, he became violently ill with diarrhea and stomach cramps, which continued through the night. To make matters worse, Taylor refused to take any of the remedies prescribed, except for a little brandy. He demurred on the basis of his acknowledged strong constitution and kept asserting that the pain would subside and the attack would pass.

Instead of abating, the illness worsened and spread. By July 6, the President had become increasingly dehydrated, despite the heavy intake of fluids. He had developed cramps in the calves of both legs. He was in the grip of a deep fever which, in the heat and humidity of Washington, reduced his strength and left him so debilitated that he could not sit up in bed without assistance. Two more Washington physicians were called in for consultation, and a specialist from Baltimore. It was already too late. On July 8, Zachary Taylor showed symptoms of massive mental distress and became incoherent. He had great difficulty breathing and was shaken by spells of vomiting. At 10:35 on the night of July 9, he died. The most likely cause was acute intestinal obstruction. The abdominal pain, diarrhea, vomiting, dehydration, and coma point to an abdominal catastrophe, such as perforation of a diverticulum of the colon or even a ruptured appendix. Sometime before the end, however, "Old Rough and Ready," as his troops called him, rallied long enough to make a final statement worthy of both a general and a president.

"I have always done my duty. I am ready to die. My only regret is for the friends I leave behind me."

The next president, Millard Fillmore, is probably best known as an example of The Great American Success Story, having risen from apprentice cloth-maker to chief executive. Luck certainly played a major role in the metamorphosis and he was so undistinguished that historians are hard-pressed to put their finger on any accomplishment except a negative one: he was a key figure in the decline and death of the Whig party.

As for his health, he was rarely sick, or even indisposed. A medical historian became so frustrated trying to uncover diagnostic facts about the President that he wrote in obvious disgust, "Fillmore is colorless, with no interesting diseases to compensate for the apparent dullness of his personality."

Not so the next in succession, Franklin Pierce. He had such a colorful—and tragic—medical history that this same medical historian was almost apologetic in trying to tone down his accounts of the President's physical, mental, and emotional problems. A clue to the situation lies in this quote from a statement made by a member of the presidential party, referring to Pierce during a postinaugural trip through New England. "I deeply, deeply deplore his habits. He drinks deep. . . . A great mistake was made in putting him in office at all."

But the story of Franklin Pierce, which deserves more than a cursory examination, will be told in some detail later.

James Buchanan, who immediately preceded Abraham Lincoln, was the only president who remained a bachelor while in office. Like Fillmore, he enjoyed steady good health, even though he took office at the age of sixty-five. In one way, he proved that a lack of stress was beneficial, since he functioned largely as a political figurehead and during the last two years in office was concerned largely with avoiding harsh confrontations and phasing out his regime. As a career diplomat, who was skillful in avoiding entanglements and emotional embroilments, he served in one unique way: he provided a sharp contrast to the next resident of the White House, to whom he gladly turned over all of his official duties and responsibilities.

"If you are as happy in entering the White House as I shall feel on returning to Wheatland," he remarked to Lincoln on March 4, 1861, "you are a happy man indeed."

However happily and auspiciously Abraham Lincoln may have entered the highest office in the land, the White House was to be the scene of prolonged affliction and agony not seen since the two administrations of Andrew Jackson. There were to be interminable periods when the failing health of the President and those around him would gravely affect the nation, as well as demand a special breed of courage on the part of the chief executive so afflicted. Some say that even the assassination had less impact on the course of events than would have occurred had he lived and been the victim of an incipient disease that would have been more devastating in the end than the quick, merciful bullet.

To see the man and the events in perspective, we turn to the late spring of 1863, a little more than two years after Lincoln had taken office. He had already issued his Emancipation Proclamation, a famous document, but one that actually freed few slaves since it exempted all areas under Union military occupation and exerted no control over the South. He was continually replacing indecisive and incompetent military commanders. He was heavily criticized for his handling of wartime mobilization, such as the Conscription Act, which touched off riots like the one in New York City, where nearly a thousand persons were killed and wounded. He was deeply disturbed, often depressed, by vicious attacks on his honor by the press. Typical was one claiming that "The people of the North owe Mr. Lincoln nothing but eternal hatred and scorn. There are 500,000 new-made graves; there are 500,000 orphans; there are 200,000 widows; there is a bottomless sea of blood . . . and these are the things which we owe Mr. Lincoln."

Such criticism was devastating to a man of Lincoln's temperament to begin with, but even more so since he was a frequent visitor to Army hospitals, where he moved from cot to cot, talking to and trying to comfort thousands of wounded soldiers.

Now he was faced with the threat of imminent invasion of the North, as General Robert E. Lee pressed forward. By June 15, Lincoln had issued a proclamation calling for 100,000 militiamen (over and above those recently conscripted) to resist the invasion. Thus far in the war, Lincoln and his administration had been labeled failures. The President was in constant anguish as he was hit from both sides. On the one hand were the radicals, called "Jacobins" (from the terrorists of the French Revolution), who relentlessly attacked Lincoln for not mounting a more vigorous offensive and pushing on to Richmond. On the other hand stood the "Copperheads," who advocated peace and a political compromise with the South, believing that it was impossible for the Union to win the war. Both sides hammered away at Lincoln —vociferously, through publications, through legislative action, and sometimes by exerting underhanded pressures. Though the President resisted all attempts—surreptitious or honorable—to budge him from the course of action that he felt was just, the toll was backbreaking.

In a bizarre sense, anguish and internal agony were Lincoln's allies rather than enemies. He endured the most brutal censure and castigation without flinching or backing away because his mind was already attuned to dark moods and foreboding outlooks. His friends, though devoted and loyal, admitted that they did not fully understand his temperament. More than one referred to his state of mind as "terrible," and his personality that of a man forever tortured by inner devils and personal misgivings. Even in the "enjoyment" of music, he turned to songs that were plaintive and sad. His favorite, for example, was a ballad entitled "Twenty Years Ago," which recounted the melancholy tale of a man revisiting the haunts of his youth and a graveyard where boyhood friends were buried.

The frustrations of the presidency, and what he often referred to as his personal failures and inadequacies, plunged him into periods of depression that today would have greatly troubled a White House physician or psychiatric consultant. Yet these depressions were not bred by his election to office.

The periods of depression that plagued Abraham Lincoln during most of his adult life have been explained in various ways, both psychologically and physiologically, by biographers and medical specialists alike. Regardless of the origins, medical implications, or diagnoses, they did play such a decided role in his life that they affected many of his outlooks and decisions while in office. And they did cause many periods of great anguish that would have immobilized a leader who was less courageous and determined.

Early in his life, these depressions were often associated with his relationships with women. The classic example—though one that has been overdramatized and exaggerated by many biographers—was his love affair with Ann Rutledge, the blonde, blue-eyed daughter of a tavern owner in New Salem, Illinois, where he had received an appointment as postmaster. The two became engaged in the spring of 1835, when Lincoln was twenty-six. But Ann became desperately ill during the summer and on August 25 died, with her fiancé at her bedside. Lincoln became so profoundly depressed, far beyond the bounds of normal grief, that he could not eat, paced the floor at night without being able to sleep, and was totally unable to return to work for many weeks. His friends described his condition as being "in the shadow of madness" and were constantly worried that he would attempt to commit suicide.

Part of his extreme melancholia has been attributed to the

fact that he was at the time being treated for chills and fever, an "ague" that was probably malaria. However, such an illness would not account for the extreme depression, nor would it account for his depressive actions some six years later, at the time of another love affair. In 1839, Lincoln met Mary Todd, of Springfield, Illinois, where he was a member of the state legislature and had a law partnership. Mary, twenty-one, was imaginative, impulsive, emotional, and a real "belle" who liked to dance and attend parties without letup. Though pert and vivacious, she could also be petulant and contrary, and always liked to have the upper hand. It seemed unlikely that she would ever be attracted to a man like Lincoln, who gave the impression of being shy and plodding, and still retaining many of the characteristics of his backwoods origins. Mary was fascinated by politics and was always outspoken in her opinions about the affairs of the day.

It was Mary, rather than Abe, who pushed the relationship from romance to engagement, and who ultimately pressed for a wedding date. The time she selected was January 1, 1841, which seemed suitable enough to Lincoln at first. But he became more and more apprehensive and dejected as the date approached. His friends attributed it to nothing more than the usual case of the jitters, since they considered that Mary Todd was a great catch for any man. The appointed date arrived. Everything was in readiness. The guests were assembled. The bride waited in an outer room, dressed in a silken wedding gown, with a veil over her face and flowers in her hair. When the time for the ceremony came and passed, the guests began to fidget and look about restlessly. Mary became alarmed when other members of the party who had gone to find out what had happened to the groom returned just as perplexed as when they left.

Not until early the next morning did his friends find him, in hiding, and looking as distraught and agitated as though he had committed a crime and was trying to escape from the police. He had no explanation, and in fact seemed totally incapable of explaining what had happened or why he had vanished without at least informing his bride-to-be that he was unable to go through with the wedding ceremony. His state of mind was so unstable that his close friends rotated around the clock in keeping a tight watch on him, for fear that he would become violent or attempt to commit suicide.

In the end, not even those closest to Lincoln were able to be of much help, as his depression stretched on for weeks, then months, and for almost a year. All during this time, he was absent from the state assembly and seemed unable to hold a regular job. Mary Todd and the members of her family considered the young man insane and purposely avoided him. In view of this, it is almost unbelievable that Lincoln finally did marry Mary Todd, on November 4, 1842. He recovered from his deep despondency largely through the efforts of Dr. Anson Henry and his intimate friend, Joshua Speed, who persuaded him to return to his birthplace, Kentucky, and convalesce. Some historians suggest that Lincoln was actually confined to a sanitarium there, but the evidence seems to be that he was largely in the care of members of the family. Ultimately, it was Dr. Henry who persuaded Mary Todd and Abe to see each other again and continue the relationship that resulted in marriage.

With this kind of mental and medical history in the background, it is no wonder that the pressures of the presidency and the anguish of wartime decisions should have exacted a high price in terms of Abraham Lincoln's peace of mind in the middle of his first term of office. How did depressions affect Lincoln's ability to function as president? The subject has long fascinated psychiatrists and other specialists in the field of mental health. Characteristic is an editorial that appeared sixty years ago in *Psychoanalytic Review,* which concluded that "Lincoln suffered lifelong from periodic depression—indeed that he never seemed entirely free from some vestiges of the more intense episodes." The illness he suffered was described as a "mental sluggishness," during which the thought processes became slow and labored, with the patient sometimes experiencing difficulty in forming sentences and selecting words and phrases to communicate what he wanted to say. During the most acute phases, Lincoln found it almost impossible to make decisions, partly because he was continually groping for facts that seemed to have slipped from his memory. Typical of the illness was Lincoln's frequent assessment of himself as being unworthy of some honor, or unequal to the great task before him. These were all characteristic symptoms of a severe depressive state, with feelings of inadequacy, poor self-image, and a "crisis of confidence." Lincoln himself recognized these pathological states and referred to them as his "hypos," presumably a contraction of hypochondria.

Consider, though, that this morbid type of illness also relentlessly pushed him into situations where his stature rose to great heights. "Lincoln was a psychoneurotic," wrote another biographer, "but that phase of his character went into the mosaic of his intensely interesting personality and was an indissoluble part of his greatness." We can almost visualize some of the phrases and messages of his most inspired speeches being formed as the man wrestled with these inner doubts and grievances and translated them in terms of what the nation and the people were facing during the war years.

Most of Lincoln's biographers refer to his periods of depression, some glancing over the evidence as though it were perhaps too personal or sensitive to inject into the profile of the man, others attempting to play the part of psychoanalyst themselves and relate the moods to "mother image" complications or the hostility he felt toward his father. But few have paid much attention to the fact that Lincoln was plagued with numerous physiological afflictions, including serious diseases and eventually ominous symptoms of an illness that would have proved fatal before the middle of his second term had he not been assassinated.

Consider the susceptible body type of the man to begin with, as described by one who knew him:

"Mr. Lincoln was wiry, sinewy and raw-boned—thin through the breast to the back and narrow across the shoulders. Standing, he leaned forward; was somewhat stoop-shouldered, inclining to the consumptive in build. His usual weight was about 180 pounds and height 6 feet 4 inches. . . . His organization worked slowly. His blood had to run a long distance from his heart to the extremities of his frame, and his nerve force had to travel through dry ground, a wide circuit, before his muscles were obedient to his will. His structure was loose and leathery, his body shrunk and shriveled; he had dark skin and dark hair, and looked woe-struck. The whole man, body and mind, worked against more or less friction and creaked as if it needed oiling. His circulation was slow and sluggish."

His ears, which were large and thick-lobed, extended at almost right angles to his long, thin face, giving rise to ridicule by some that he was "horse-faced." There is no doubt that his appearance helped to develop him from early youth into a person who was acutely sensitive. His appearance was all the more open to comment because of his speech, which usually emerged as a slow, drawling monotone, and because of his very deliberate manner and seemingly sluggish mental response. Those who met him never forgot him. His voice was rasping and high-pitched, tending to become shrill and squeaky whenever he became emotional. From a medical viewpoint, he was afflicted with permanent nervous lesions, or deficiencies that were detrimental both to his voice and his manner of speaking. From a political viewpoint, he had everything against him as a person who throughout his lifetime had to rely on public speaking to further his career and gain his objectives.

Lincoln was also afflicted with serious defects in his vision. His left eye had a tendency to turn upward, leaving more white, or scleral, surface exposed and giving him a staring effect that was all the more grotesque because it was only in the left eye. This has been diagnosed as hyperphoria, or weakness of the muscles, and was exaggerated into a severe cross-eyed look whenever Lincoln became excited or agitated. This condition, more than simply an inconvenience, had to be compensated for by almost total dependence on the right eye for general vision and reading. It contributed intensely to Lincoln's frequent nervous attacks, characterized not only by burning eyestrain, but by sick headaches, indigestion, and nausea. When he became president, Lincoln installed a couch near his desk so that he could lie down with a cold compress over his eyes whenever one of these attacks got the better of him.

The disability in the left eye, along with a weakening of the facial muscles on that side and probably some of the other physical and mental ailments, seem to have originated with an accident that Abe suffered when he was ten years old. The boy had been assigned the job of tending a horse that was hitched to a circular mill for grinding corn. When the horse slowed down, young Lincoln gave her a whack with a stick. Unfortunately, she kicked back, striking him in the head and knocking him unconscious. When he was found stretched out on the ground, he was thought to be dead. Despite the severity of the blow, which left a permanent depression in his forehead, he received no medical attention, revived, and was apparently all right. Years later, when Lincoln sought medical help for headaches and melancholia, a doctor questioned him about the injury, but without being able to make any specific diagnosis. Today, medical opinion holds that the skull had been fractured at the point of impact, deeply enough so that there was brain damage. It is likely that a subdural hematoma developed, a swelling of considerable size filled with blood from ruptured vessels. The damage to the left frontal lobe played a part in the nature of his personality, as well as in causing physical and mental imbalances.

It was characteristic of Abraham Lincoln as president—as it had been throughout his earlier career—that injuries, stresses and strains, disabilities, and serious illnesses served more as catalysts activating him on the road to historic eminence than as deterrents. Because of his problems with vision, for example, and because he had to read voluminous texts as both attorney and statesman, he unconsciously schooled himself in rapid-reading and scanning techniques that were not perfected by educators for several generations after his time. Finding it too tiring, and often painful, to reread lengthy documents as most of his colleagues did, he developed an extraordinarily retentive memory. Oftentimes, when he appeared to be withdrawn and slow-witted, he was in fact mentally retrieving some of the information he had rapidly stored in his mind.

Lincoln often "saw" things in ways that were especially meaningful to him, almost as a mystic. His outlook was not entirely mental or spiritual, however, but to some extent based on physical aberrations. Consider, for example, the way in which he mystically interpreted his first experience with diplopia, or double vision. The date was November 6, 1860. It was Election Day, and a time when he was under great mental and emotional strain. He had spent most of the day at his office in the state house and although he appeared outwardly calm, one of his friends later described him as being "nervous, fidgety, intensely excited." He was, in effect, setting himself up, unconsciously, for the unique experience that was to take place. This is best described in Lincoln's own words:

"It was just after my election in 1860, when the news had been coming in thick and fast all day and there had been a great 'Hurrah boys!' so that I was well tired out and went home to rest, throwing myself upon a lounge in my chamber. Opposite to where I lay was a bureau with a swinging glass upon it, and in looking in that glass, I saw myself reflected nearly full length; but my face, I noticed, had two separate and distinct images, the tip of the nose of one being about three inches from the tip of the other. I was a little bothered, perhaps startled, and got up and looked in the glass; but the illusion vanished. On lying down again, I saw it a second time, plainer, if possible, than before, and then I noticed that one of the faces was a little paler, say five shades, than the other."

Lincoln was unable to shake this vision from his mind, despite the activity and excitement of the election. "When I went home," he recalled, "I told my wife about it and a few days after I tried the experiment again when, sure enough, the thing came back again, but I never succeeded in bringing the ghost back after that, though I once tried very industriously to show it to my wife who was worried about it somewhat. She thought it was a 'sign' that I was to be elected to a second term of office, and that the paleness of one of the faces was an omen that I should not see life through the last term."

This note of foreboding pinpoints a factor that was to affect the President's outlook and mental health increasingly during his years in the White House.

Lincoln had to contend not only with his own depressions and discouragements, but increasingly with the mental problems and personality changes that seriously afflicted his wife. At the time of their marriage, Mary Todd Lincoln had been an inspiration, a girl with everything that her peers envied: liveliness, charm, good taste, and if not beauty at least a special vivacious-ness that made her seem pretty and pert. By the time Lincoln reached the White House, his wife had become an unbelievably changed woman, the result of a strange metamorphosis that had started to take place after their children were born. Her steady nature had turned into stubbornness and constant demand; her pep changed to pepper and sarcasm; her love degenerated into an insane jealousy.

Even shortly after their marriage and for the first decade of their marriage, the Lincolns showed evidence of incompatibility. There was a strain to begin with, since Mary's parents had made it clear that their daughter had not shown good judgment in marrying a man who had not only displayed severe emotional instability but was far below her socially. During these years, Abe relied heavily on his wife to motivate him, to drive him toward a career that he was unsure of, and to keep him on the right track. But after the children were requiring both her attention and constant effort, the situation reversed itself. Mary seemed to be less and less competent to handle household and family problems, while Abe continually had to set aside his own work and take over duties that should have been handled by his wife. Whenever Mary did not get her way, she became agitated, often resorting to tantrums and sometimes to physical assaults on her husband. Neighbors reported instances in which Abe was seen scurrying from the house, often with a child in tow, while Mary stood in the doorway screaming after them and occasionally brandishing a makeshift weapon. There were times, too, when she would greet her returning husband after such an episode by pouring a bucket of water on him from an upstairs window as he reached the front door.

Lincoln faced the steady disintegration of Mary's personality with the kind of sad stoicism which was to become symbolic of his later personality. He never retaliated or showed emotional outbursts himself. Instead he would try to soothe the irritation by remarking, "Now, Mother, calm down. Calm down."

By the time Lincoln had proved himself in politics and was nominated for president by the Republican party in May 1860, Mary should have been riding the crest. She had a fine family, a wide circle of acquaintances, and a reasonable income. She had always been interested in politics and ambitious to be at the forefront of the action. On the surface, everything seemed to be going exactly the way she had dreamed about many years earlier. Instead, she was dissatisfied and irascible. In addition to the marked change in personality that relatives and friends alike had observed in her, she was afflicted with physical ailments, some of which were undoubtedly the consequences of her mental state. She had developed headaches that were persistent and recurrent, and at times unbearable. Not infrequently, they necessitated her confinement to bed for days at a time. The situation had long since become so bad that Abe was no longer able to sacrifice his own time and had to count on one of Mary's cousins to stay at the house and take care of the children.

Very few people realized it at the time, but when Lincoln was elected president, he had to face the staggering challenge of entering the White House with a wife who was no longer able to handle even the most commonplace family emergency. Her conduct was erratic and unpredictable. She was acutely sensitive to criticism and unable to respond positively to practical suggestions or advice. Those who began to associate with the President in taking over official duties tried to avoid her, as a violently complaining termagant whose tantrums were often so severe that they turned into frightening convulsions. She was also developing obsessions, compulsions, and signs of paranoia, exhibiting wild changes of mood that were sometimes dangerous to her own person, as well as to anyone else who happened to cross her at the time. She could be pouting and tearful, sulking by herself and seemingly desirous of having no contact with anyone, then all at once starting to make demands hysterically and screaming at servants and family members alike. She did have "good days," when she seemed to be effusive with good cheer, planning picnics with the children in the countryside or selecting guests for a dinner party, but these periods became fewer and further between. "The hell-cat gets more hell-catical every day" is the way the White House servants expressed it.

By 1863, as Abraham Lincoln was facing some of his most mind-wrenching military decisions, he was also trying desperately to cope with another pathological development that afflicted his wife: delusions of grandeur. Her extravagances increased geometrically with the change in her mental state. She acquired an overwhelming passion for lavish gowns and would spend many days and hundreds of dollars on shopping sprees in New York City. Her bills became monstrous, despite the continuing pleas of the President, since she was obsessed with the idea that she could surpass wealthy socialites of the rich Eastern cities only by outdressing them. She was so aware of the power of money that she devised a scheme for selling the manure from the White House stables in order to acquire extra cash.

Mary's delusions and obsessions were the result of numerous disturbances, physiological and mental alike. Later in life she became the victim of "a cerebral disease" and intense neuralgia which made her cry out on occasion that she had "hot wires being drawn through her eyes" and "steel springs in her head." At one time she moaned that her "brain was on fire with pain." These attacks brought on periods of irrational thought and behavior. She was constantly worried about plots to kill her. She heard voices and had numerous hallucinations. A typical complaint was that she had been seized by an Indian who was pulling wires out of her head.

In one sense, Mary's deteriorating health was as debilitating to Abraham Lincoln as though he were suffering some of these afflictions himself. It is certain that her outbursts and her pain diverted his attention frequently and disastrously from the affairs of state and the immense problems of administration during the Civil War. In another sense, though, his wife's irrational demands and vicious behavior served to increase his own strength and endurance. By the time he was half-way through his first term and facing some of the bitterest decisions that ever had to be made by an American president, he was more than equal to the task. He had acquired infinite patience and self-control, so that the angriest outcries of his detractors and the most brutal editorials of an often antagonistic press did not throw him off balance or force him to swerve from his convictions.

Nevertheless, it required a special kind of courage for a man in Lincoln's position to meet his day-to-day responsibilities while these marital storms were raging all around him. Mary constantly attempted to interfere with the President's decisions, even to the point of accusing him of being influenced by other women. She was uncontrollably jealous, as has been documented in numerous biographies.

Typical was the instance in early 1864 when Mary Todd Lincoln insisted on accompanying her husband on one of his frequent inspection tours of Union headquarters camps in the field. When they arrived at the headquarters of General Ulysses S. Grant, whom Lincoln had just commissioned as the highest ranking officer in the army, Mrs. Grant was also there. Mary Lincoln became visibly upset when the general's wife came over and sat beside her and made it quite clear by her words and actions that she considered this a serious affront and that she was to be—literally—accorded the same treatment as a queen.

On another presidential visit to troops in the field, Lincoln inadvertently reviewed the ranks of officers and men while accompanied both by the commanding officer, General Ord, and Ord's wife, who was an experienced horsewoman. Mary, who had been left on the sidelines in the security and comfort of a carriage, was livid when she saw the inspection party returning —with a *woman*. Mary screamed insults at Mrs. Ord, accused her of having intentions on her husband, and was so vile in her language that the astonished lady burst into tears and was upset for several days.

The effect of this episode, and others, on the President was marked. He is said to have borne the outbursts "as Christ might have done . . . with supreme calmness and dignity." On such occasions, he would often call her "Mother," and attempt to soothe her by explaining that no one had meant her any affront. His words might or might not have the desired effect, but if she once heard him trying to apologize to anyone who had been the target of her stinging tongue, she would erupt all over again, until he had to turn and walk away. Often he would cover his face so that those present could not see the extent of the emotion that overcame him.

The tragedy of it all was that Mary's violent eruptions and personality changes had nothing to do with the President's capabilities as a husband and father. She was a very sick woman.

There is every likelihood that she had general paresis of the insane or luetic infection of the central nervous system—to put it bluntly, central nervous system syphilis.

No matter how Lincoln tried to hide his feelings after one of Mary's fits, he could not conceal the melancholy that engulfed him for days afterward.

His depressions were deepened by the tragic cases of their children, William and Tad. William died of typhoid in February 1862. His mother, who had refused to enter his room when he was dying, collapsed and suffered convulsions upon hearing word of his death. She lay in bed for days, occasionally arising to wander about the White House in the nude. She had illusions that someone was trying to murder her and began having visions in which she saw her dead son approaching in the company of other relatives who had long since died. She could barely eat and was terrified of going to sleep. The President tried to calm her and guide her back to reality, reluctantly admitting to those closest to him that he thought her to be at least partially insane. But Lincoln himself was fighting an inner battle, gripped by a deep melancholy that he could not entirely shake for several months.

Thomas Lincoln played a part in the medical story of the President in an entirely different way. Nicknamed "Tad" because, as an infant, he had an oversized head and resembled a tadpole to his father, he was a clear example of the hyperactive child syndrome. As is common in this puzzling disability, he was emotionally unstable, given to temper tantrums, abrupt changes in mood, and impulsiveness. He was constantly disturbing other children, including his older brothers, Robert and William, who were even-tempered and bright. Tad, who was eight at the time his father took office, was described as a "veritable whirlwind." On the day of the inauguration, he displayed characteristic behavior by circulating among the bystanders and pointing out other men as "Old Abe" to credulous strangers. On another occasion, when the President wanted to introduce his sons to a visitor, he threw himself on the floor like a doormat and refused to budge. In the White House, he was described as having a "mercurial temperament," not unlike his mother's. He whittled the furniture, broke mirrors and china, and squeezed paint all over the walls from some tubes being used in the completion of his mother's portrait. He possessed a devilish imagination, which on one occasion inspired him to drive a team of goats through the house, pulling him behind them on a chair. On another occasion, he almost precipitated a riot by spreading a large Confederate flag on the White House lawn, and later by firing guns from an upstairs window.

Throughout it all, Lincoln displayed an almost saintly restraint and remarkable endurance. In fact, he really showed great love and compassion for this strange child whose behavior, in those days, was considered nothing less than demonic. Tad resembled his father in many ways, except for his speech, which was garbled by a cleft palate. Time and again, the President commented that Tad's outrageous acts and antisocial conduct played a part in brightening the gloomy halls of the White House and the somber lives of its principal inhabitants.

These were some of the disorders that attacked the President from the outside and which intensified those inner conflicts from which he could not escape through any medication or treatment then known to the medical profession. Many of the physical ailments he brought with him to the White House were minor in nature, and not uncommon to the general populace—such as chronic constipation, corns and callouses, insomnia, low blood pressure, various fevers, latent tuberculosis, and gradual hardening of the arteries. Yet they contributed to the overall clinical portrait of a president who literally lived and functioned in anguish, a man who—like some of the world's greatest poets—derived inspiration from maladies of body and mind that would have disabled most other human beings.

The Gettysburg Address is a classic example.

By mid-1863, when the sounds and smells of battle were not far from Washington itself, and when the challenges of being both a civilian and military chief were at their peak, Lincoln was at his finest level of performance. The Battle of Gettysburg, from July 1 to 3, was proving to be the turning point of the Civil War and certainly one of the costliest for both sides in the numbers of troops killed, wounded, and missing. When Vicksburg, Mississippi, was captured with its garrison of 20,000 men on July 4 after a six-week siege and Port Hudson, Louisiana, a few days later, the Confederacy was split. The situation was drastically changed from that day one year earlier when Lincoln had such great despair that he later said, "Things had gone from bad to worse, until I felt that we had reached the end of our rope on the plan we had been pursuing, that we had about played our last card, and must change our tactics or lose the game." He had been tormented by congressmen, senators, cabinet members, and others who were endlessly trying to pull him in opposite directions. Worse still, he found it all but impossible to find military leaders with leadership and command abilities, and by the end of the year had to remove General George McClellan from the field.

Abraham Lincoln was, in the summer of 1863, a different man. Though still sad, contemplative, and evidencing periods of melancholy, he had emerged from two years of continuing indecisiveness and become recognized as a world statesman. Half a year had passed since he had issued the famous Emancipation Proclamation, which abolished slavery in the Confederate States of America and established his firmness in taking a stand on vital issues.

By the fall of 1863, Lincoln had decided to visit the battlefield at Gettysburg to participate in the dedication of the cemetery on November 19. By this time, the significance of the battle for the North had been recognized by both sides and the President's attendance would be symbolic.

Lincoln almost canceled the trip.

Several days before, Tad had been confined to bed with aches and a high temperature, which the doctor had diagnosed as scarlet fever. Actually, it was smallpox, from which he soon recovered. By the time the President left Washington on November 18, he had also contracted the disease and was in the incubation period. As a result, his mental and physical capabilities were already in that state of limbo we experience prior to illness, a condition that may have had something to do with the brevity and tone of the address. During the trip back to the capital on the nineteenth, Lincoln suffered a severe headache, accompanied by heavy perspiration and a feeling of great exhaustion. He found little relief by dousing his head in cold water and lying down in the drawing room of his private railway car. As soon as he arrived at the White House, he went to bed, aching all over and so obviously ill that his personal physician, Dr. Robert K. Stone, was called in. The diagnosis ranged from at first a bad cold to "bilious fever," then to scarlet fever, and finally to smallpox when his skin began to break out in the telltale signs: red spots, pimples, and water blisters. Dr. Stone feared most that the blisters would become infected, a frequent occurrence in smallpox, since Lincoln's constitution was not very rugged at the time and he had been subjected to great stress over a long period.

Even more alarmed was the nation's press when the news leaked out that the President had smallpox, then a much-dreaded disease. Reports, though not enlightening, were grim and speculative. The news spread with surprising rapidity abroad, where it was received with even more gravity and dire predictions. The *London Spectator*, considered a reputable voice in English-speaking countries, but apparently without many facts to tap, made the unfortunate editorial decision to consider how the death of the President might affect America's critical civil war. Who would take over the leadership of the country? After searching out and publishing a brief biography of the little-known vice-president, Hannibal Hamlin, the editors concluded that the "substitution of a Hannibal for an Abraham" would be devastating to the affairs of the world, let alone the United States.

The uneventful recovery of the patient, with an enforced period of more than three weeks of rest, proved to be a boon for Lincoln. For the first time in many months, he was able to escape the hounding politicians and favor seekers whom he was never able to turn from his doorstep without feelings of guilt that he might overlook someone really in need. When asked how he had felt when he contracted the highly contagious smallpox, he remarked with a refreshed sense of humor that now he had something that he could give to everybody! By mid-December he was completely back on his feet, his spirit bolstered also by news at the end of November that General Ulysses S. Grant had won a decisive victory at Chattanooga, Tennessee.

The Gettysburg Address is, without question, one of the

great historical documents. Historian Allan Nevins attributed to it a far broader insight than that which related to the United States and the Civil War. Abraham Lincoln, he said, "chose to speak not to his country alone but to aspirants for freedom in all countries, and not to his own moment in history but to the centuries. The proposition that all men are created equal was a truth for the ages, and if America, under God, achieved a new birth of freedom, it would stand as an object lesson to all nations."

The speech is also a reflection of the man, the sense of a melancholy of historic proportions that was both his and the nation's. It was not a speech born of healthful exuberance or robust optimism or vigorous assertiveness. It was an expression of all the anguish and agony, the heartache and despair, and the classic illnesses from which America itself was recovering.

During 1864 and into 1865, the military dominance of the North continued upward, a fact that would seemingly have given Lincoln some relief from the continuous strain he had been under. Yet his face seemed to grow more haggard and his eyes more sunken as the months progressed. He participated in the campaign for reelection in the early autumn of 1864 with the gloomy prediction that he would be defeated because of the number and viciousness of his enemies. Some of his friends hoped that he would be, for his own sake. An old friend, Noah Brooks, who had not seen him for a couple of years, commented that the way he had aged in that time span was appalling. The renowned editor, Horace Greeley, recalled him as being so "weary and haggard" when he saw him in early 1865 "that he seemed unlikely to live out his term." Augustus Saint-Gaudens, one of the world's great sculptors, who was shown a life mask of Lincoln's face that was made by another sculptor at about this time, insisted that it must have been a "death mask," made after the assassination.

Historians, as well as psychics, have placed considerable significance on the fact that Abraham Lincoln prophecied on numerous occasions that he would not survive his second term. He was a great believer in dreams, which sometimes gave him premonitions of death. A characteristic example was the one that occurred several weeks before the assassination. He dreamed that he was hearing distant sobs in the White House and was wandering from room to room trying to find the people who were making them. Entering the East Room, he was startled to see a funeral bier on which lay a corpse draped in vestments. Soldiers stood guard, surrounded by mourners. When he asked who was dead, he was told that it was the President.

Although he mentioned assassination on this and other dream-related occasions, it is possible that this morbidity originated more from the failing state of his health than from the actual fear of being killed. On the morning of March 14, 1865, the President was so tired, that he could not get out of bed and carry on his customary matinal activities. Dr. Robert K. Stone was again called in and, after preliminary examination, diagnosed the illness as "exhaustion, complete exhaustion." Surgeon General Joseph K. Barnes, noting that Lincoln's skin looked very sallow, that his eyes seemed more sunken than ever, and that he was quite emaciated, feared that the President was "on the verge of a nervous breakdown." The *New York Herald Tribune* published an editorial asserting that if steps were not taken at once to preserve the President's health more effectively, he would never survive his term.

The *Tribune* and a few of the individuals who noted with alarm the indications of declining health were more perceptive than they could possibly have realized, based on evidence that was not even researched until the 1960s. In its issue of May 1972, *California Medicine* published an article on Lincoln entitled, "The Declining Health of the President," in which the following finding was made:

> The health of Abraham Lincoln in his last year of life was such as to preclude completion of his second term of office even if he had not been assassinated. Understandably, in the absence of a known organic basis for that unfavorable prognosis, the decline in the physical well-being of the President has been attributed to emotional factors attendant upon the burdens of office and a tragic war. . . .

The report presented conclusions that Lincoln had suffered for at least two years prior to his assassination with aortic insufficiency (poor functioning of the valve of the aorta carrying blood to all parts of the body) and that this disability was but one of several complications of a disease that was always fatal called "Marfan's syndrome." Some of the symptoms of this disorder, which is genetic in origin, are heart and eye problems, poor skeletal growth, and spidery, somewhat uncoordinated legs—all of which were present in Lincoln.

The author of the article, Dr. Harold Schwartz, an authority on Marfan's syndrome, more recently published an article in the *Western Journal of Medicine*, in which he made some specific and startling comparisons to prove his diagnosis. Lincoln had disproportionately long arms, hands, and feet; his middle finger was nearly half an inch longer than that of an ordinary hand; he squinted with his left eye; he complained often about poor circulation in his extremities—all symptoms of the disease. Dr. Schwartz, in his painstaking research, uncovered a unique piece of evidence disclosing that Lincoln had a specific cardiovascular problem associated with Marfan's: imperfect closure of the valves of the aorta. This disorder disrupted the flow of blood through the arteries, typically causing the vessels to throb excessively.

The most dramatic clue was a photograph of the President taken in 1863. His legs were crossed and the left foot, held off the floor, was blurred. This seemed curious, since the rest of the photograph was in sharp focus. Lincoln himself was perhaps the first to notice this seeming imperfection. When he asked his friend, Noah Brooks, whether the photographer might have made a slip of some kind, Brooks suggested that the blur was caused by throbbing arteries instead. Curious, the President sat down and crossed his legs in a similar pose. "That's it! That's it!" he exclaimed, pointing out that the foot was indeed throbbing.

The story was a favorite of biographers for a hundred years before anyone thought to question the reasons for the throbbing itself. That was when Dr. Schwartz stepped in with his surprising diagnosis. "Aortic regurgitation," he said, was the result of the disease. Supporting this contention were statements made by Lincoln shortly before his death that suggested that he was suffering from congestive heart failure in its early stages. One of these was his references to cold hands and feet; another his increasing frustrations over becoming so often and so easily fatigued, a condition that should not have been experienced by a man of fifty-six, who neither smoked nor drank, and was in the position—rare to the presidency—of facing *declining* stresses and pressures with each passing week.

The editorial in the *Western Journal of Medicine* was convincing enough to be featured in an article in *Time* magazine on May 22, 1978, with this statement: "Had John Wilkes Booth not fired the fatal shot on April 14, 1865, Lincoln would have died within a year from complications of Marfan's syndrome—for which there is still no cure."

If true, that would have condemned the President to anguish and suffering and the American people to trauma and conflict far more intense than anything that was triggered by the assassin's pistol at Ford's Theater in Washington on that tragic Good Friday evening.

6

Living with Demons

"The victims of it are to be pitied and compassionated just as the heirs of consumption and other hereditary diseases."

The statement was made by Abraham Lincoln, referring to the problems and tragedies of people who could not control their drinking. In this, he was a century ahead of his time, for it has been only within the two decades or so past that alcoholism has been recognized as a disease, even by the medical profession.

Not a few presidents were known for their proclivities as tipplers on occasion, both before and during their terms in the White House. Andrew Jackson was seen under the influence of alcohol on occasions and under circumstances that frequently led to brawls and injuries. Andrew Johnson is said to have hit the bottle more than he should have from time to time. Martin Van Buren, while always a gentleman, was known for his love of fine wines and vintage champagnes. And the old general, William Henry Harrison, while making campaign claims that he never drank anything more potent than hard cider, had a special penchant for strong Barbados rum.

Yet it is little known to most readers of American history that two presidents were alcoholics. Lincoln was undoubtedly aware of the first case, that of Franklin Pierce, who had left the White House only four years ahead of his arrival. He must also have been aware of the problems of Ulysses S. Grant, whom he appointed to the highest military post as general-in-chief in March 1864, and who would become president just four years after his death.

The alcoholism rate in America's top position—five percent —is comparable to the percentage of problem drinkers in the

United States as a whole, based on statistics that are generally, though not totally, reliable. The implications are, of course, much more horrendous. Who can envision a greater drinking problem than that of a *president* hitting the bottle every time he faced a crisis or difficult decision or was to appear in public as the spokesman of his country? We do not have to speculate or conjecture, for Pierce and Grant provide clear-cut pictures, though they are surprisingly different.

Franklin Pierce's drinking problems started while he was still a student at Bowdoin College in Maine in the early 1820s. During his sophomore year he joined a group of liberal students who sat up much of the night planning ways for improving their college, the country, and the world. Since he had to compete with some of the most lucid and outspoken voices on campus, including those of Nathaniel Hawthorne and Henry Wadsworth Longfellow, he occasionally turned to liquor to help loosen his tongue and sharpen his wits. He found that his oratory improved, a revelation that was to shape his drinking habits later in life, when he entered politics.

When Pierce was elected to Congress in 1833, his occasional need for alcohol was increased by the very nature of his environment. He lived in a boarding house with other bachelor lawmakers who were solid drinkers. Since he was known for his penchant for getting along with people and being a convivial companion, he could never refuse a social invitation or leave a party early, no matter how much of a workload he might have scheduled for the following day. Realizing that he did not hold his liquor well, he frequently ended up in drinking bouts with some of the harder drinkers, just to prove that he could compete on their level. His friends were considerably relieved when he married Jane Means Appleton, whose father was a Congregational minister and president of Bowdoin. They felt—mistakenly —that the effect of this relationship would most certainly be a beneficial one in the matter of his consumption and his behavior.

As is frequently the case with problem drinkers, he was driven more toward the bottle than away from it when his habits were disparaged. Jane's outlook was puritanical. To make matters worse, she was shy and retiring, so that she often took disturbing escape routes rather than attacking the problems openly. Pierce found himself more and more in the position of having to make excuses. He drank because he had been brought up in a gregarious society in which his home was an informal tavern and his father the tavern keeper. If he drank to excess, it was mainly because his mother was a heavy drinker and some of her weaknesses were passed along to the son.

Marriage proved an ineffective deterrent to his drinking for another reason: during the years from 1833 until 1842 when he served first as a congressman, then as senator from New Hampshire, his wife spent much of her time back at their home in Hillsborough. She hated Washington, D.C., was extremely uncomfortable at functions, whether social or official, and could not stand the climate, which affected her tubercular constitution adversely. So Franklin Pierce was largely left to his own devices—which often took the form of partying with his old drinking companions.

He was constantly making a fool of himself, as typified by the following account, which is mentioned in most of the sparse profiles and biographies that have been written about the man: one evening he and two friends decided after a few too many rounds of drinks to go to the theatre. As it turned out, their box was next to that of an army officer with whom they had already had some noisy disagreements. They became so boisterous that the play had to be stopped in mid-performance. When the officer tried to evict them from the theater, they threatened him with a pistol. The confrontation eventually developed into a street fight. Pierce was not seriously injured, but did end up in bed with a throbbing hangover and a severe case of pleurisy. The illness, which continued for several weeks and was accompanied by a deep depression, was undoubtedly aggravated by the suicidal pace of Pierce's dissipations.

In 1842, after constant nagging by his wife, he resigned from the Senate and returned to New Hampshire to continue his law practice. Establishing himself with considerable success, with only one period of upheaval when he accepted a temporary army command to fight in the Mexican War, he seemed to be more stable than he had been in many years. But the relatively happy years from 1848 to 1851 were suddenly cut short when some of his political friends, impressed by the good name he was making for himself in Concord, New Hampshire, where he practiced, induced him to return to the political scene. When he protested, they pointed out that it would all be strictly on paper—nothing even his wife could object to. They simply wanted to place his name before the Democratic convention as a presidential candidate, but only to be acted upon in the highly unlikely event that the convention should be deadlocked. He was titular head of the Democratic Party in New Hampshire, a position that was largely passive, and as such it would be a great honor for him to be recognized, and would certainly give a boost to his law practice. Knowing that the choice lay between James Buchanan, a strong contender, and Lewis Cass, a senator from Michigan, Pierce agreed, on condition that they keep it a secret from his wife, no matter how slim the chances were.

Buchanan and Cass, however, were so equally supported by the delegates that vote after vote failed to gain either the required two-thirds majority. Pierce's name was finally entered when the battle was still deadlocked after the thirty-fourth ballot. Fifteen ballots later, the convention reluctantly gave Pierce the necessary margin, as the only dark horse who could possibly keep the party from a disastrous split.

The news reached the future President as he and his wife were driving quietly in their carriage and a courier on horseback was dispatched to find them. Pierce could not believe what he was hearing. As for his wife, she fainted from the shock. Later, he tried with dismal failure to convince her that he had never sought the nomination and that, even so, there was little chance that the voters would choose him over a strong Whig candidate, General Winfield Scott, who had won honors on the field of battle in the fight against Mexico.

Jane Pierce was due for a second shock when her husband beat Scott in a surprising electoral landslide and she saw little hope of avoiding the hated capital, as she had been able to do when he was in Congress. Then in January 1853, less than two months before the inauguration, the Pierces were struck by a grim and cruel tragedy. They were traveling on a campaign train from Boston to Concord with their only son, Benjamin, eleven, when their railroad car was suddenly derailed. They escaped with slight injuries, but the boy was thrown against rocks along the embankment and killed before their horrified eyes. The President-elect was overcome with grief and, shortly, with remorse when his hysterical wife began proclaiming that the tragedy had been the will of God, punishing the father for having neglected his family in favor of worldly office.

Pierce's confidence and hopes were demolished, especially when his wife refused to attend the inauguration or even set foot in Washington for a long time afterward. History records that two years passed before she participated officially in any White House social affairs. Pierce's arrival on the scene was pathetic. He and his male secretary wandered through cold, dark halls, eventually sleeping on the floor in their coats, shivering and uncomfortable. For months, Jane kept her distance. In the meantime, Pierce began turning back again, more and more, to his earlier form of solace: the bottle. Not long after he began his term, he sought this means of escape during a tour of New England. A few of those who accompanied him on that occasion reported privately that they were greatly disturbed about the manner which the President was drinking to excess.

The President had, if nothing else, plenty of excuses for drinking in order to alleviate his frustrations. During the entire first half of his administration, he found it almost impossible to enact any significant legislation because there was such division in the ranks of his own Democratic party. He was badly shaken by the death of Abigail Fillmore, wife of the former president, who had befriended him, barely a month after entering the White House. He was acutely depressed by the death of his vice-president, Rufus King, who became fatally ill with tuberculosis while in Cuba and never took office. He made serious errors of judgment in supporting "involuntary servitude" and compromise measures in the matter of slavery. He failed in attempts to "expand" the western reaches of America through a poorly devised plan to purchase a large block from Mexico, and was equally unsuccessful in efforts to acquire Cuba from Spain.

How many of these failures were a direct result of his drinking and consequent retreats from reality? No one will ever know, since the records are unclear and since many of his intimate associates managed to cover up for him again and again. Although his health otherwise remained fair during his term of office, he suffered from chronic bronchitis. This was attributed to unknown allergies. Sympathetic doctors blamed it on the cold, damp atmosphere in the White House, or possibly on latent tuberculosis, caught from his wife. Others just laughed and joked that the only "allergy" he suffered was alcohol.

By the time Mrs. Pierce moved into the White House, she was almost too far gone, mentally, to give him any of the kind of support he needed to abstain from his hard drinking. Instead, she only gave him further cause for turning to drink. She stayed in her bedroom most of the time, a pitiful, emaciated being who endlessly scribbled notes of endearment to the son whom she could not believe was dead. When an official function called for a hostess, Pierce had to enlist the aid of wives and daughters of some of his cabinet members, who remained strangely loyal to him. One of his few accomplishments was indeed unique. He is the only president who served a full term without replacing a single member of his cabinet.

Franklin Pierce kept trying to stay dry, but each time he achieved short periods of abstinence they ended abruptly with some personal or political crisis that triggered his drinking again. He so deceived himself, that when the Democrats met to select candidates in the convention of June 2, 1856, he was certain that he would again get the nomination. But the party had suffered enough and quickly bypassed him—this time in favor of James Buchanan of Pennsylvania. Pierce's life after leaving the White House was even more of a tragedy, but fortunately no longer one which the nation had to share. The best that could be said for him was written by a despairing friend, who wrote, "My heart bleeds for him, for he is a gallant and generous spirit." Yet even he admitted that the man was overshadowed by his office and "crushed by its duties."

As his wife lost her battle with sanity, broken in physical health as well, he simply drank more and more to try to compensate for his personal burdens. He suffered liver damage, diagnosed as alcoholic or nutritional cirrhosis of the liver with ascites (called abdominal dropsy at the time) and finally hepatic coma. Although he gave up drinking during the last few years of his life, he did so only out of fear of death. It was too late and his constitution was simply overwhelmed by the accumulated disorders that had resulted from his addiction to alcohol. Even more pitiful was the anguish caused by the almost total desertion by his friends and former associates. Nathaniel Hawthorne alone remained loyal, understanding better than any of his contemporaries the real nature of alcoholism. When Hawthorne died, Pierce simply went to pieces.

He left such a bitter trail behind him that he was almost completely shunned in New Hampshire, where he had hoped to find peace in retirement. Feelings were so strong that his native state did not even dedicate a statue in his honor for more than fifty years after his death in 1869.

The story of Ulysses S. Grant had an almost equally tragic and agonizing conclusion, but for different reasons. Fortunately for him, as well as the nation, his two terms in office did not parallel the experiences of his alcoholic predecessor.

Grant started his career—or, more accurately, a succession of careers—with every evidence that he would make little impact on his country or his times. With a domineering father and a mother who showed him little affection, he grew up a shy, awkward youth who was considered by his peers and elders to be dull, if not stupid. Local jokesters liked to refer to him as "Useless" Grant in the town where he spent his youth, Georgetown, Ohio. Most of the neighbors were surprised when his father succeeded in procuring an appointment for him to attend the Military Academy at West Point, where he was a sloppy, indifferent student who was perpetually tired and could never get enough sleep. Two things helped him survive the ordeal, despite a constant accumulation of demerits and detentions: he had a natural aptitude for mathematics and he was a superb horseman.

Grant's other affinity, a craving for alcohol, began after he received his commission as a second lieutenant and was assigned to active duty in the Mexican campaign. Most of the other officers drank, sometimes heavily, but they did so boisterously in the company of each other. Grant became a solitary drinker, withdrawing into an alcoholic seclusion because he felt uncomfortable and awkward when trying to make jokes and carrying on a light conversation with others. When he returned from Mexico, he married Julia Dent, whom he had met four years earlier. Julia was as plain as a mud pie, and cross-eyed to boot. Yet she possessed a sweet disposition and in her unconcealed devotion to Ulysses imbued him with a confidence he had never felt before.

By this time, Grant was aware enough of his inability to handle liquor that he joined the Sons of Temperance at Sackett's Harbor, New York, where he was stationed in the military barracks. There is much controversy among his biographers as to how often he drank, and how much. Two facts, however, do emerge: the first was that even small amounts of hard liquor affected him more than was normal. The second was that he seemed incapable of abstaining for long and was forever taking pledges, then breaking them. The situation grew worse after his regiment was dispatched to Fort Vancouver on the Pacific Coast and he had to leave his pregnant wife and infant son for two years. Once more, in his loneliness, he sought alcohol as an escape. When Grant, then a captain, appeared before his troops several times while still "under the influence," he was asked to resign his commission.

Returning to the East with the only career he knew totally destroyed, he moved his wife and children to a piece of land that had been given to them as a wedding present by Julia's father. He managed to build a crude log cabin, named the farm "Hardscrabble," and attempted the life of a farmer. A combination of malaria, tuberculosis, and liquor proved to be adversaries that he could not beat and he finally had to admit failure and sell the farm at auction. He proved to be equally unsuccessful at selling real estate, despite the assistance of one of his wife's cousins, and at clerking in a store run by his younger brothers in Galena, Illinois. Thus, at the age of thirty-nine, penniless and with no evident abilities, he seemed to be living up to the nickname so cruelly pinned on him many years earlier: Useless.

It was little wonder that he sought the comfort of the bottle.

The outbreak of the Civil War wrought an incredible transformation in Grant. When it arrived, he was little more than a bum, always broke, dirty, unkempt, dressed in cast-off clothes and remnants of old army uniforms. At one point, he had even tried—unsuccessfully—to sell off some slaves belonging to his wife's family. Old friends deliberately avoided him on the street, while relatives were embarrassed to have his name brought up in conversation. His first break came when he was placed in command of a rag-tag army unit that was on the point of mutiny. In his old clothes, sloppy in bearing, and with a dirty beard, he was just the person to establish the right rapport and motivate the troops.

He was so successful that he was promoted to the rank of colonel and given a more impressive command. Before another year had passed, his record, plus the fact that he was one of the few West Point graduates available, elevated him to the position of brigadier general, and two years later he was appointed by Lincoln as General of the Armies. Though his rise was meteoric and all of his latent skills were suddenly activated, he did fall back on his liquid crutch on a number of occasions, sometimes with disturbing results. The situation might have been disastrous had he not appointed an old friend, John A. Rawlins of Illinois, as his chief of staff. Rawlins was exceptionally strong-minded, and a teetotaler to boot. Knowing Grant's weakness, one of the first steps he took in his new position was to make him pledge that he would not drink a drop of liquor while in wartime service. To lessen the opportunities for a slip, he banished all liquor at army headquarters and even went so far as to make it known confidentially to staff officers whose commands the General would be visiting that the offering of drinks was forbidden.

Grant broke the pledge from time to time. On one occasion he is said to have barely missed capture by the Confederates when he passed out on a small scouting vessel and did not give the order to follow a certain course that was less dangerous. Following his important victory at Vicksburg, he is said to have celebrated to such an extent that reports had to be circulated that he had contracted severe migraine headaches and was recuperating in his tent. On several occasions, too, when he achieved victories but suffered severe casualties, he was roundly criticized for having pressed the battle beyond the point necessary to defeat the enemy—and that he did so only because he was under the influence of alcohol and did not fully comprehend what he was doing.

In the spring of 1868, with the Civil War long since over and Grant basking in the rosy glow of heroism, he was unanimously nominated by the Republican Convention on the first roll call as candidate for the presidency. His drinking habits were, by then, well known, if not thoroughly publicized. Many of the stories were exaggerated, yet most of his contemporaries agreed that they were based on the truth. No biography seems complete without relating the comment by President Lincoln—probably apocryphal—when he was begged to relieve his General of the Army during the war for reasons of intemperance.

"Do you know what brand of whisky Grant drinks?" Lincoln is supposed to have asked. "I would like to get barrels of it and send them to my other generals."

No matter where the real truth lay, the voters, as well as the delegates, apparently agreed that Ulysses S. Grant had his drinking problems now under control and that they would not surface while he was in the White House. In this they were absolutely correct. Grant had many serious shortcomings as president, including the appointment of many cabinet officers who were inept, crooked, or both. But the record seems clear that he never imbibed to excess during his eight years in the White House and in all probability was an almost total abstainer. How did he manage so successfully to sublimate his craving for strong drink for such a long period when he had never been able to do so previously? One answer is that "the opiate of power took the place of intoxication by alcohol."

Another answer is Julia Dent Grant, a loving wife who refused to give up on her husband. His family and friends all deserted him at one time or another, but Julia stuck it out and gave him the support he badly needed. The love and respect between them was of a special quality, maturing with the years. At the time of their engagement, Ulysses was an awkward, ill-at-ease lieutenant. As for Julia, she was so plain in looks and manner that, when Grant came to ask for her hand, Mr. Dent thought that the young man was referring to his younger, and more physically attractive, daughter.

Julia's eyes crossed so badly that she had to turn her head ninety degrees and peer out of the corner of her eyes to avoid the kind of distorted vision that caused her to bump into chairs and tables when she walked across an unfamiliar room. As a result of this deformity and her attempts to compensate for it, she developed a crab-like sideways scuttle that helped her to move in and out of rooms without tripping. At most White House functions, Julia remained quietly in one place, or moved about only on an escort's arm.

One day, toward the end of Grant's first term, Julia appeared downstairs at the Executive Mansion with bags packed and announced that she was entraining for New York City to have her eyes operated on. The President was horrified, protesting that there was no need for this. "I met you and fell in love with you the way you are," he said, "and, anyway, I'm not such a handsome fellow myself."

Although Julia inspired him to stay away from the bottle, a more probable reason for his continued abstinence was the fact that he was fundamentally a person with an overriding sense of duty. He had great courage, but his bravery—whether under fire on the field of battle or facing civilian enemies—was simply an instrument of duty. He could not control his drinking while serving as an officer because he usually started imbibing on occasions when he did not need to be alert. As for his earlier civilian life, he held such inconsequential positions that the state of his sobriety made little difference to any particular outcome. As president, he abstained because he knew that it was a twenty-four-hour-a-day job and that at any hour of the day or night he might be called upon to act or make a decision.

His administration, unfortunately, did not reflect his diligence. It was described by at least one historian as a "sink of corruption," and in equally damning terms by other writers. His predecessor, Andrew Johnson, referred to Grant's selections for the cabinet as "a sort of lottery, those getting the best places that

paid the most. . . . Offices were disposed of at various prices from
$65,000 down to a box of segars." Numerous officials were ex-
posed for dealing illegally in the stock of the Union Pacific Railroad, which was the recipient of substantial federal subsidies.
Five federal judges and two members of the cabinet were forced
to resign ingloriously in order to avoid indictments for bribery.
The Whiskey Ring flourished, a conspiracy that bilked the government of millions of dollars by avoiding excise taxes on liquor.
And Grant's own brother-in-law was revealed as the source of
illegal inside information that was helping the financier, Jay
Gould, make a killing on Wall Street.

The President himself was not involved in any fraud or bribery. If he accepted gifts from his supporters, they were modest
and not out of line with what had long been deemed traditional
in the White House. The people believed in him and not only
voted him back into the White House for a second term but
showed evidence that they would also have supported him for a
third. He refused, quite frankly admitting that he shared the
blame, because of political ineptitude and lack of executive experience, for the mistakes and errors of judgment that had been
made.

He was to prove further his lack of experience, and particularly his weakness for naively trusting others, after he retired
from public life in March 1877. After a globe-girdling trip of
almost three years' duration, during which time he was ac-
claimed by the peoples and leaders of many countries, he returned to Galena, Illinois, and finally moved to New York City.
There he invested his entire savings, some $100,000, in a banking
firm headed by one Ferdinand Ward, who turned out to be more
speculator than businessman. Grant ended up penniless. As one
of his biographers, W. E. Woodward, sadly recounted, "The
great adventure of Ulysses Grant . . . the epic of the marching
men . . . the triumphs and the adulation . . . all had come to an
end in poverty and despair."

Grant could well have been excused at this low point in life
had he returned to the bottle. But he did not. Instead, he began
a major undertaking, the writing of his memoirs, which had been
commissioned by none other than Mark Twain. Grant desper-

ately needed the money, not only for current expenses, but to provide for his wife who, he knew, would soon become a widow. Doctors had informed him that a persistent, stabbing pain in his throat, which he first noticed in the spring of 1884, was caused by a malignancy. Although Dr. John Hancock Douglas, one of the nation's foremost throat specialists, was at first hopeful that he could treat the disease successfully, he soon had to admit that chances of recovery were poor. The probable cause of Grant's cancer of the throat was recorded as his heavy addiction to smoking cigars. Not so openly mentioned, but suggested, was the effect of alcohol during his periods of heavy drinking, even though they had occurred many years earlier.

For the next year the former president labored with increasing difficulty and agonizing pain to complete the memoirs and meet the contract for the publishing firm, Charles L. Webster and Company, of which Twain was part owner. His work was constantly interrupted by the necessity to spray his throat with solutions that were of dubious benefit and spitting out accumulations of foul-smelling pus as the cancer spread. When he could no longer dictate to a stenographer in a cracked, husky voice, he had to sit up in a chair, propped with pillows and write with a shaky hand. This, too, became increasingly difficult because of fevers and chills that made it difficult for him to hold pen and paper and that frequently made it necessary for him to huddle under heavy capes.

It was, quite literally, a race with death.

On April 7, 1885, an artery in his diseased throat ruptured, causing such severe hemorrhaging that it seemed certain he would not last through the night. With the help of digitalis for the heart, cocaine solutions, and morphine injections, he was saved, at least temporarily. But he was emaciated and steadily losing weight and was so grotesquely swollen around the neck that he wore a heavy scarf to conceal his deformity whenever he was expecting visitors.

In late June, he was moved to Mount McGregor, near Saratoga Springs, New York, where it was felt that he would be more comfortable during the heat of summer. But he realized that there was no real relief for him any more and that death was imminent. He died quietly at 8:08 in the morning of July 23, 1885, at the age of sixty-three. He had won the race by a matter of days and was, in fact, still making refinements in the manuscript two days before. The memoirs were so successful that his widow eventually received royalties of more than $440,000.

Dr. John Hancock Douglas paid him what was probably his finest tribute:

> Nine months of close attention to him have only endeared him to me. I have learned to know him as few have known him. The world can know him as a great general, as a successful politician; but I know him as a patient, self-sacrificing, gentle, quiet, uncomplaining sufferer, looking death calmly in the face and counting almost the hours in which he had to live, and these hours were studied by him that he might contribute something of benefit to some other fellow-sufferer. If he was great in his life, he was even greater in death.

It was quite a eulogy for a man who had started out life as Useless, who had drunk himself into near-oblivion, and who served for eight years in the White House as a recovered alcoholic.

7

The Ultimate Ordeal

We think of a presidential assassination as perhaps the most traumatic single event that can occur in the United States. John F. Kennedy, gunned down, died almost instantly. Abraham Lincoln expired in a matter of hours. Yet, after the initial shock, a new president is sworn in and the nation continues—has to continue—its unending course. But what about a situation that is even more horrendous: the case of a president who is *critically disabled,* not killed? Senator Birch Bayh asked the question succinctly, shortly after the shootings in Dallas:

> Concerning the recent national tragedy, what if John Kennedy had been seriously and permanently injured—rendered a helpless cripple, physically or mentally unable to perform the duties of President?

In the century that has passed, most Americans have either forgotten or paid little attention to the desolate period in history when James Abram Garfield hovered for months between life and death and the United States was totally immobilized. Exactly twenty years later, the country was again paralyzed when William McKinley was mortally wounded. It could happen again, and with far greater implications if there were a military disaster in an era when every major nation had to be on the alert, not only around the calendar but around the clock. To be frozen in inaction, even for hours, invites tragedy.

The case of James A. Garfield is not only an object lesson, but a study in anguish, the ultimate ordeal that can face an individual, let alone one who also bears the burden of guiding the nation.

It is also the story of a president who finally ran out of courage and could no longer fight back.

Garfield, a self-made man and the last President to have been born in a log cabin, had served in Congress for an unbroken period of seventeen years when he was nominated by the Republicans and elected twentieth President of the United States, in 1880. He had also served as a teacher before entering politics, during which time he had married a former classmate in Ohio, Lucretia ("Crete") Rudolph, and had been an officer in the Civil War, rising from the rank of lieutenant colonel to major general.

The young Garfield had grown up with no father and was constantly rebelling against his mother. He once looked back on his childhood as ". . . wild, chaotic, unrestrained." He recalled the lack of guidance as harmful to his development. His mother gave up trying to discipline him and the rest of the family were unable to.

In his early twenties he became intensely religious, attending a school run by the Disciples of Christ. After a few years, he found that the principles of this church conflicted with his rising political and social drives. Whereas his religious tenets told him to be selfless, quiet, and contemplative, his ambitions thrust him into increasingly active social and political intercourse.

He tried to relieve this dichotomy by denying that he was seeking community acceptance, yet in devious ways he was involving himself more and more in public activities. A prime example was his behind-the-scenes maneuvering to become president of the Western Reserve Eclectic Institute at age twenty-three. Making deals, undercutting his opponents, spreading rumors, yet all the time denying that he was seeking the position, were successful gambits. Even rumors that he was philandering while engaged to Crete did him little damage. A final deal with the faculty to establish a committee to run the school and later name him president gave him the job. His first political campaign had paid off handsomely.

In his personal life he learned early that his social and sexual urges were not compatible with the rules of his church and society, so he consequently clung to Lucretia Rudolph, the daughter of one of the church's founders. But her typically conservative, parlor-conversation, church-meeting activities were too mild to satisfy him. He therefore involved himself in frantic love affairs and travels with unattached women—sometimes two at a time.

James A. Garfield became more and more self-seeking and hypocritical. With the outbreak of the Civil War, he quickly saw how important it was for him to become involved. Some small successes in the field led to his appointment as chief of staff to General Rosecrans. He handled this promotion so adroitly that he was able to associate himself with the accomplishments of the general and at the same time divorce himself from certain actions that led to the general's downfall. After conspiring behind the old general's back and becoming a general himself, he quit the army to run for the U.S. Senate. He was described at this time as being mercurial, subject to depression, restless, self-indulgent, and moody.

With his entry into politics, Garfield found his niche in life. A good speaker and a man with proven administrative ability, he was able to impress other politicians and become a leader among them. Operating from a solid Republican base back home in Ohio, he was returned to the Senate four times and in 1880 became the Republican candidate for the presidency. His capture of the nomination was a typical Garfield maneuver. He had anticipated that the delegates would trip all over themselves trying to agree upon one of three equal contenders—Sherman, Blaine, or Grant. With shrewd dealing and aggressive bargaining, as he saw the voting heading toward a deadlock, he slipped his name through the back door and within two ballots won the nomination.

Garfield had enjoyed excellent health during his boyhood and up to the years of the war. He was strong and athletic, with an abundance of energy. From 1861 to 1863, while in service with the 42nd Ohio Regiment, however, he was plagued by one illness after another, including dysentery, disorders of the digestive tract, and jaundice, which gave him an excuse to resign his commission before the end of the war. By the time he entered the White House, his damaged constitution had recovered somewhat, yet he was the victim of a persistent insomnia and recur-

rent depression, which made it difficult for him to take on the
heavy load of appointments he was expected to fulfill each day.

James Garfield had been in office barely four months at the
time he was leaving Washington to attend commencement exercises, twenty-five years after his own graduation, at Williams
College. At 9:30 on the morning of July 2, 1881, he entered the
Baltimore and Potomac railroad station in the company of Secretary of State James G. Blaine. As they walked toward other
members of the presidential party, neither one noticed the presence of a man who was short and stocky, dressed in a blue suit
and derby and, but for a light mustache, generally undistinguished in appearance. When they were within a few feet of the
stranger, he suddenly faced them abruptly, whipped out a .44-
caliber pistol, known as an "English Bulldog," and fired two
shots in quick succession.

The assailant, later identified as Charles Guiteau, thirty-
eight, was obsessed with the idea that God had commanded him
to eliminate the President as a betrayer of his party. He had
vainly hoped to be appointed to a job in the new Republican
administration. Guiteau was seized before he could fire any of the
three bullets remaining in the chamber.

At the sound of the first shot, Garfield half turned and started
dropping to his knees. "My God, what is this?" he cried as the
second shot was being fired. The first shot passed without harm
through the left side of the President's traveling coat. The second
entered the right side of his back, fracturing two ribs, and vanishing somewhere within his six-foot, 205-pound frame in the vicinity of the lower thorax. What followed is not entirely clear, since
there is great variation in the accounts recorded at the time. But
one reliable eyewitness later described the President as falling
forward near the wall of the room. As blood began oozing from
the wound, Garfield pressed one hand against his side and began
vomiting. He remained conscious, but faint and pale.

The first physician to reach the scene, perhaps five minutes
after the shooting, was Dr. Smith Townshend, health officer of
the district. "From the pulse at the wrist, I thought he was
dying," he was quoted in the *Medical Record* of July 16, 1881. "I had
his head lowered and administered aromatic spirits of ammonia

and brandy to revive him." When the President showed signs of reviving, he was asked by Townshend where he felt the most pain. He replied that he had a "prickling sensation" in the right leg and foot. "He rallied considerably," said Townshend, and I proceeded to examine his wounds. I found that the last bullet had entered his back about two and a half inches to the right of the vertebrae."

Doctors—even laymen—are horrified today when they read the next comment. "I introduced my finger into the bullet wound, some hemorrhage followed. After examination of the wound, the President looked up and asked me what I thought of it. I answered that I did not consider it serious. The President groaned, 'I thank you, doctor, but I am a dead man.'"

Townshend was only the first of several doctors—all eminent and respected physicians—who explored the cavity with their naked fingers. In the early 1880s, the subject of antisepsis was still a theory that was debated controversially within the medical profession. The British surgeon, Joseph Lister, had published his findings on his successful use of antisepsis in the prevention of infection of injuries, wounds, and tissues exposed during surgery. But American doctors were skeptical and at the time of the attack on Garfield remained so. In addition to fingers, the wound was subjected to examination by an instrument called a Nélaton probe which, while "clean," was not washed with antiseptics.

After Townshend's initial examination, the President was placed on the only substitute for a stretcher available, a mattress, and carried awkwardly to a room on the second floor of the station. By this time, a number of other doctors had been hastily summoned, including Surgeon-General J. K. Barnes, Dr. J. J. Woodward of the United States Army, Dr. Robert Reyburn, and Dr. D. W. Bliss, a prominent Washington surgeon who had been summoned by Secretary of State Blaine. Bliss, who had also served for a short time as the President's personal physician, immediately took charge, apparently at the express wish of Garfield, who was still conscious and able to talk coherently.

The President's pulse was weak, his respiration slow, and his face pale. He was plainly in shock, yet able to describe how he felt. At 10:30, he was transferred by ambulance to the Executive

Mansion, where the first official bulletin was issued at noon: "The President is somewhat restless, but is suffering less pain. Pulse 112. Some nausea and vomiting have recently occurred. Considerable hemorrhage has taken place from the wound." The bulletin was issued by Dr. D. W. Bliss.

At this stage, President Garfield had become something of a medical curiosity, an object of interest to every well-known physician, surgeon, or specialist in Washington who could make his way to the White House and gain entrance. It was reported that, among others, Surgeon-General Philip S. Wales of the Navy arrived and "introduced his finger to its full extent into the wound and declared that the liver was perforated." (This would mean that Dr. Wales's finger was seven inchs long!) Dr. J. J. Woodward "introduced his finger sufficiently deeply to determine that the eleventh rib was broken," and Dr. Bliss "passed several probes, but made no comment." Garfield was even examined in mid-afternoon by a homeopathic physician, who added his own fingers to the succession of digits that had already probed the suffering patient and exclaimed, "My God, General, you ought to have surgical advice!"

The answer that Garfield is supposed to have given illustrates the state of affairs: "There are about 40 of them in the adjoining room—go and consult with them."

Since the consensus of the doctors was that there was a considerable amount of undetected internal hemorrhaging and that the President was dying, the attempts to locate the bullet were discontinued. By late afternoon, it was decided that the best course of action was to make the patient as comfortable as possible. Strange though it seems, it was recorded that his clothing was not removed until 5:00 P.M., indicating that he had been subjected to so many examinations that there had not been time to change him into a gown. At about this time, too, Garfield's wife arrived from Elberon, New Jersey, where she had been recovering from a serious attack of malaria and depression. She had been sent there to escape the humid, unhealthy climate of the nation's capital. Later, the President was catheterized to relieve his bladder, which appeared to have some kind of obstruction, and was given a sedative and some medication to relieve his nausea and frequent vomiting.

By July 3, after a restless night which no one thought he would survive, Garfield astounded the medical experts by appearing to be greatly improved. His bladder and bowels were functioning normally. He reported less pain in his feet and ankles. There were few signs of bleeding. Dr. Bliss stated in his bulletin, issued shortly after noon that day: "The improvement in the President's condition, which began early in the evening, has steadily continued up to this hour. His temperature and respiration are now normal, and his pulse has fallen to 120. The attending physicians regard all his symptoms as favorable, and a more hopeful feeling prevails."

The "attending physicians" referred to had now fortunately been reduced to a small team made up of Bliss, Surgeon-General J. K. Barnes, and Drs. J. J. Woodward and Robert Reyburn. All of the others were dismissed by Bliss, who then sent for Dr. D. Hayes Agnew of Philadelphia, reputed to be "the outstanding surgeon in the United States," and Dr. Frank H. Hamilton of New York City, also a famous surgeon. Not all of the doctors left without protest and in some cases feelings ran high. The situation became particularly tense when, at about nine-thirty that morning, Dr. Bliss was informed that there was a doctor waiting in the anteroom who insisted on seeing the patient. He was Dr. John H. Baxter, who had served the Garfield family as its personal physician for many years. The following conversation was reported:

Baxter: I have come to ask you to take me in to see the President.

Bliss: Well, I don't see the necessity of your seeing the President. I wish to keep him quiet.

Baxter: [Astonished] I make the request as the President's physician. I have, for years, been his physician.

Bliss: Yes, I know your game. You wish to sneak up here and take this case out of my hands.

Baxter: I wish nothing, Dr. Bliss, except what I am entitled to. If the President prefers that you should take charge of his case, I haven't a word to say.

Bliss: Well, you just try it on. I tell you that you can't do it. I

> know you are sneaking around to prescribe for those who
> have influence and will lobby for you.
> Baxter: [Springing up] That is a lie!

After being threatened with forceful eviction by Dr. Bliss's son, Dr. Baxter decided not to press the issue and walked out. Dr. Bliss, though now the physician-in-charge without further contest, was severely criticized by many for the high-handed manner in which he had dismissed so many prominent doctors and selected consultants on his own authority. As the President continued to hold his own during the days and weeks that followed, and the case turned into a gruelling ordeal, few people in the medical profession envied the role that Bliss had assumed. He remained at his eminent patient's bedside day and night, supervising every aspect of his care down to such minute details as the amount of water he drank and the frequency with which the bed linens were changed. Yet he was just at the beginning of what was ultimately described as "the longest house call on record"—constant attendance for ten weeks.

From the start, the most frustrating and agonizing challenge was that of trying to locate the bullet. Not only were the incessant probings—with fingers, the Nélaton probe and a long, flexible silver probe—completely unsuccessful, but they made at least one false channel in the internal tissues which later caused even more confusion when it deceived doctors newly called in for consultation. There was hardly a doctor in the country who did not express personal theories about where the bullet lay. Newspapers and magazines published articles on how to determine where the ball had lodged and whether it was dangerous to leave it in place. Letters of advice flooded the Executive Mansion, from private citizens, scientists, and inventors. Some of the imaginative schemes for implementing the search included suction machines, large magnets that could react on the lead, a device for flushing interior passages with a powerful jet stream that would wash out foreign substances, and the application of all kinds of psychic and hypnotic powers.

These schemes were not rejected as crackpot ideas. Several were tried, the most notable being that of the famous inventor of the telephone, Alexander Graham Bell. Armed with an electromagnetic apparatus, which operated on the principle of "induction balance," he attempted on two separate occasions to locate the bullet. The hoped-for "balance," which would reveal the exact location, was never achieved, leading Bell to the conclusion that the metal was too far from the surface of the body to have enough impact on the magnetic field. He had failed to take into account the metal bedsprings upon which the President lay, which interfered with his experiment.

Another, somewhat more gruesome, expedient had been tried about four days after the shooting. Dr. Faneuil Weisse, publicity-seeking anatomist, professor of anatomy at the New York Medical College, set up cadavers borrowed from the morgue in the position that he thought Garfield had been in when shot. A British Bulldog revolver like Guiteau's was used for these tests. Basing his experiment on facts that had been readily revealed by the assassin, he loaded the revolver with twenty grains of powder and a ball of two hundred grains' weight. By firing bullets repeatedly into each cadaver, he thus attempted to determine the type of wound produced, the depth of penetration, and the manner in which the ball was deflected by muscle and bone. At the conclusion of this experiment, an anatomical chart was prepared for use by Dr. Bliss and his colleagues to show the results of the test. It proved to be clinically interesting, but of no practical value.

During the days from July 2 on into the heart of the summer, the affairs of the United States hung in suspended animation. It was fortunate that the climate in the nation's capital was so intolerable during the summer that many government activities were suspended anyway. The members of Congress and the cabinet, along with other officials, traditionally escaped the heat and humidity of Washington from late June until September. So the President's disability did not cause the kind of panic it might have had the shooting occurred while Congress was in full session, or at a time when the government was engaged in fighting enemies, internal or external. The intensive search for the bullet also had one result that was positive: it so fascinated the press and the public that it took peoples' minds away from public matters and gave them little opportunity to become panicky.

But these very factors—the oppressive weather and the lack of medical progress—created an ordeal of proportions never experienced by any other American president, before or since. The heat of Washington, generally over 90 degrees, and several times exceeding 100, was unbearable to persons who were in good health, and certainly worse for a man who frequently had fevers, suffered from bed sores, and was confined to one room. Suggestions that he be moved to a cooler climate, perhaps in the mountains, were repeatedly rejected. It was claimed, for one thing, that the journey alone would kill him, and for another, that he would be too remote from the kinds of medical attention he needed during the frequent crises that occurred.

Reading about the President's sufferings from the heat, Americans again responded—this time with suggestions and inventions for keeping their leader cool. Not the most extreme by any means was the suggestion that the patient's bed would remain much cooler if a hugh pan were suspended over it, filled with several hundred pounds of ice. One proposal was scientific enough so that it was put into operation, with good results. The brainchild of an engineer named Jennings, of Baltimore, it consisted of a cast-iron chamber filled with hanging strips of terry cloth—some three thousand square feet in all. Iced water was constantly sprayed on the strips from an overhead pipe, through hundreds of tiny perforations. A pipe with an exhaust fan drew air through this unit and into the President's bedroom. Though makeshift and ungainly, the unit was efficient enough so that air sucked in from the outside at a temperature of 99 degrees could be cooled to 54 and when diffused throughout the bedroom maintained it at a constant temperature of 75, day and night—a forerunner of modern air conditioning!

From mid-July until the twenty-second, the condition of the President was little changed. He lay in bed, had few conversations, conducted no business and worst of all, began to lose his desire for food. The Garfields had previously turned White House repasts into models of good nutritional meals since Crete was interested in food and nutrition. Thus the appearance of anorexia in the patient was an ominous sign. On July 22, Dr. Bliss became concerned when he noticed a discharge of pus from the open wound, accompanied by fragments of bone and shreds of cloth that had been carried in by the bullet at the time of impact. The next day the President started to vomit and showed other signs that he was in considerable distress. His temperature rose suddenly to 104 degrees, enough so that his condition was described in bulletins as "critical." Doctors Agnew and Hamilton, who had returned to their homes, were hastily summoned. On July 24, Agnew made an incision three inches below the wound. Although he used no ether and the tissues were extremely painful to the touch, he reported that Garfield withstood the operation well. The surgeon also inserted a catheter for a distance of some seven inches to irrigate the wound and force out more of the pus and foreign matter.

The President showed gradual signs of improvement day by day thereafter, so that by the end of a week his condition was reported as "excellent." Nevertheless, the infection did not seem to have been adequately countered. So, on August 12, Agnew again resorted to surgery, extending the previous incision by some three inches. Because Garfield was much stronger than he had been on the previous occasion Agnew was able to use ether for anaesthesia. Another incision was made just below the twelfth rib, in an area where it was suspected that the bullet had passed. The President withstood the surgery, with only mild fever, but on August 15 began spasmodic vomiting that continued for three days and made it impossible for him to take any nourishment by mouth. He was given "nutritional enemas," with mixtures of eggs, beef extract, and whisky, which were completely useless but at the time were thought to provide real nourishment.

On August 18, a disturbing symptom was noticed: extreme, painful swelling of the right parotid (salivary) gland just in front of, and below, the ear. The seriousness of the patient's changing condition was further evidenced by paralysis on the right side of the face, noticeable restlessness, and wandering of the mind. Since the swelling indicated the spread of the infection and the possibility of blood poisoning, Dr. Hamilton subjected the President once more to surgery, this time making an incision in the right side of the face and squeezing out a small amount of pus.

Since the cut was small and close to the surface, no ether was given.

For the first time, Garfield's spirit seemed to be breaking and his mental condition deteriorating. He was lethargic during the day, often talking incoherently or skipping dreamily from one subject to another. By this time, some seven weeks after being shot, he had lost eighty pounds, and was losing more each day. He seemed to be completely exhausted by the various infections that were besetting him and was constantly in great discomfort, both from pain within and from the presence of increasing numbers of pustules and boils all over his lower back and buttocks, and even in his armpits. Many were opened and drained, but without affording much relief.

The President's tolerance finally broke down at the end of August. The turning point was possibly the occasion on August 28 when the increasingly painful abscess in the parotid gland ruptured and discharged pus through the mouth and the right ear. He was already in misery because of spreading bronchitis and congestion of the lower lungs. For two agonizing months he had endured the depressing heat of Washington, along with the constant probing and cutting and draining and catheters and enemas and flushings and examinations with strange instruments and more lack of privacy than any human being could stand— or be expected to stand. Now, he said, he was fully resigned to the fact that he would not survive. His only plea was that he be given permission—medical permission—to quit the depressing and demoralizing confines of the White House and the oppressive atmosphere of Washington and be taken to the place where he had intended to be for part of the summer: the New Jersey coast.

Dr. Bliss and his colleagues assented (relented would be a more fitting word) and proceeded with plans the first week in September to have the President transported to a private cottage at Elberon, New Jersey, near Long Branch, where he had his summer home. They were none too soon, for the day before the move, September 6, was reported as the hottest day of the year in the capital. Garfield was transported in a specially designed bed aboard a private car furnished by the Pennsylvania Railroad, and from the station to Francklyn Cottage by carriage. Although the day was sweltering—almost as hot along the Jersey shore as in Washington—the President was in excellent spirits, delighted with the prospect of a change.

Four days later the heat wave was replaced by a cold, easterly storm that blew in from the Atlantic. Dr. Bliss, still sticking by the presidential bedside like a bodyguard, was apprehensive. In the first place, his patient had developed a hacking, exhausting cough that would undoubtedly be aggravated by raw, wet weather. In the second place, he had been so optimistic about recent improvements in Garfield's condition and his cheerful outlook that he had relieved Drs. Barnes, Reyburn, and Woodward of their immediate responsibilities and sent them back to Washington. The President himself had requested the reduction in the medical staff as a form of self-defense against the continual invasion of his privacy and, to prove that he was right, had insisted on sitting up in a chair for half an hour or so on two successive days, but then had become too weak to continue.

For one week in mid-September, Garfield continued in what today would be referred to as a "stable" condition. The bulletins during this period were guardedly optimistic, while editorials proclaimed that the fresh salt air of the seacoast was doing wonders for his health. Then on the seventeenth, he suffered a sudden, severe chill, followed by a rapid pulse and rise in temperature, a feeling of weakness, and a rasping cough. Within two days, his pulse had become weaker and his temperature higher. After dinner, he fell into a restless sleep from which he awoke at 10:10 to cry out suddenly, "Oh, how it hurts here!" He clutched an area just above his heart, then fell back on his pillow in a coma. Dr. Bliss and Mrs. Garfield raced to his side but were unable to revive him. At 10:35 P.M., his respirations slipped off into inaudibility. The President was dead.

When an autopsy was performed, the doctors and the public at last had their answers. The bullet had entered Garfield's back, broken two ribs and a vertebra (slightly injuring the spinal cord and producing the initial pain in the feet and ankles), and had come to rest below the pancreas, out of harm's way. Infection had followed the bullet in, evidenced by an abscess cavity along the bullet's track. This undoubtedly had been aggravated by the many probings with fingers and unsterile instruments. The wound alone was not fatal, and had more attention been paid to proper sterility and antisepsis, and had the patient been able to maintain his nutrition by eating, he would have survived.

Garfield was actually killed by a nick in the splenic artery that had been produced by the passing bullet. This nick turned into a weak spot in the wall of the artery, which turned into an aneurysm which, ten weeks after the bullet had produced it, ruptured. The President complained of severe pain at this time, lapsed into a coma and bled to death internally. Nothing could have saved him then.

Ironically, almost all the doctors who predicted the course of the bullet were wrong—even Dr. Weisse of the cadaver experiments. This led to a medical editorial in one of the journals of the day which whimsically stated, "Where ignorance is *Bliss*, 'tis folly to be *Weisse.*"

Another irony lay in the complete failure of government leaders to circumvent the drama being played in the sickroom and get back to their official duties and the business at hand. During his entire period of disability—some eighty days—James Abram Garfield completed only one official act: the signing of a relatively minor State Department paper. Yet there were a number of key issues that needed executive attention, including a series of frauds that was incapacitating the Post Office Department, inter-American relationships that were to have been resolved in a Conference of American Republics, and measures to develop a proposed Nicaraguan canal. Vice-President Chester A. Arthur was the target of many demands that he assume the role of acting president, as an accumulation of problems began to bother senators, congressmen, and other officials who were involved in the issued being neglected. Members of the cabinet were particularly agitated, yet there was great disagreement among them. Four of the seven secretaries insisted that if Arthur, whom they detested, were to exercise the powers of the chief executive he would then remain president, no matter how completely Garfield might recover. The Attorney General took this viewpoint and did not share the assumption of the minority of the cabinet that Garfield could return whenever he was able again.

The suggestion was made that the President himself be consulted on the matter. But the secretaries were either too timid or too apprehensive that the discussion might come as a shock and cause a setback to the patient. The cabinet met with Chester A. Arthur on only one occasion, and then with such hostility pervading the atmosphere that they did little more than acknowledge his presence. (There was some suspicion at one point that Arthur's supporters might have been behind the assassination plot, and although this was completely disproved, the hostility lingered.)

Finally, when the post office situation became intolerable and mail service was at the point of crisis, the cabinet dispatched Postmaster General Thomas L. James to New York, where Vice-President Arthur maintained his office. Even the suggestion that he step into Garfield's shoes temporarily brought an instant rebuff. Under no circumstances, said the Vice-President, would he take on the responsibilities of the office while the President was still alive.

He held to his decision and the nation simply drifted until James Garfield's historic ordeal was over and there was no alternative.

Twenty years later, in September 1901, the same ordeal was almost repeated. On September 5, President William McKinley (also from Ohio) traveled to Buffalo, New York, to make a public address at the Pan-American Exposition. He was warmly received by the crowd, for he was almost universally admired and had received a larger plurality of popular votes when reelected in 1900 than any previous chief executive. At seven minutes past four on the following afternoon, he stood in the Temple of Music shaking hands with supporters, when he was approached by a man who had his right hand wrapped by a white handkerchief, making it appear to be bandaged. As the President started to greet him, the man fired two bullets at point-blank range from a short-barreled .32-caliber revolver. McKinley, his face distorted in astonishment, staggered backward, but was prevented by a guard from falling to the floor. The first bullet was partially deflected by a metal button and caused only a superficial scratch over the breastbone. The second penetrated the upper abdomen slightly to the left of the midline. The President bent forward, clutching his white vest, and gasped, "Cortelyou, be careful. Be careful how you tell Ida." A dazed George B. Cortelyou, his private secretary, helped him to the nearest chair.

The Ida referred to was his wife, Ida Saxton, the once beautiful and popular girl he had married in Canton, Ohio, in 1871. He had settled in that town after his discharge from the Grand Army of the Republic as a major in the Ohio Twenty-third.

Shortly after returning home, he walked into the local bank, where he first saw Ida, who was working as a teller. Rather than sit at home and await suitors, like most young ladies of her era, she had convinced her father, president of the bank, that she should be working for him. She and William fell quickly in love, and after a whirlwind romance were married. The wedding was the social event of the season and the young couple became the most popular pair in town. McKinley rapidly made a name for himself as an attorney and a speaker on the Chattauqua circuit and his law practice flourished. Ida soon gave birth to a beautiful blond daughter, and for the first few years of their marriage things could not have been better.

Then tragedy struck. Within two years, Ida became pregnant again and produced a sickly baby. Shortly, both children died. Ida, who never recovered from the birth of her second child or the shock of the two deaths, remained in the hospital an especially long time. Consultants in obstetrics and nervous disorders were imported from Buffalo and New York to see her. When she finally did leave the hospital and returned home, it was to sit in a darkened room, moaning and pretending to rock with a baby in her arms. She developed severe phlebitis in both legs and was unable to walk without assistance. She had headaches, so severe that she could not stand the weight of her hair and had it all cut off. Most tragic of all, she developed epilepsy.

Grand mal, petit mal, and what are now called absence seizures, plagued her constantly. She never knew when she would be besieged with fits, which ranged from convulsions, with frothing at the mouth and incontinence, to little grimaces, snorts, and smacking movements of the lips. Frequently she would lapse into an absence state in the middle of a conversation. She became a whining, brain-damaged woman, demanding more and more attention from her husband and refusing to be left alone for more than a few minutes.

It is not quite clear what the medical explanations were for her condition, but whatever the cause, the results were catastrophic. The McKinleys descended from the heights of Canton society to the depths of despair. William McKinley, undaunted, became an expert in the care of his wife and taught himself to be a fine psychiatric and neurologic nurse. He fed her, patted her, soothed her, read to her, and nursed her day and night. Hours were spent holding hands in a dark room because Ida could not stand light, hours given to reading poems aloud because Ida liked the sound of his voice, and hours devoted to gentle rubbing and massage of the tortured head. Although Ida became more demanding, William seemed to grow to love her more each year.

When he left Ohio for Washington and the White House, he took Ida along as his hostess, and though she often greeted guests at the door by grabbing their jewelry and disappearing into the back rooms to clean and polish it, he refused to allow anyone else to take over her responsibilities. She turned out pairs of knitted slippers by the gross—in a sort of early occupational therapy.

The President insisted on her presence at state dinners even though her conversation left much to be desired. He had learned over the years how to handle his wife's fits with great aplomb. Her sudden attacks were always telegraphed by a sharp, prolonged, rapid inspiration of air through pursed lips, almost a whistle. If the whistle presaged a grand mal epileptic attack, McKinley would whisk her off to a quiet part of the White House and soothe her until the convulsions had stopped. If, on the other hand, he felt that this was going to be a short-lived petit mal episode, he would whip out a damask napkin and throw it over her head and allow her to sit there grunting, drooling, smacking her lips or whatever, until the attack had passed. The darkness and quiet under the napkin seemed to soothe her and shorten the attacks. When she had quieted down, the napkin was removed and dinner continued.

No wonder that William McKinley's first concern after being shot was for his wife.

The first doctor to arrive on the hectic scene of the shooting was George M. Hall, listed as serving on the "Sanitary Staff" of the Pan-American Exposition. He called for the electric-powered motor ambulance. It quietly transported the wounded president to the nearest medical facility, the small Exposition Hospital, little more than a first-aid station. Equipped only for emergencies on the grounds, it was staffed by a handful of nurses, interns, and senior medical students, serving in rotation.

The first surgeon to arrive, at about 4:45 P.M., was Dr. Herman Mynter, a Dane who had lived in Buffalo for about twenty-five years. McKinley was fully conscious. One report states that he recognized Mynter as a doctor he had met and carried on a conversation with the day before. "Doctor," he said weakly, "when I met you yesterday, I did not imagine that today I should have to ask a favor of you."

Mynter required only a brief examination to see that the wound was deep. He felt that the situation required immediate surgery, but withheld a professional decision until other opinions could be obtained. The question was quickly resolved with the arrival of Dr. Matthew D. Mann a few minutes later. Mann was quickly selected as the doctor in charge, perhaps because he had an air of supreme self-confidence and was well known and respected in Buffalo. Educated in the United States and abroad, he was described, at fifty-six, as being "at the height of his career."

Mann announced that he was ready to operate, with Mynter as his assistant. He did so, knowing that the lighting was poor and the surgical equipment rudimentary. But he argued that immediate surgery under these limitations was preferable to taking the time to move the heavy-set patient to the Buffalo General Hospital, though it had a brand new operating room. This major —and soon to be controversial—decision was directly influenced by the outcome of the Garfield case. Mann was acutely aware of the outcry, "Why don't they *do something?*" that pursued Garfield's doctors as they poked and prodded indecisively. He was determined not to get caught in that kind of crossfire.

Shortly after 5:00 P.M. ether was administered successfully. Mann opened the peritoneum, the membrane lining the abdominal cavity, and located the two bullet holes, one in the front wall of the stomach, and one posteriorly. He then had difficulty, because of the uncertain light and the protuberance of the stout patient's abdomen, in tracing the wound and was unable to find the bullet. He was operating at the end of what he referred to as "a big hole," and without the proper instruments. He then decided, with the concurrence of his assistants, to probe no further. He made the deduction that the lead ball had lodged in a place where it could do no further damage (echoes of the Garfield case!) and announced that he could see no evidence of damage behind the stomach. After trimming some of the torn tissues in the wound cavity, and irrigating the stomach with a warm saline solution, he closed the holes in the stomach and the surgical incision with sutures. He made no allowance for drainage.

There now appeared on the scene one of the most eminent surgeons in the United States, Dr. Roswell Park, of the University of Buffalo, with a reputation for being unusually skillful with the knife, and ambidextrous at that. He had long studied and lectured on gunshot wounds and had spoken out his opinion that the Garfield case had been badly bungled. He held the theory that patients were in great jeopardy if surgery did not remove all of the tissue injured or contaminated along the entire track of the bullet. It was also critical, he asserted, to allow for complete drainage.

But for the fact that Park had gone to Niagara Falls to treat a patient with cancer, he would have been the first choice in the McKinley case. As it was, when he arrived at the Exposition Hospital he could do little more than offer some postoperative assistance. He declined to comment on the decisions and procedures, although later it was evident that he felt that the operation should have been delayed until the President could be taken to the Buffalo General Hospital. The hospital had excellent equipment, including one of the first X-ray machines, the use of which would probably have shown the position of the bullet.

In any case, the first medical bulletin on the evening of that fateful Friday, September 6, was "cautiously optimistic." The President had, by this time, been moved to the home of John G. Milburn, a prominent Buffalo attorney and president of the Pan-American Exposition, who had been hosting him during his stay in the city. Except for some obvious pain during the transfer to the large bedroom he was to occupy, the patient seemed to have come through the exploratory operation well enough. By this time, Dr. Park had been put in charge of postoperative care by the President's personal physician, Dr. Presley M. Rixey, although Park seemed reluctant to intrude. His attitude was in sharp contrast to that of another doctor who suddenly appeared on the scene on Sunday and, astonishingly, seemed to take it upon himself to act as the official spokesman. He was Dr. Charles McBurney of New York City, who did not hesitate to let it be known that he was one of the country's leading consultants in abdominal surgery. After examining the patient, he stated unconditionally that there was no evidence of peritonitis or any other complication. Moreover, he told members of the press (and anyone else who cared to listen) that the recent operation marked "the epoch of the century in surgery."

Doctors Mann and Mynter tried to counteract this rash gush of overoptimism by cautioning reporters that their patient was not yet out of the woods and that, in fact, he had a disturbingly rapid pulse and a high temperature. "Hogwash," interrupted McBurney, diverting the discussion to his plans for moving the President to the White House at the earliest opportunity. When, on September 11, Vice-President Theodore Roosevelt, asked McBurney for a report on his chief, the news was so glowing that "Teddy" left the scene and made plans for a hunting trip into the Adirondack wilderness. The members of the cabinet who were anxiously standing by also took their departure, comforted immensely by McBurney's proclamation that the door had been bolted against the "grim monster of death" by the skillful hand of modern medicine.

After issuing Bulletin no. 26, describing the "excellent" response of the President and the manner in which he was eating with great relish, McBurney himself departed for Albany on the Empire State Express. Even as he did so, the other doctors who remained in attendance were growing increasingly worried about signs that all was not as rosy as it had been made out to be. For one thing, the patient was *not* eating heartily and seemed in so much distress that a stomach specialist, Dr. Charles Stockton, was called in for consultation. For another thing, his heart sounds were weaker and he kept moaning, "I am tired, so tired." This was not like McKinley, who until then had been suffering with great fortitude and lack of complaint.

On Thursday afternoon, his condition worsened to such a degree that his secretary began what was to be a frantic search to try to locate Mr. Roosevelt in his forest retreat. Friday the Thirteenth loomed as ominous as its traditional implications. The bulletin issued at 6:30 P.M. announced that "The end is only a question of time." Ironically, Dr. McBurney returned to the scene at about this time, having heard that the President's condition had deteriorated badly. He was there in the darkness and gloom when, at 2:15 A.M., George Cortelyou descended the steps, his head cast down.

"Gentlemen," he said in a choked voice, "the President has passed away."

One further irony came to light in the issue of *American Medicine* that same day, September 14, 1901. "The surgical aspects of President McKinley's case are of the greatest interest to the entire medical profession . . ." said the lead editorial. "President McKinley's injury seems to be one offering exceptionally favorable prospects of recovery."

The editors failed to report that the prospects for recovery were poor because the President had been operated on in a first-aid station with improper equipment, no electric lights, and amateurish assistance, when the fully equipped operating room of the Buffalo General Hospital was barely twenty minutes away; or that the attending surgeon, "at the peak of his career," was an obstetrician and gynecologist who had never before operated on a male or a patient with a bullet wound.

McBurney led his own profession astray with his strange, inexplicable bursts of optimism. Some said he had been sent by

J. P. Morgan to try to prevent a drop in stock market prices.

When an autopsy was performed it was clear that no healing had taken place, the perforations in the stomach had reopened and the pancreas had become inflamed. The bullet was never found. Although Dr. Roswell Park tried not to criticize his colleague, Dr. Mann, it was obvious that he held the opinion that the surgery and the lack of drainage violated good practice. Two factors supported his position: first, he had been teaching and lecturing about the care of gunshot wounds since Garfield's assassination twenty years earlier and had become a recognized expert in the field. The second factor was more bizarre. It happened that, several days after the shooting, a lady who was mentally unbalanced was reading about the problems of locating the bullet and decided she would make a personal sacrifice to help the doctors. She marked a spot on her abdomen at the location where the bullet had entered the President's belly. She then aimed a .32-calibre revolver she had bought for the purpose and shot herself—right at the mark. She was taken to the Buffalo hospital, where she was placed immediately in the care of Dr. Park. He operated successfully, drained the wound properly, and saw his demented patient on the road to physical, if not mental, recovery with no complications.

The lady's "sacrifice" has been used ever since as an indication that McKinley also would have recovered had his medical treatment been different. Whether or not the comparison has any validity is a moot question, but the self-inflicted wound was of no value in helping to determine the course of the assassin's bullet.

Dr. Roswell Park's final tribute to McKinley is a touching bit of medical writing and certainly captures the essence of the character of the President who never lost his courage. "He bore his illness and such pain as he suffered," wrote Park, "with beautiful, unflinching and Christian fortitude. . . . No harsh word of complaint against his assassin was ever heard to pass his lips. . . . Up to this time I had hardly ever believed that a man could be a good Christian and a good politician. His many public acts showed him to be the latter, while the evidences of his real Christian spirit were most impressive during his last days."

William McKinley's physical sufferings and mental anguish

were over in less than nine days, as compared with the eighty-day ordeal of James A. Garfield. Abraham Lincoln and John F. Kennedy did not suffer at all, for they were rendered unconscious within seconds after their assassins squeezed the trigger. Yet it is one of the undesirable demands of leadership that every American president sees the threat of death hanging over him from the day he begins running for the nation's highest office. No matter how well protected he may be by guards, secret service men, last-minute changes in routes and schedules, and various other detection methods and devices, he is constantly in the minds of a small group of people who are considering or activating plots against his life. Many of these would-be assassins are paranoid, imbued with the obsession that they have been ordained by God to eliminate a tyrant. Only a few have been identified as political fanatics or revolutionaries.

But they are out there—waiting. And every president accepts the risk as part of that continuing test of courage that comes with the office. Many threats were made against the earliest presidents—Washington, Jefferson, Monroe, Madison, the Adamses—but the first real assassination attempt involved the irascible Andrew Jackson, who escaped injury or death only because his attacker's pistols misfired. Few people recall that Theodore Roosevelt came very close to being killed, though it was three years after he had left office. He was shot from only six feet away by a fanatic, John N. Schrank, while entering his car in Milwaukee to be driven to a speaking engagement. The bullet fractured his fourth rib and lodged in his chest, near the right lung. What saved his life was the fact that the bullet first passed through his metal glass case and his fifty-page speech (folded double) and was almost spent by the time it pierced his flesh.

Franklin D. Roosevelt escaped an assassination attempt in Miami in February 1933, when bullets were fired at him by a man later committed as insane. The occasion was tragic, however, for one of the bullets killed one of the companions with him, Anton Cermak, the Mayor of Chicago and a close political ally; four others were wounded.

Harry S. Truman was the only chief executive to be the target of terrorists. Two members of the Puerto Rican nationalist movement tried to shoot their way into Blair House, where the Trumans were temporarily in residence. They failed to get near the President, but did wound two of his guards and kill a third. Gerald Ford was threatened on two occasions by would-be assassins—both women and both mentally unbalanced.

It is fortunate for the nation that, while presidents are subject to all of the other ills of mankind, they seem to suffer not at all from what is commonly referred to as "being afraid for one's life." Some, like Andrew Jackson and the two Roosevelts, who were well aware of the threat of assassination from firsthand experience, were indifferent, almost contemptuous, in their attitude toward the lone enemies. The threat of the "ultimate ordeal" seems not to have made a single president change his routine, cancel a speech, or avoid the public in any way. If we judge by the records, presidents as a class are so cool to dangers that they have often tried to thwart plans for their own protection, and they spent little time pressing for defensive legislation. Not until August 1966, during the administration of Lyndon B. Johnson, was it even made a federal crime to kill or kidnap the president.

8

The Presidency in Limbo:
The Tragedy of Wilson

The frail, scholarly-looking gentleman with the lantern jaw and pince-nez glasses slightly askew was almost feverish in his intensity as he shoved and tugged on bulky upholstered chairs, heavy mahogany tables and other pieces of living-room furniture. Blotches of perspiration sprouted on his sallow, clean-shaven cheeks, as much from inner agitation as from physical exertion. Over and over, he kept muttering to himself and two distraught companions something about French spies at work and forces of evil conspiring against them.

The chief character of this bizarre drama was the twenty-eighth President of the United States, Woodrow Wilson. During that spring of 1919, he was not only at the apex of his career, but idolized by the people of Europe and America. He was the foremost head of state in the entire postwar world.

The strange scenario and frantic activity represented no mere outburst of exuberance. Unfortunately for America and the world, the furniture moving had been triggered by Wilson's fixation that the French were scheming against him and that spies were stealing, and rearranging, furniture in the embassy and other locations where the President was staying during the Paris Peace Conference. And the fixation, in turn, was one of a number of outward indications that Wilson was so physically and mentally ill that he would, within a matter of weeks, reach a state of complete collapse.

On December 4, 1918, the President had sailed from Hoboken, New Jersey, for France, having announced two weeks earlier that he would attend the Paris Peace Conference. Some legislators felt that the trip was unnecessary. Wilson had guided the nation through the critical years of World War I and was needed at home as America began reverting to a peacetime economy. Furthermore, the President was already an international hero and stood to gain little by involving himself in matters that were fundamentally European and best left to European leaders to settle.

Few reckoned with the President's overriding determination to see the blueprint for peace include his own most ambitious plan: a League of Nations that would virtually assure the abolishment of war. Those close to the President were deeply concerned about the very intensity of their chief's involvement. Although he was obviously buoyed in spirit by the defeat of Germany and the part the United States had played in the victory, and although he seemed stronger and healthier than he had for many months, he *did* have a history of serious disabilities, some of which had reduced him to long periods as an invalid, going back to his boyhood.

Nothing could dissuade Woodrow Wilson from plunging ahead. Never again would there be, in his mind, such an opportunity for presenting his case to the acknowledged world leaders of the day. He had meticulously created and defined "Fourteen Points" as the basis for peace in Europe, the most important one being his concept of the League of Nations.

The concerns about his health soon seemed to be totally weightless. When Wilson arrived in France in mid-December, the first American president to visit Europe while in office, he was greeted by cheering crowds and prominent statesmen. It now seemed evident that his decision to participate was wise after all and his chances of success great. The President addressed the opening session of the Peace Conference on January 18, 1919, and was greatly encouraged when his plan for the League of Nations was included on the agenda one week later. He was able to convince the other three members of "The Big Four"— Georges Clemenceau of France, David Lloyd George of Great Britain, and Vittorio Orlando of Italy—that the League incorporated many of the elements required for the peace plan. Yet Wilson's points were soon blunted as he found that he had to make major concessions in order to plead his case.

The European leaders grew more and more obdurate as Wilson attempted to convince them that his plan held the greatest assurance of lasting peace. To his way of thinking, they did not even care as much about peace as they did about punishment and revenge for the sufferings the Germans had caused during the long war. Frustration, nourished by a steadily building resentment, caused Wilson to suffer attacks of heartburn and indigestion. These ailments in turn made him more irritable, and more impatient to establish the League and have done with it. He seldom left the conference table without severe headaches, an upset stomach, and increasingly painful muscle spasms in his head, shoulders, and neck.

His physical problems intensified as he devoted longer and longer hours to work—early in the morning before the negotiations continued, and late into the night. Since he was unable to sway the other members of the conference during discussions, he constantly wrestled with the substance and wording of his Fourteen Points, to see how he might adapt them to propositions that Clemenceau, Lloyd George, and Orlando would accept. The strenuous commitment to work accomplished nothing in the end, and only served to make him weaker and undermine his health.

This kind of gradual collapse came as no surprise to those who knew Wilson intimately. It was, in fact, true to a pattern that went right back to his youth and continued throughout his days as a student at college, and later during his career as a professor and on into his rising years in the field of politics and government. From the time he was born in Staunton, Virginia, on December 28, 1856, until he was well into his thirties, Woodrow Wilson led a most sheltered life, dominated by his father and shielded by his mother. His father, Dr. Thomas Wilson, was a Presbyterian minister who almost completely neglected his son's physical growth as he concentrated on developing the boy's mind, spiritual perception, and religious belief. The bond between the two was so strong that one biographer later wrote, "His passionate love of his father was the core of his emotional life." When they were separated, even for short periods of time, they wrote what were described as "love letters," and they kissed each other with great emotion whenever they met.

As a boy, Wilson was a pathetic figure. He was constantly sick and weak, suffered the pain of indigestion and headaches, had poor eyesight, and was often referred to as "nervous." He was also indecisive in the extreme, and is said not to have made an important decision until after the age of forty without first seeking his father's advice. His mother, lacking vitality herself, coddled him constantly and was forever warning him about such dangers as rich food, drafts, and dampness. Under such circumstances, he could hardly have grown up without the certainty that he was prey to innumerable disorders.

At the age of seventeen, he had an opportunity to escape the dominance of his father and get out from under the wings of his mother when he enrolled at Davidson, a small Presbyterian college, in North Carolina. But this environment offered little improvement. The food upset his stomach so that he was constantly in the grips of heartburn, nausea, constipation, or "nervous indigestion." He suffered from various allergies of uncertain origin. By the end of the first year, he gave up and returned to the shelter of his family, where he convalesced for the next year and a half, devoting most of his time to reading and study on his own.

In 1875, by the time he had reached nineteen, he was sufficiently recuperated to enroll at the College of New Jersey, later to be renamed Princeton, where he qualified for free tuition because of his father's position as a clergyman. This was probably the most productive and fortuitous step he ever made. Poorly prepared, scholastically as well as constitutionally, he had to struggle hard the first year to avoid dropping out. What saved him was his passion for public speaking, debating, and courses in government, in which he was to excel. In effect, he became so absorbed in his speaking and writing that he seems to have been able to ignore the physical ailments and inner fears which had heretofore sent him into frequent retreat.

For the first time, too, his father's nagging insistence on clarity of expression and selection of words and phrases was a motivating force. "Study *manner*, dearest Tommie, as much as matter," the father had advised in one of his frequent letters to his son, "Sentences ought to resemble bullets—that is, be compact and rapid, and prepared to make clean holes." Wilson followed instructions precisely and soon became known as the most effective speaker and writer on government in his class, if not the entire college. It was typical of his life that success bred success and he was able to maintain an average well over 90 and graduate as one of the most promising young men on campus.

The momentum carried him easily and naturally into the University of Virginia Law School, where he continued during the first year to maintain his position as a student leader and speaker. He read prodigiously and wrote articles on government and politics, two of them published in the *University Magazine.* Then came the slump, at first mental, then physical. The warning sign was his growing opinion that the details of the law, which he was forced to study, were "as monotonous as hash." Boredom with mandatory courses led to a distaste for drudgery and a feeling that what had once been stimulating was now lackluster. Again, it was a familiar pattern in the Wilson cycles of health and disability. As winter set in during his second year at Virginia, Wilson contracted a severe inflammation of the respiratory tract, acute indigestion, and general fatigue and nervousness that he attributed to overwork. These flare-ups of symptoms that incapacitated him, and always seemed to be associated with respiratory infections, would seem in retrospect, to be exacerbations of acute, and then chronic, nephritis. It is certain that before too many more years went by he began having the more serious symptoms that denoted chronic nephritis and coincident hypertensive cardiovascular disease.

"How can a man with a weak body arrive anywhere?" he asked in a letter to a friend, expressing his profound distress at having to capitulate to the weaknesses of the flesh. He also excused his dropping out as "the most prudent step I could have taken," explaining that his doctor had found "my digestive organs seriously out of gear and has confirmed me in the belief that, had I remained at law school, and there continued to neglect systematic medical treatment of myself, I might have confirmed myself in dyspepsia and have fixed on myself a very uncomfortable future."

To his credit, he did continue his studies at home in such a diligent manner that he was able to pass the bar exams in 1882 with high honors. A year later, having failed to produce any income as a lawyer, he decided to shift into teaching on "subjects whose study delights me." He enrolled at Johns Hopkins University and signed up for courses in government, constitutional history, economics, and international law. Once again, his health took an upward swing, greatly fortified by his all-consuming preoccupation with the writing of a book, *Congressional Government: A Study of Government by Committee*. The book, which occupied much of the two years he spent at Johns Hopkins, was not only accepted by the university as his doctoral thesis, but was highly praised after its publication. Significantly, it was the first time in American history that a comprehensive study of the presidency was written by a man later to hold that office.

Woodrow Wilson's journey through life was marked by medical milestones of increasing severity, each one more damaging to his health than the previous ones. Thus, by the time he was sixty-two and at the Paris peace table, the attacks of ill health were crippling rather than simply distressing and inconvenient. It required immense fortitude and backbone to ignore the warning signs. On February 15, 1919, Wilson interrupted his participation in the talks to sail back to the United States for a brief confrontation with members of the Senate and House Foreign Relations committees. If his efforts on behalf of the League of Nations were faring poorly in Paris, they were even less promising at home. In retrospect, Wilson had made a serious political blunder. When he decided to go to Paris, he undertook almost the entire burden himself, with most of his proficient advisors left out, and with only a skeleton crew of experts. This placed far too many details on his own shoulders. More significantly, though, the omission rankled with many legislators and officials who felt they should have been included, and all but doomed the mission to failure from the start.

Wilson, already becoming shaky from his exertions and obsessed by the frustrations, was not ready for a further blow to his ambitions when he read a statement of opposition, rejecting the League, signed by thirty-seven Republican senators and two senators-elect. There were distinct indications that he was under-going an emotional crisis, marked by feelings of betrayal and abandonment. His speeches, in which he used phrases like "drunk with this spirit of self-sacrifice," revealed that he was losing touch with reality, even attempting to place himself in the role of a martyr to attract supporters.

After little more than a week in the United States, he faced, with rising impatience, the long voyage back to Europe. Arriving in Paris on March 14, he learned that the situation there had deteriorated badly. The French, in direct opposition to every-thing he had pleaded for, were making severe demands on the enemy, including reparations for war damage to French prop-erty and the Allied occupation of the Rhineland. Wilson insisted that there would be no treaty without his League of Nations. He was not simply insistent, but increasingly obsessive, asserting that he was being betrayed and that enemies, both at home and in Europe, were plotting against him. More and more, his exhor-tations to the British, the French, and the Italians contained religious overtones, suggesting that God had chosen him as His messenger to establish peace among men.

On March 27, Wilson's handful of associates were fearful that a nervous collapse would occur at any moment. During the meet-ings, Clemenceau reiterated his demands that the Rhineland should be occupied and the Saar annexed. Wilson exploded at the conference table, almost in tears as he attacked the Frenchman in a verbal tirade, accusing him of fabricating selfish demands that had never previously been considered in the peace talks.

"You are pro-German, Mr. Wilson!" replied the French leader, "You are seeking to destroy France."

"That is untrue and you know it is untrue," replied the President bitterly, adding a little later, "If France does not get what she wishes, she will refuse to act with us. In that event, do you wish me to return home?"

"I do not wish you to go home," remarked Clemenceau in a tone of resignation, perhaps realizing that the American was a sick man, "but I intend to do so myself." With that, he plunked his hat on his head and walked out of the room.

For Wilson, this was really the end of the road in Europe.

Although he struggled to consolidate a position and even delivered one more speech that was moving and aroused great sympathy for the man, his cause was disintegrating.

By April 3, it was obvious that Woodrow Wilson was seriously ill. He was so overcome by convulsive fits of coughing that he was scarcely able to breathe. His lungs were heavily congested, his stomach unable to take nourishment, and his bowels afflicted by constant diarrhea. Although "food poisoning" was the initial diagnosis, this was quickly changed to influenza.

Woodrow Wilson was another victim of the pandemic of influenza that swept over the world in 1918 and 1919. Estimates are that four million Americans died of the disease and that perhaps twenty million people died world-wide. Wilson may well have been the most important man to have caught the disease and his illness certainly affected world events and the future of Europe and America more than could have been known at the time. Wilson was fighting Clemenceau, Orlando, Lloyd George, and swine influenza.

The sudden onset of high fever and headache, with insomnia, vomiting, diarrhea, myalgias, sweats, chills, and severe malaise, was typical of the epidemic "flu." The initial fear that he might have been poisoned was quickly discounted by Dr. Cary Grayson. Bedrest and the standard antiflu measures of the time were sufficient to bring down his fever and see him into a period of convalescence within a week. Yet subtle changes had taken place that did not promise an early—or even a complete—recovery. One was the return of his old headaches with such increased severity and persistence that viral encephalitis could even have been a contributing cause. There was evidence, too, that he might have suffered viral myocarditis, which would seriously affect a heart already damaged by long-standing hypertensive cardiovascular disease. This may have been evidenced by the beginnings of a serious disturbance in his breathing, which occurred only at night and was associated with a real shortness of breath. A cough persisted, resistant to all of the remedies tried.

Most alarming, however, were the appearances of distinct personality changes in the President. His suspicions that spies had invaded the American embassy and were moving and stealing furniture and his frantic rearranging of tables and chairs were clearcut evidences of these vagaries. During the nights when he could not sleep, nagged by coughing and weakened by shortness of breath and headaches, he would awaken an aide, whisper that he had heard the spies at work, and insist on sneaking downstairs and moving the furniture into what he thought was the proper place. This frantic activity was not only alarming to the few Americans who knew about, and guarded, the secret, but left him exhausted and debilitated.

Another bizarre change in personality, which carried over into his return to the United States was the "motor car syndrome." The President had long enjoyed a passion for motoring, a form of relaxation that should have been most beneficial while he was convalescing. But he was no longer to enjoy his sojourns on the highway. The instant another automobile passed the presidential limousine on the open road, he would become highly agitated. He would demand that the offending motorist be arrested and tried for speeding. On at least one occasion, he wrote to his Attorney General to inquire whether the president of the United States had the legal power to arrest a motorist, acting in effect as "a justice of the peace."

Even for those close to Wilson, who had lived through the hours when he writhed in his bed with the flu, vomiting, fighting for breath, and discharging bloody urine, the mental disintegration was the most frightening of all. They were amazed that he was able to recover, at least in part, and enough so that he could attend sessions at the Peace Conference and continue fighting for his Points right up until the signing of the Treaty of Versailles on June 28, 1919.

On June 29, Woodrow Wilson sailed for the United States, intent on submitting the covenant of the League of Nations with the Treaty of Versailles to the Senate for ratification. He was already depressed by the fact that he had been forced to make so many concessions to the other members of The Big Four, and that he had been accused by the Germans of assisting in framing a treaty "dictated by hate." Now, the only ray of hope lay in convincing America to participate in that greatest of all newly formed institutions for peace: the League of Nations.

After his very first session with the Senate Foreign Relations Committee, he must have realized—though he tried to conceal his doubts—that his personal battle was just starting, not coming to a conclusion. He must have realized, too, that he was neither physically nor mentally ready for such a battle. As one who knew him well wrote, "When the President returned to America in July, 1919, he did not resemble the man who had left barely seven months before, radiating strength and self-confidence. His shoulders sagged, weariness and anxiety had deeply gnawed into his face that looked gray and drawn."

Even a president in top physical condition would have faced almost insurmountable odds. The Senate was against the League of Nations, with individual opinions varying from simple reservations about the workability of the concept to outright hostility. One of the leaders, Hiram Johnson of California, went so far as to denounce the League as a "gigantic war trust." Wilson was strongly opposed, too, by Senator Henry Cabot Lodge of Massachusetts, who had served for more than three decades in Congress and who, as chairman of the Senate Foreign Relations Committee, not only considered the President weak as an internationalist, but "egotistical, unprincipled, and narrow-minded."

When Wilson realized that he was not winning Congress over to his side, he announced that he would take his case directly to the people. Travelling across the country by train, he would speak from the rear platform at every whistle stop, stopping over in the cities for meetings, speeches, and other public appearances. His wife, Edith Bolling Galt Wilson, whom he had married after the death of his first wife, was stunned. The effort would be nothing short of suicidal. Wilson's personal secretary and a man of considerable influence, Joe Tumulty, tried to dissuade him. His personal physician, Admiral Cary Grayson, literally forbade the President from making such a trip.

They were concerned as much about his past medical history as by his more recent bouts with flu and other diseases. Even as far back as the days when he was a professor, living a quiet and sheltered life on campus, he was constantly suffering from one illness or another. In 1890, he had begun one of the healthiest

Andrew Jackson photographed before he left Washington in 1836, age 70.

—Culver Pictures, Inc.

Franklin Pierce shortly after his inauguration, March 4, 1853.

Abraham Lincoln in 1863. See text regarding apparent motion of foot.

—Culver Pictures, Inc.

Ulysses S. Grant.

A contemporary drawing of the attack on President Garfield—July 2, 1881.

—Culver Pictures, Inc.

When it was discovered in 1884 that "Grover the Good" had fathered an illegitimate child, Republicans flooded the country with this cartoon captioned: "Ma! Ma! Where's my pa? Gone to the White House, Ha! Ha! Ha!"

William McKinley photographed at his desk in the White House.   —Culver Pictures, Inc.

Thomas Woodrow Wilson pictured as a student, as a professor at Princeton University, and as an ex-president.

"You're the only woman I know who can wear an orchid. Generally it's the orchid that wears the woman," said President Woodrow Wilson of his second wife, Edith Bolling Galt.

—Culver Pictures, Inc.

Warren G. Harding, throwing out the first baseball of the 1922 season.

—Culver Picutres, Inc.

Churchill, Roosevelt, and Stalin pictured at Yalta.

Culver Pictures, Inc.

John F. Kennedy, the picture of youthful vigor, photographed on the steps of the White House.
—Culver Pictures, Inc.

periods in his life when he accepted a professorship at Princeton, teaching jurisprudence and political economy. But five years later, in the autumn of 1895, he had begun to suffer periods of intense nervousness, touched off by hostilities and conflicts with other members of the faculty. He agonized through a dreadfully long winter with a succession of splitting headaches and violent stomach pains. These ailments were caused by both indigestion and nervousness. The spring of 1896 found him in even greater misery when he contracted an excruciating form of neuritis that made it impossible for him to use his right hand.

These and other long-enduring bouts of illness established a certain pattern of determination and courage—almost an aggression—that was to characterize his presidency. After the greatest periods of physical pain and mental agony, after the most crushing political defeats, after the kinds of pressures that would have forced many leaders to throw in the sponge, he always bounced back fighting, and often more aggressively than ever. Almost nothing seemed to make him admit personal defeat. In the spring of 1899, he underwent such a severe breakdown that he had to retreat temporarily to the British Isles to get hold of himself. In 1906, when he was just fifty and by then serving as president of Princeton University, he awoke one fateful morning to find that he was completely blind in his left eye. The shock to his system was overwhelming. His first wife later wrote that he had hardening of the arteries and was "dying by inches and incurable." The blindness was diagnosed as a thrombosis of an ophthalmic artery. At the same time, he experienced the weakness in the right hand that had affected him earlier. The most likely explanation is that he also suffered an occlusion or clot of blood in one of the small vessels in the brain, which seems probable in view of the subsequent course of his diseases. At about the same time, it was also noted that he had what was called "albumenuric retinitis," diagnosed by the ophthalmologist treating him. This term was used to describe the appearance of the retina, when viewed through an ophthalmoscope, of patients suffering chronic kidney disease.

Although Wilson suffered no further illnesses pointing to diseases of his central nervous system until he became ill during the Paris Peace Conference, thirteen years later, it seems probable that the sudden blindness indicated that he suffered a series of small strokes, a most common warning of impending trouble. The term, made popular by Dr. Walter Alvarez in the 1950s, is used to describe any of the multiple minor disabilities that afflict people as they age. Usually explained by a diminished blood supply to the brain, with spasms and sometimes the occlusion of small blood vessels of the brain, these small strokes may go unnoticed by all but the most careful medical observers. However, when they are obvious even to the layman, as in the case of Wilson's blindness or the partial inability to use a hand, they can hardly be brushed aside as something a person has to put up with in the process of growing older.

Wilson was what the medical profession refers to as *anosognosic*—a person who overlooks, even denies, illnesses and disabilities. Although he continued to have problems with his eye for the rest of his life, along with the "writer's cramp" and other failings, he simply ignored the consequences. When he became involved in a series of internal faculty disputes at Princeton and failed in his efforts to assume the increased powers that he felt the president of the university should be endowed with, he decided to enter politics. His name had already been mentioned as presidential timber when, in July 1910, he agreed to run for the governorship of New Jersey.

His role as governor was too limited—barely two short years —to provide much evidence of his qualities as a political leader. By the time he reached the White House, in March 1913, he had certainly acquired a most unusual medical history, especially for a man who was to be called upon to lead the nation through some of its toughest and most critical years. His constantly recurring headaches were leading him to ingest large quantities of aspirin, phenacetin, aminopyrine, and the like. These, in turn, were aggravating his chronic renal disease, as well as his usually sensitive stomach. Thus, in order to start each day with less distress, he had acquired the habit of swallowing a stomach tube and flushing his stomach with a soothing liquid. Although this procedure was more harmful than beneficial, it apparently brought about a certain peace of mind, the conviction that he had temporarily at least rid himself of "poisons and toxins" that were invading the membranes of his stomach.

It was surprising, if not miraculous, that Woodrow Wilson enjoyed almost normally good health during his first administration and into the beginning of his second. This was in part the result of the practical counsel of the White House physician, Dr. Cary Grayson, who for example put an end to the use of the stomach tube. It was also to a large extent the happy result of Wilson's intense absorption in the duties and responsibilities of the presidency, to such a degree that he literally had no time for concern about personal ailments and symptoms that might earlier have triggered some of the old aggravations—nervousness, indigestion, fatigue, and general debilitation.

The greatest blow to his health and spirit came in August 1914, when his first wife, Ellen Louise, died. Emotionally, he fell apart, even to the extent of expressing the hope that he himself would die, or even be assassinated. Since 1885, he had relied on his wife, the former Ellen Louise Axson, for emotional security, counsel in times of stress, and maternal, as well as connubial, love. "To an extraordinary extent," wrote one of his biographers, "she protected him, guided him, established the environment in which his intense nature could best function," and shielded him from the erosions of his personal prejudices and hatreds. Once he was away from his mother and father, she was the only person on earth with whom he could bear to share his innermost problems and tensions.

Ellen Louise Wilson had served, in effect, as a vital relief valve for the pressures that reached explosive proportions within the President. Although he was inclined to overlook some of the really serious symptoms of disease, he was constantly prey to lesser physical annoyances. He leaned on Louise to help him become less intense, or to be more careful about overstraining his eyes, or to soothe his headaches and nerves. Many who were close to the President predicted that the death of his wife would trigger a physical, as well as emotional, slump from which he would never recover. One of his physicians, Dr. S. Weir Mitchell, a noted neurologist from Philadelphia, had already expressed the belief that Wilson could never survive the presidency. His prophecy might well have come true, had it not been for the strength of his wife and the diligence and understanding of his White House physician. Dr. Cary T. Grayson was a young officer in the Navy Medical Corps when first appointed, later to be promoted to the rank of admiral.

The most critical, and certainly a most unique, role in American history was to be played by a lady who did not appear on the scene until the middle of 1915. She was Edith Bolling Galt, a widow of forty-three when, in April of that year she was invited to the White House to have tea with a member of the staff, Miss Helen Bones, who was a cousin of the President. Quite inadvertently, the ladies ran into Wilson at the elevator and were invited to have their tea in the Oval Room.

The chemistry was just right. The President showed his interest by sending Mrs. Galt copies of some of his favorite books, then by inviting her to the White House so that he could read passages of particular interest to him and enjoy her reaction. This communication led very quickly into more serious discussions about the problems of the presidency and matters of state. It was not long, wrote one of Wilson's biographers, Ray Stannard Baker, before he was "opening his whole mind, seeking her suggestions and opinions, as he continued to do as long as he lived. It soon became a relationship based upon the deepest understanding and sympathy."

As Baker pointed out, "All the Wilson family, and the nearest friends, from the beginning looked with the warmest approval upon the new friendship. The loneliness that followed the death of the first Mrs. Wilson had been desolating. His friends feared for him."

It is significant that friends and relatives, including the President's own daughters, nourished the relationship. Encouragement of the friendship just a few months after Ellen's death, and during an era when the "proper" interval of mourning was at least one year, indicates how gravely concerned Wilson's intimates were about the state of his health. Even Stockton Axson, a brother of the first Mrs. Wilson, expressed his complete approval, saying that he was "thoroughly thankful that the great man doesn't have to keep on being a *lonely* great man."

There was no doubt that Woodrow Wilson's health during

the summer and fall of 1915 was at a peak. His anxieties and nervous stomach seemed to be matters of the past. He no longer dwelled upon the loneliness and futilities of the presidency. More importantly, the very real physical disabilities he suffered, such as partial blindness and muscle cramps, were almost totally ignored as he subconsciously and automatically compensated for them in other ways. By the time Wilson and Mrs. Galt were married on December 18, 1915, the President was considered by Admiral Grayson to be totally fit and ready to face almost any contingency.

From that crucial period until late in 1918, Woodrow Wilson walked a medical tightrope, managing to hold himself in physiological balance, yet always susceptible to a sudden and devastating downfall. Keeping him in balance mentally was his wife, who skillfully kept him from stumbling on his own neuroses. Maintaining the physical balance, Admiral Grayson supervised every aspect of the President's regimen—diet, exercise, rest, work habits, and life style. Wilson became known as an extremely hardworking world leader, with a record of immense accomplishment. Yet, incredibly, under Grayson's dictate, he invariably enjoyed nine hours of uninterrupted sleep, spent many relaxing moments on the golf course or motoring in the countryside, and was seldom at his desk for more than four hours each day. He lived in a bubble of isolation that is today almost beyond imagination for a chief executive, seeing very little of Congress or his own cabinet.

The warning signs, however, were ever-present. On practically every occasion when he was subjected to a heated confrontation with a congressional leader (or even a member of his own White House staff) over an issue, he was tortured by "sick headaches" or indigestion—perhaps for two or three days thereafter. His two alter egos made most of the contacts, disposed of day-to-day business with the outside world, and absorbed the shocks of disagreement and challenge, long before they could impact on the President. They were Joseph P. Tumulty, his faithful and long-suffering White House secretary, and Colonel Edward M. House, Wilson's closest advisor and the man on whom he most relied for the drafting of the points in the Treaty of Versailles and the League of Nations. It was characteristic of Wilson that his closeness to these two faithful aides eventually disintegrated under the corrosion of the neuroses that afflicted the President, as did all of his intimate relationships with people, with the notable exceptions of his two wives.

The long period of stable, if not robust, health continued right through until the end of World War I, during a critical period in both American and world history. If it was threatened by Wilson's participation in the Paris Peace Conference, it was even more seriously menaced by the ill-considered decision he was to make in the mid-summer of 1919. When the President arrived home on July 8, after the signing of the Treaty of Versailles, he was a sick man, only partially recovered from the influenza that had struck him down in April. In his biography of Wilson, Herbert Hoover wrote that his predecessor had suffered far more than flu, never fully recovered, and that "the previously incisive, quick mind became a slow and more resisting mind."

Under these circumstances, and with his history of cerebrovascular disease (which so often precedes the major catastrophe of a stroke), Wilson's decision that summer was inexplicable, if not irresponsible. When it seemed apparent that Congress was not going to ratify the Treaty of Versailles and support the concept of the League of Nations, Woodrow Wilson was furious. Having battled for six months in Europe—literally fighting himself sick—to see his brainchild become a reality, he was determined that his enemies in Congress were not going to thwart his dream of a League in which America would play a basic role. He announced that he would embark on a coast-to-coast speaking tour of the United States, a personal campaign during which he would convince voters and legislators alike that the United States should join the League of Nations, and thus assure lasting peace.

The decision to embark on a crusade that could have no positive effect on the outcome, and that posed an obvious threat to the health of the chief executive, certainly ranks as one of the greatest blunders ever made by an American president.

Dr. Grayson, Joseph Tumulty, Colonel House, Edith Wilson, and members of his cabinet tried to dissuade the President, from the standpoint of both health and diplomacy. But Wilson was adamant. If the Senate was not going to confirm the Peace Treaty for which he had fought so long and hard, he would take his case to the people, who would understand and would rise up in their clamor for approval. On September 4, 1919, he embarked on a railroad train for a speaking tour of the West that was eventually to cover almost 10,000 miles, twenty-nine cities and countless whistle stops in between. The only concession he made to his wife and doctor was to spend a week or two beforehand in quiet and rest, to build up his strength and resistance.

Wilson ranks close to the top of American presidents in the ability to speak clearly, convincingly, and eloquently. And he knew it. He was so skilled in the selection of the right phrases and words that someone once remarked that he "was born half-way between the *Bible* and the dictionary." It was obvious as the train pulled out of the Washington station and the President was seen to be in unusually high spirits as he waved in departure, that he was really "up" for the tour. There is no doubt that he was convinced that his message to the people would force Congress to reverse its stand on the League of Nations.

When Wilson's wife, secretary, and personal physician all pleaded with him not to attempt the cross-country tour, Wilson fully revealed that he was aware of the possible consequences to his health. He was not only fighting for the treaty, but *against* his enemies in Congress, the most notable being Senator Henry Cabot Lodge. It was not stretching the point to say that he would willingly have died in order to defeat Lodge and see the United States join the League of Nations.

"I know that I am at the end of my tether," he asserted at the time, "but my friends on the Hill say that the trip is necessary to save the treaty and I am willing to make whatever personal sacrifice is required, for if the treaty should be defeated, God only knows what would happen to the world as a result of it."

He countered Grayson's protests by saying bluntly, "I *hope* it won't have any bad effects, but even if it does, I must go. The soldiers in the trenches did not turn back because of the danger and I cannot turn back from my taks of making the League of Nations an established fact."

Though statements like these sound histrionic and exaggerated, if not overemotional, there seems to be little doubt that Wilson was entirely serious about the extent of the sacrifice he was willing to make. As one historian, Karl C. Wold, expressed it, "He was a casualty of the Armistice as much as thousands of soldiers were casualties of the war, and his fall was perhaps even more tragic than theirs in its implications."

The President might have lowered the odds against his health had he headed north instead of south. The first two days went well, but then he found himself in the midst of a heat wave, unable to sleep soundly, plagued by headaches, and with his speaking effectiveness greatly reduced by shortness of breath. Worse yet, the breathing also began affecting his lungs when he was lying down, interrupting his sleep and sometimes forcing him to try to rest in a sitting position at night, after spending long hours on his feet. Although the lung condition was diagnosed as asthma at the time, it later seemed evident that the attacks were actually symptoms of heart failure—orthopnia and paroxysmal nocturnal dyspnea.

The physical and emotional strain of the President's schedule and demands would have taken a severe toll of a *healthy* man in his early sixties, let alone one who had recently had a bout with influenza and had a long-standing medical history of hypertensive vascular disease and probably viral myocarditis. One of the most aggravating symptoms, and perhaps the most distressing for a man of Wilson's mentality, was a failing memory. He began to find difficulty in recalling what he had intended to say. The right words kept eluding him. His delivery became more ranting and emotional, and less effective in defining the reasons why America should play a key role in the League of Nations. Sometimes he became so overcome by the emotional implications of what he was trying to say that he was moved to tears, although his listeners appeared to be little touched, or even restless.

Even more of an indignity was the development of a twitch in his cheek muscles, accompanied by a drooping of the left side of his mouth and occasional drooling. His hands trembled noticeably, and did not seem to be coordinating with his brain, giving him the appearance of fumbling or being unprepared. More often than not, he concluded speeches with irrelevant bits of information, as though he had forgotten the intended ending and was rattling off whatever else came to mind.

The inevitable crisis occurred on September 26, near Pueblo, Colorado, where the heat had been registering 103 degrees during the day and not much cooler at night. On that occasion, he suddenly began fumbling for words, his speech slurred, then ceased abruptly. His face twitched uncontrollably and his eyes became flooded with tears. Mercifully, his aides half-carried him quickly from the rear platform of the train to the inside of the Pullman car. Someone apologized for the President's "indisposition," and the crowd dispersed with the impression that he had suffered from nothing more than a heat stroke.

Edith Wilson knew, better than anyone else present, that the President's great humanitarian effort was over. With the obvious facts staring him in the face, Wilson desperately rejected the idea of giving up his private crusade. That night, his breathing was so labored that he could sleep only when sitting upright in a chair. By morning, he was having difficulty holding himself in position, panting erratically, and perspiring profusely. His speech had thickened noticeably. When he overheard his wife, secretary, and doctor making plans for an immediate return to Washington, he was overcome with tears and tried feebly to stand up and take control of the situation. It was now noticed that his left side was partially paralyzed and that he could not stand up unsupported, much less walk.

It took three days for the train to run the return trip from Colorado to Washington. At the start, Dr. Grayson made plans for emergency stops at hospitals en route, in the event that the President's condition should worsen. Yet Wilson amazed everyone by his incredible powers of recuperation, as he had done during past illnesses. The three days of complete rest and the knowledge that there were no speeches to be made, no crowds to greet, no deadlines to meet, did wonders for his condition. By the time the train pulled into the Washington station at 11:00 A.M., Sunday, September 28, his speech had returned to normal and the paralysis on the left side had been reduced to little more than an undetectible annoyance.

The few people who knew of the arrival time and met him

at the station were all but convinced that the President had
suffered a minor indisposition and found it advisable to cancel
the trip in order to be on the safe side. Wilson emerged from his
private car unassisted and strode down the platform to his waiting limousine. It was during the ride to the White House that
reporters first noticed something amiss. Wilson was bowing and
waving to empty sidewalks, almost as though he had pro-
grammed himself into a pattern of behavior upon arrival and was
mentally incapable of accepting the fact that his return had been
kept quiet and there were no crowds on hand.

Although he appeared to be a great deal better and was certainly stronger, he was now in such great pain that he was unable
to hear clearly, to think, or to focus his eyes. "All the rest of the
day," wrote Mrs. Wilson of the homecoming, "my husband wandered like a ghost between the study at one end of the hall and
my room at the other. The awful pain in his head that drove him
relentlessly back and forth was too acute to permit work or even
reading."

By October 2, the President seemed more relaxed, as his wife
observed his sleep almost hourly. But at eight that morning she
woke from a fitful nap to find him sitting on the edge of his bed,
trying unsuccessfully to reach a bottle of water on the nearby
table. As she handed it to him, she noticed with alarm that his
left hand was hanging loosely.

"I have no feeling in that hand," he explained. "Will you rub
it?"

As she started to massage the sickly pale flesh, he interrupted
abruptly, "First, help me to the bathroom."

Taking his arm, she quickly realized that even his smallest
movements were made with great difficulty and that each effort
induced spasms of intense pain. "It was so alarming," recalled
Mrs. Wilson, "that I asked if I could leave him long enough to
telephone the doctor."

The President nodded assent, but by the time his wife was
on the phone, she heard a muffled thump. Rushing into the bathroom, she found him spread out on the floor, unconscious. This
time he had suffered a complete stroke, paralyzed on the left side

from head to toe. In medical terms, he had suffered a cerebral thrombosis of the right middle cerebral artery, producing infarction of the brain and resulting left hemiplegia.

The unconscious form was gently lifted onto the big bed that had once been used by Abraham Lincoln. Dr. Grayson was immediately summoned from Philadelphia. When he saw the President's condition, he called in Dr. Francis X. Dercum, a noted specialist in internal medicine, Rear Admiral E. R. Stitt, of the Naval Medical Corps, and Dr. Sterling Ruffin, of Washington, who was Edith Wilson's family physician. Later, Dr. George de Schweinitz, a pioneer in ophthalmology, was brought in, to determine what kind of prognosis could be made through an examination of the patient's eyes. These specialists decided that the best course of action was to keep him in the White House, where he could be kept in quiet and isolation, rather than run the risk of exposing him to the distractions of a hospital, where it would be difficult to shield him from noise, germs, and the prying eyes of the press. There, for several days, his life hung precariously in the balance. By the end of the first week, however, full consciousness had returned and Wilson was beginning to chafe at his enforced imprisonment. He was becoming obsessed with the idea that he had to get back on his feet and continue fighting for the cause of the League of Nations. Much of the time he was rambling and incoherent.

One of the questions that constantly arose—and is still the subject of discussion by biographers—was this: how could a man of Wilson's intelligence and extensive education be so persistent in ignoring the signs warning him that his health, even his life, were in great jeopardy? Referring to the headaches, dizziness, and nervousness that disabled him during his futile tour across the country in September 1919, the *Journal of the Oklahoma State Medical Association* voiced a common reaction in an issue several months after the President's attack.

> These symptoms conjoined with the fact that for a long time he had high blood pressure were danger signals which no physician would dare neglect. It is legitimate to infer that his physician apprised him

and counselled him accordingly. Despite it, he persisted until nature exacted the penalty and by so doing jeopardized his own life and the equilibrium of affairs of the country.

The medical journal pronounced Mr. Wilson not only obstinate but both selfish and cruel. These judgments were made largely because Wilson had dismissed one of his cabinet members, Secretary of State Robert Lansing, for having scheduled several cabinet meetings without his knowledge or authorization. Wilson may certainly have been obstinate, selfish, and cruel—and much more—in the accepted sense of the words. More importantly, though, he was so convinced that it was his ultimate destiny to lead America, and the world, back on the road to peace that he was willing to endure any torment and anguish to achieve that objective. His was a special kind of courage that would be damned by most and interpreted as heroic by very few. Most readers probably agreed with the editorial assessment of the medical journal that "future candidates for the Presidency should be submitted to psychological tests to determine their intellectual and emotional coefficients. Those who do not measure up to a certain standard shall be eliminated."

Logical though such a suggestion may be—and it has been proposed during just about every election campaign over the past century—it would have classified many of our most eminent presidents as unfit to run.

At some point during the first two weeks of disability—no one will ever know just when—a critical decision was made that was to affect the course of the nation for the next year, and beyond. Dr. Grayson and the other specialists who were brought in made it clear that the President's recovery hinged delicately on how successfully Wilson could be relieved of even the most minor concerns and responsibilities. The obvious solution today would be to let the vice-president and cabinet take over completely, and for whatever length of time was necessary to see the patient completely out of danger.

But Vice-President Thomas Marshall, though a respected administrator, and formerly Governor of Indiana, was totally incapable of taking action. Secretary of State Robert Lansing, already out of favor with Wilson for trying to persuade him to compromise on the points he had demanded for the peace treaty, was the only official of importance who ventured a solution. He went directly to Joseph Tumulty and, in as diplomatic a manner as possible, read him clauses from the United States Constitution, including the following statement:

> In case of the removal of the President from office, or his death, resignation, or inability to discharge the powers and duties of the said office, the same shall devolve upon the Vice President.

Tumulty's reaction was cold, even indignant.

"Mr. Lansing," he said flatly, "the Constitution is not a dead letter with the White House. I have read the Constitution and do not find myself in need of any tutoring at your hands of the provision you have just read."

When Tumulty asked bluntly who should assume the responsibility of determining that the President was "disabled" to the extent required by the Constitution, he was told that he himself could make that decision, or Dr. Grayson. "You may rest assured," replied Tumulty angrily, "that while Woodrow Wilson is lying in the White House on the broad of his back I will not be party to ousting him. He has been too kind, too loyal, and too wonderful to me to receive such treatment at my hands."

At this point, Grayson entered the room, was asked the same question, and made it clear that he would under no circumstances certify that the President was too disabled to remain in office. The matter was closed when Tumulty informed Lansing that if anybody outside the White House circle attempted to establish constitutional "disability," both he and Grayson would stand together and repudiate the assertion.

In retrospect, there were elements of conspiracy in Wilson's case. The patient was never hospitalized, never tested to determine the extent of his mental functions, never checked to define the nature and location of the brain lesion resulting from the cerebral trauma. Despite the outward show of indignation on the part of Tumulty and the obvious reluctance of Grayson to pronounce his friend and leader incompetent, it is reasonable to suppose that they would eventually have given in to reality as the weeks and months wore on and Wilson remained a complete invalid. But the course of history often hinges on individuals, and in this case the real catalyst was Edith Bolling Galt Wilson.

She had already been told by her own doctor and by the medical specialists who were consulted that the President's recovery was in her hands. She had, first of all, to protect him from stressful situations and worries. She not only had an iron will of her own, but she was intimately aware of the way he reacted—and would have reacted—to every item of business on the White House calendar. From the start, she jealously guarded him from all visitors—even the Vice-President was never once admitted to his chief's bedroom. She literally stood at the door, permitting occasional bulletins to be issued to the effect that Mr. Wilson had been exhausted by the Peace Conference, the extended trip out West, and other matters, and that he was tired and suffering from frayed nerves.

For a couple of weeks, the press and the public accepted these reports. But in mid-October newsmen became suspicious that there was more to the medical story than they had been told when they observed a number of well-known specialists being ushered quietly into the White House. The reason for their presence—though never publicly announced—was that Wilson was in great pain, suffering from a prostatic obstruction that was blocking his bladder. On October 17, Dr. Hugh Young of Johns Hopkins, considered the top urologist in the country, was summoned in the emergency, bringing with him five other consultants.

The situation became critical after Young and his team repeatedly failed in their attempts to dilate the muscles of the urethra and insert a catheter. Since the bladder was becoming increasingly distended with urine, the only other way it could be drained was through surgery. Without relief, kidney damage would occur, soon followed by uremia that would be fatal. Although the doctors were in agreement that the operation should be performed, and at once, they could not proceed without the permission of Mrs. Wilson. When she was informed that surgery involved great risk, she refused to grant her approval.

The President's temperature rose alarmingly. His pulse became weak and erratic. It was obvious that he was in great pain, even though he was semiconscious. The only possible treatment was the application of hot-water bottles in the affected area. Two hours passed, then three. At the moment when Dr. Young was about to insist that the operation, dangerous though it might be, was the only hope, the muscles of the urethra suddenly relaxed and the crisis was over.

That was the only time during a period of several months that the outside world seemed to have any real suspicion about the serious nature of the President's health. Today, it would be impossible for a week to elapse without congressional, press, and public clamor for official reports. Yet it was not until at least three months had gone by from the date of Wilson's hasty return from the West that Congress decided that a review of the situation was in order. Motivated by some private investigations by Senator George Higgins Moses, a Republican of New Hampshire, the Senate moved to appoint a committee to visit the White House and determine the true state of the chief executive's health. Moses had stated unequivocally that the President had suffered a serious stroke. Congress was prodded into action, too, by the increasing outbursts of rumors, including one that Wilson had contracted syphilis in Paris, that it had affected his brain, and hence had to be treated in complete privacy.

The committee was duly appointed and the members, following an official request, were invited to meet with the President. At the appointed hour, Joe Tumulty ushered them into the patient's bedroom, where they were also greeted by Mrs. Wilson and Dr. Grayson. It was obvious from the start that the members of the committee were embarrassed and ill at ease. Beyond the usual meaningless comments about health and appearance, no one had much to say. Wilson enjoyed an obvious advantage. Having been well rehearsed by Mrs. Wilson, he was able to make a few humorous quips, inquire sensibly about the status of a couple of bills that were pending, and even appear to be physically alert. He had been placed in an upholstered chair, propped erect by the judicious placement of pillows, and had his left arm and hand partially covered by a shawl so that there was no indica-

tion of paralysis. The room was arranged in such a way, too, that
the official visitors viewed the President from an angle that minimized the droop of his jowls and the slump of his shoulders.

Unknown to the committee, Woodrow Wilson was in such
poor mental condition that he had an attention span of about
fifteen minutes. If forced to concentrate beyond that limit, his
mind wandered. He would become forgetful and repetitive, and
not sure what he was doing. Fortunately, since the senators were
at a loss as to how to proceed anyway, Mrs. Wilson was able to
cut the visit off well within that critical time span and see that
the visitors were politely ushered out so that the President could
get on to some other "pressing business" that was on his mind.

As a consequence of this visit, the committee reported that
the President's health seemed to be stable enough to preclude
further investigation or congressional concern.

Recovery from the prostatic obstruction seemed to provide
a noticeable, if brief, spur to Wilson's activities. He engaged in
a flurry of letter writing, dictated memos to his staff, and even
vetoed one bill. When his wife and the doctor helped him to move
his limbs, he referred to them as being "lame," never paralyzed.
The phrase "brain damage," which the doctors clearly recognized, was never used by either Wilson or his wife. Moreover, the
President was almost obsessive in asking how long it would be
before he could start walking again. His mental outlook was such
that, in addition to refusing absolutely to consider the idea of
resigning, he actively sought support for his nomination for a
third term. In the following summer, when the Democratic party
nominated James M. Cox of Ohio as its candidate, Wilson dismissed the selection as a "joke" and refused to believe that he was
being told the truth.

The only person in Washington outside the White House
who remained suspicious was Senator Moses. He had established
some kind of pipeline, never revealed, to the inner circle and
repeatedly warned any who would listen that Wilson was totally
incompetent to run the country because of severe brain damage.
He even went so far as to proclaim that the President was a mere
puppet and that the nation was really in the hands of Edith
Wilson, who was the puppeteer, pulling the strings. Despite his

arguments and presentations of medical evidence, no one listened, for it was well known that Moses was a long-time critic of Mr. Wilson. His public and private statements were discounted as pure political animosity.

No government leader today could remain so ill for such a long time and still masquerade as being competent. But affairs of state moved slowly in that postwar period. Moreover, after a few months, Wilson was able to control his muscles and limbs well enough so that he could walk with a shuffling gait. The process of recovery was agonizingly slow and would have caused most men to have admitted defeat. But not Wilson. He had lived with disabilities so long during his lifetime that his own ego forced him to believe that the maladies did not really exist. He might even have made rational decisions and taken constructive actions had he not been subject to massive outbursts of emotional instability. These were not observed by members of Congress, kept outside the closed doors, but they did serve to alienate, one by one, the members of his cabinet.

It was not until April 13, 1920 (some six months after his near-fatal attack) that Wilson actually held a formal cabinet meeting. He was described then, at sixty-three, as "old, worn, and haggard." He was unable to lead the meeting, acting more in the capacity of an auditor. In a later account, D. F. Houston, Secretary of the Treasury, remarked that the first incident that struck him as peculiar was that each cabinet member was announced by name as he entered the room. Was it possible that the President was unable to remember their names? Or perhaps that his vision was so affected that he could not see them clearly? Houston reported that "It was enough to make one weep to look at him. One of his arms was useless. In repose, his face looked very much as usual; but when he tried to speak, there were marked evidences of his trouble. His jaw tended to drop on one side, or seemed to do so. His voice was very weak and strained."

At the moment the meeting was supposed to commence, there was silence. The first subject at hand was the situation regarding the reorganization of the railroads for peacetime travel. Wilson seemed to have difficulty concentrating on the issues, even after several of the others present tried to outline the points covered. Dr. Grayson peeked in the door several times, obviously concerned about his patient. Finally, after an hour had passed, with little to show for it, Edith Wilson came in. Although she could not hide the disturbed expression on her face, she resolutely called a halt to the proceedings with the remark that the President had been subjected to enough exposure, considering that this was his first cabinet meeting in many months.

Despite the lack of any accomplishment during this historic session, Houston was deeply impressed by Wilson's "brave front," by his heroic efforts to ignore his disabilities, and even by his ability to crack a few jokes.

Was there really any improvement? Houston did report that the President looked "rather better" when a second cabinet meeting was attempted two weeks later. However, Secretary of the Navy Josephus Daniels pointed out that Edith Wilson was always close at hand with a ready excuse for entering the room if Mr. Wilson seemed to be losing touch. He had his good days and his bad ones, yet even at best he was seldom able to devote more than an hour or two to official business.

Admiral Grayson was with his patient almost constantly, though he gave no advice on any subject besides medicine and health. Tumulty saw his chief less and less, and other members of the White House staff almost never. So in effect the office of president was held for some eighteen months by a woman: Edith Wilson.

During the period when the President was "recovering," some twenty-eight bills went unsigned, although, as noted, he did manage to veto one: the Volstead prohibition enforcement bill. His ability to make decisions or provide any kind of leadership in absentia was impaired by his emotional instability, which in many instances took the form of extreme sensitivity to criticism, or imagined criticism. When his wife, personal friends, and advisors urged him to accept compromises, he stubbornly refused. As a result, when the final vote on the League of Nations came on March 19, 1920, the League was rejected and Wilson defeated.

In the late spring of 1920, Wilson's health improved to the point where he was able to sit up in a wheel chair in the garden or on the sunlit South Portico. He was described in the press as dictating to his secretary or studying congressional bills and other documents of state. He was confused, illogical, given to emotional outbursts. When Franklin Delano Roosevelt, then Assistant Secretary of the Navy and one of the few who had accompanied Wilson back from the Paris Conference, visited the President that summer, he was aghast. This man whom he had been led to believe was winning his battle for life, was unable to utter more than a few barely coherent words.

It was an ironic, as well as historic, meeting. For Roosevelt, who had just been nominated for the office of vice-president by the Democratic party, was within weeks of being stricken by the poliomyelitis that was to make such an incisive mark on his own life and his years as president.

Wilson survived for three years after the end of his term, failing steadily until his death on February 3, 1924—deaf, almost blind, and unable to speak or move without assistance. The tragedy of Wilson's illness was not that he suffered multiple strokes at a time when he most needed all of his physical and mental powers to accomplish his great aims. Rather, it was the fact that he stubbornly continued to deny the critical nature of his disabilities, even though to do so placed in jeopardy the very cause of peace for which he had fought so long and so persistently. Had he died in Paris at the peace table, at a time when he was idolized by foreigners and countrymen alike, he might well have been classed as one of America's three greatest presidents.

Yet it is astonishing that Wilson ever reached the presidency at all, when one considers the nature and extent of his physical and mental disabilities during his lifetime. Between the summer of 1875, when he was eighteen, and the beginning of his final illness in the spring of 1919, he had no fewer than fourteen critical breakdowns, lasting from two months to a year, and not including the final four years as an invalid. To aspire for the nation's highest office and to continue the battle required a certain kind of courage that is almost beyond comprehension.

9

Guts and Bondage

Woodrow Wilson's months of total disability have been of greater interest to readers of history than have his years of well-documented accomplishment. This fascination with presidential illnesses has been equalled in some instances by a curiosity about the marital lives of the occupants of the White House. Even Wilson, considered a model of propriety during his years as an educator and on into politics, set a few tongues wagging over his friendship with the lady who was to become his second wife so soon after his first wife had been laid to rest.

The interest in Wilson's personal life was mild when compared with that concerning some of the other presidents. Public attention has always been triggered by anything that would suggest activities or conditions beyond the norm. In the case of the chief executive, however, "beyond the norm" does not necessarily imply sexual deviations as much as involvements that people may not consider proper or expected of the man in the Executive Mansion.

Dwight D. Eisenhower, who had become something of a steadying father figure to America, found his image chipped when it was widely rumored that he had almost divorced his wife, Mamie, to marry an attractive British WREN who had been assigned to drive his Jeep while he was directing the military invasion of the European continent. It did not matter that the incident was past history and that his conduct in office had been exemplary. On the other side of the coin, crusty old Harry Truman was the object of considerable admiration when a White House maid leaked the inside information that he and his matronly wife, Bess, had broken through the slats of their bed one night because of the vigor of their unexpected action on the mattress.

Examination into the sexual lives of the men who have held the presidency reveals them as representative of a cross-section of persons their age, with a not unexpected number of variations and real, or suspected, aberrations. There were, first of all, a proportionate number whose sex lives were limited or even nonexistent. Three men typify this group: James Buchanan, William McKinley, and William Howard Taft. Buchanan was the only president who was a bachelor all of his life. Although he has attracted scant biographical interest and is little remembered today, people almost invariably are curious when told that he never married. What were the reasons? Why was his name romantically linked only once with any woman during his long public life?

From the time he concluded military service during the War of 1812 until his election to the presidency in 1856, he followed an active political career. In 1819, he was engaged to marry a young lady named Annie C. Coleman, but her brothers considered Buchanan to be beneath them socially and circulated rumors that he was unfaithful. The heartbroken Annie not only broke the engagement but became so emotionally upset and unstable that she died, apparently by her own hand. Buchanan, who could hardly shoulder the blame heaped upon him and who was undone by the tragic outcome, was not even permitted to attend the funeral. He immediately fell into a deep depression and was so shaken by the affair that he never permitted himself to become romantically involved for the rest of his life. The episode came back to haunt him thirty-seven years later, when he was running for the presidency. An opposition newspaper depicted him as unfit for this high office, by virtue of his instability, claiming that he, too, had attempted suicide at the time of his broken romance. As proof, the editors pointed out that Buchanan bore the scar of an aborted hanging, since he had a twisted neck and carried his head at a curious angle. In truth, he was afflicted with a "wry neck," caused by a birth injury and accentuated by nearsightedness in one eye and farsightedness in the other. To compensate for this physical defect and the fact that one eye was actually positioned higher than the other, he held his head at an angle that permitted him to see more clearly.

The second president to find his romantic life curtailed was William McKinley. When he was honorably discharged from the 23rd Ohio Volunteers after serving through the Civil War, he was reportedly the only man in the regiment who had completed his hitch without ever having uttered a profanity, gotten drunk, or lost his virginity. He did eventually get married, to an attractive young lady named Ida Saxton. He was certainly virile enough to produce two children during the next four years. But it ended abruptly after the birth of the second child, when Ida became desperately ill. When she was finally discharged from the hospital, it was obvious that she had suffered severe brain damage. For weeks, she was able to do little more than sit in a rocking chair in a semidarkened room, with swollen legs, excruciating headaches, tearful depressions, and fits of epilepsy. The death of her infant, whom she was permitted to hold for short periods of time, shattered all hope of recovery.

McKinley's personal life became badly disrupted. As in the case of several other presidents, he turned away from his life as a husband and toward a career. He devoted more and more of his time to politics. Yet he continued to care for his invalid wife, not only calming her outbursts with consummate patience, but becoming a highly experienced neurologic and psychiatric nurse. Moreover, he insisted that she accompany him to the White House after his election and serve as his official presidential hostess. He considered it a real triumph when he could escort her into the dining room for a state dinner, even though she was likely to have an epileptic seizure or act out some bizarre performance that certainly disconcerted, and sometimes terrified, high-ranking guests. If social intercourse was almost impossible, sexual intercourse was nonexistent. Yet McKinley—unlike Lincoln or Pierce—was not shaken by his wife's disruptive infirmities. Rather, he seemed to gain personal strength through being able to cope and, in fact, continued to show real devotion and love right up to the moment of his untimely death.

William Howard Taft is included in the group of asexual presidents by virtue of his immense size and prodigious overweight. A fatty who tips the scales at 315 pounds and has a touch of narcolepsy* is hardly a choice partner in bed. Mrs. Taft is said to have prodded her husband, against his will, into running for the presidency. "I would prefer to be on the Court," he used to say. Yet it is unlikely that she was able—and probably had little incentive to try—to push him into any elephantine sexual activities.

Most presidents fall into a "normal" group whose sexual opportunities and accomplishments would have been predictable. George Washington, though not able to produce a child of his own with Martha, was notably attracted to the opposite sex. Thomas Jefferson was thought to be attracted to the half-sister of his late wife. John Tyler needs no commentary on his sexual virility, since he produced fourteen children with the help of two wives. In general, the majority of American presidents seem to have enjoyed perfectly normal sex lives—even though affairs of state often curtailed normal marital relationships.

There are no hints in the history books that any president experienced an abnormal love life. Yet at least one evidenced a serious interruption in the normal pattern, with consequent behavior that could be called "aberrant." He was Rutherford B. Hayes, who as a child was smothered with affection by his mother and an aunt and—most notably—by his sister Fannie. She cared for him, fed him, played with him and became the prime object of his affections. Several episodes in his early adulthood indicate an unusual emotional relationship with Fannie, including his almost total collapse when his law practice forced him to establish an office at some distance from his beloved sister. Depressed and confused, he finally moved to a new location, close enough so that he could lunch with her every day.

Later, his courtship of and marriage to Lucy Ware Webb were constantly interrupted by visits from Fannie for both approval of his actions and comfort in times of doubt. Fannie even accompanied the young couple on their honeymoon. And she herself, married, openly admitted that Rutherford, not her hus-

*An uncontrollable urge to fall asleep.

band, was "the love object" of her dreams. Fortunately for the political career of Hayes, this intimate relationship ended long before he sought the nation's highest office. Fannie died in her thirties, after the birth of stillborn twins. Hayes was as grief-stricken as any lover upon the death of a mistress, but he compensated for the loss in an unusual way. Turning to his wife, Lucy, he declared, "Now you must be what my sister was to me."

Finally, in the pattern of presidential intrigues, there is one group whose sexual exploits and appetites have drawn enormous public interest, whether rightly or wrongly. Democrat Grover Cleveland found himself embroiled in the subject at a most embarrassing time—just when he was in a close race for the presidency in 1884. Rumors were flying that he had been somewhat promiscuous and had fathered a child by a young lady named Maria Halprin. "What shall we say to the public," groaned his campaign manager, "to answer these charges?"

"Tell them the truth!" replied Cleveland, who was still a bachelor, though he married while in the White House.

The Republicans had thought they had the race won when they turned up Maria Halprin in Buffalo and heard her claim that her child had been fathered by the affable Cleveland. With this in mind, they mounted what was surely one of the most lurid campaigns in presidential history. Across the country, they chanted:

"Ma, Ma! Where's my Pa? Gone to the White House, Ha! Ha! Ha!"

The last laugh was obviously Cleveland's as he entered the White House. He had made such a clean admission of the affair and such an acceptance of responsibility for the child's education and upbringing that the public voted him into office as "Honest Grover." Even in that Victorian era, the exploits of a swinging bachelor in Buffalo were acceptable to most of the voting population. Curiously, the child's mother was never certain whether the child had really been fathered by Cleveland or by his good friend and carousing companion, Oscar Folsom. To solve the dilemma, she named the infant Oscar Folsom Cleveland Halprin. While president, Grover Cleveland became the guardian of Folsom's sister, Frances, fell in love, and married her in one of the most publicized weddings ever to have taken place in the White House. Proof that he rates as one of the top performers lies in the fact that he enjoyed a long and active married life—which he did not mind talking about—and produced five children.

John F. Kennedy has been widely personified as a great ladies' man, particularly during the days when he was a bachelor in Washington. Yet there is no medical evidence to support some of the claims of hypersexuality or activity beyond what would be normal for a man of his age in a job combining both unique opportunities and great pressures. On the contrary, it would be astonishing—almost medically unique—if Kennedy could have lived up to his billing in light of his physical condition, the excruciating problems he had with his back, and the necessity for constant treatment by powerful drugs. (This will be discussed later.)

For the classic portrait of sexual involvement and an abnormal drive that was actually a severe illness, we have to turn to a man who should never have reached the White House and who was the first to admit it: Warren Gamaliel Harding.

The year was 1921; the season, mid-spring; the location, one of the most insignificant rooms in the White House—actually a large closet, barely six feet by eight feet, adjoining the President's office. It was dark, airless, and without furniture, used largely by previous occupants of the Executive Mansion for the storage of umbrellas, coats, and a variety of articles inadvertently left behind by visiting dignitaries. During the Harding administration it was to have an astonishing, almost unbelievable, purpose as a *chambre d'amour* into which the President could retreat for ten or fifteen minutes to gratify himself with a sensual young mistress half his age. His most frequent partner was Nan Britton, with whom he had been sleeping for several years prior to his election as president. The crisis that Harding feared most had nothing to do with the national economy or the image of America abroad. He was terrified that "the Duchess," his wife, would discover his private brothel.

The closet had two entrances, the first accessible directly

from his office and the second leading to a corridor. Harding minimized the chances of being caught in the act by his wife through the simple expedient of assigning two of his secret service men to guard these entrances under orders that the President was not to be disturbed. On this occasion in 1921, he had a very close call when Mrs. Harding, growing suspicious that her husband was carrying on affairs under her nose, came running down the stairs. At the outside entrance to the anteroom, she was momentarily stopped in her tracks by a tall, husky guard named Jim Sloan, who stated firmly, but politely, that Mr. Harding would fire him if he permitted anyone to enter. When the Duchess scurried down the corridor, obviously intent on entering her husband's office, Sloan banged out a quick warning on the door. By the time Mrs. Harding had run out into the Rose Garden, where the corridor led, and into the Oval Office, "Wurren," as she called him, was already strolling across the floor, straightening his tie and asking sweetly, "What's the matter, Duchess?"

Was it really worth the trouble, the risk, and the chance of a national—if not international—scandal for a few minutes of illicit pleasure? Definitely it was not. But Warren Harding was driven by an uncontrollable urge that was every bit as much an illness as the stroke that had crippled his predecessor in office in October 1919. He was a victim of satyriasis, the abnormal, unmanageable desire for sexual intercourse that is to a male what nymphomania is to a female. Far from being a vigorous sexual pleasure, it was a form of agonizing bondage from which he found neither release nor relief. This illness was not as lethal as the other diseases that were to ravage him during his brief tenure in the White House, yet it was possibly the greatest cross he had to bear.

Harding showed no real signs of developing illnesses in his youth in his hometown, Marion, Ohio. He started a career in good stride when, at the age of only twenty-one, he became editor of the *Marion Star*. He attracted the opposite sex like a magnet through the unbeatable combination of youth, influential position, and smashing good looks. He would have been an attractive model for some of the advertisements he solicited: just over six feet, with finely chiseled features, skin with a permanent suntanned look, thick, dark hair, a sensuous mouth, and a commanding voice whose resonance would have held audiences spellbound on the stage.

Curiously—though perhaps because he quickly became typed as a hail-fellow-well-met and the epitome of youthful success—he became chronically restless in his early twenties, travelling as often as he could. In 1888, he took an active part in the presidential campaign as a delegate to the Republican State Convention. Shortly afterward, he suffered an emotional breakdown and made the first of five visits to Battle Creek Sanitarium. He was only twenty-three at the time. He referred to the occasions as "nervous breakdowns." The symptoms described are those of anxiety, hypomania, and psychoneurosis. He and his associates always knew when he was heading for trouble when they noticed him becoming overactive, extremely restless, and unable to focus his talents on his publishing business. He tended also to depend more on liquor, but not to the extent of having any alcoholic problems.

His friends had mixed feelings when, in 1891, at twenty-six, he married Florence Kling De Wolfe, an attractive and capable divorcee. She was five years older than Harding, which led some to believe that her maturity might be a steadying influence and assuage his restless spirit. Those who were dubious more accurately pegged his nature as that of a man who would soon tire of the "older woman" influence and seek out the sexual comforts of younger and less serious females. Nan Britton came on the scene not too much later, an impressionable, romantically inclined nymphet who, as it turned out, had been smitten by the handsome editor of the *Star* when she was a schoolgirl. Within a few years, they were meeting secretly in hotel rooms in New York, Chicago, and then Washington, as he traveled about, first as an editor and later as the lieutenant governor of Ohio, a speaker on the Chautauqua circuit, and then as senator.

The first indication that marriage may have been anything but a solution for his emotional difficulties came shortly after his wedding. He began to complain of gastrointestinal disorders, which were manifested largely as heartburn, indigestion, cramps, and gas. He became so totally indisposed for such a long period that the Duchess had to take over the management of the newspaper, a job that she relished so much that she kept at it for some fourteen years. "Mrs. Harding in those days ran the show," wrote one of her former newsboys many years later. "Her husband was the front. . . . He was . . . very affable, very much of a joiner and personally popular."

That ex-newsboy was Norman Thomas, later to be a candidate himself for the presidency.

Warren Harding partially alleviated his restlessness through a different form of "travel," from one bedroom to another. In 1902, he became physically attracted to Mrs. James (Carrie) Phillips, who responded eagerly and in like manner. They first met as neighbors and managed to carry on a blossoming affair without the knowledge of either spouse. When Jim Phillips contracted tuberculosis, Harding obligingly helped to pack him off to Battle Creek Sanatorium, thus making the liaison easier. He could hardly believe his luck when the Duchess was also hospitalized, with a kidney infection, eliminating most of the risks of a continuing affair. Their sexual relationship lasted for fifteen years, most of the time without arousing the suspicions of the cuckolded spouses. That is not to say that the Duchess was so naive and dense as to think that her husband was faithful to her. She was well aware of his lack of control in emotional matters and was tortured by unsuccessful attempts to stifle her mounting jealousy. For her, work was only a partial escape.

Harding's libido was not quenched by the overlapping affairs with Carrie Phillips and Nan Britton. By the time he reached Washington as a senator from Ohio in 1914, at the age of forty-nine, he was deeply involved with several other women as well as his old standbys, Carrie and Nan. He displayed an unusual sexual quirk, perhaps because of his earlier development as both writer and editor, not found in most men with satyriasis: he lived his libidinous experiences all over again by authoring long, rambling love letters to his sex partners. The letters frequently ran to thirty or forty pages, they included details that were often explicit. They provided useful fodder for an exposé, *The President's Daughter*, written by Nan Britton and published in 1927. The book was a sensation, but did not help Nan in her lifelong efforts to win a share of Harding's estate for herself and the child she claimed was his illegitimate daughter.

These letters almost drove to distraction Harry M. Daugherty, the small-town lawyer who spent years trying to urge Harding to prime himself as a presidential candidate. When he finally succeeded in 1919, over Harding's objections that he much preferred to remain a senator, he came face to face with the realization that his chosen candidate had all but broadcast his adulterous records to the public at large. Frantically, he sought out and destroyed every letter he could lay hands on, sometimes at considerable expense and occasionally by threatening blackmail in reverse.

Daugherty had to contend with another, equally frustrating, drawback: although he had been priming Harding for some twenty-one years, his protege had a real dread of the possible outcome. "The only thing I really worry about," Harding admitted, "is that I am going to be nominated and elected. That's an awful thing to contemplate."

The noted historian, Samuel Hopkins Adams, was astonished to be told by one of Harding's closest friends, George B. Christian, that "He had no taste for politics. Never had."

"But he liked to be a Senator, didn't he?" asked Adams.

"No, he didn't like being a Senator," replied Christian, making a point that summed up Harding's whole political outlook in a few words. "He liked being in the Senate."

Many people, including William G. McAdoo, who had served as secretary of the Treasury under Wilson, wondered in astonishment why the Republicans had nominated Harding. "He was, as every one knows, soft and pliable and easily managed," wrote McAdoo, noting that Harding was always amenable to a deal. "The possessor of an adjustable conscience, which could be altered to fit every changing circumstance, Harding went through life with good cheer and gusto, believing thoroughly that a man can get along very well if he can fool some of the people some of the time."

What astounded every politician, Republican and Democrat alike, was that this amenable and sociable fellow who preferred defeat over victory won with a plurality of more than seven million votes, a new and dramatic record. Looking back on the phenomenon, some political specialists have concurred that perhaps it was not so surprising after all. The election of 1920 marked the first time that women had the vote—so the turnout was bound to be much greater than in the past and comparative figures more dramatic.

When Harding carried his sexual exploits into the White House, after his inauguration in March 1921, his illicit affairs were so well known to those at the top that there was very little shock effect. William Allen White summed it up succinctly when, in a profile written in 1926, he referred to America's twenty-ninth President as a "He-harlot."

Harding's sexuality was as much a symptom of other disabilities and weaknesses as it was an illness itself. He wanted to continue enjoying the same pleasures he had discovered as a senator, if at a higher level. He often expressed the opinion that he did not expect to be the best of presidents, but he hoped that he would be one of the *best-liked.* More than twenty years earlier, he had acquired a reputation for what he called in his editorial jargon "harmonizing." He was probably the only Chief Executive in history who was as warmly liked and enjoyed by the opposition party as by his own. He ruffled few feathers. Even when he made speeches, which he loved to do, his oratory was mellifluous, filled with fine-sounding words which actually said nothing. Reporters assigned to cover these speeches came away with nothing but frustration to show for their attentiveness, completely unable to identify any issues or even report clearly what it was that the President had said.

The Harding administration was characterized by poker parties in the White House, attended by the more fun-loving members of his cabinet and inner circle, and well lubricated by liquor and other refreshments. What Harding apparently was not aware of until it was far too late was that the real game of poker went on at a different level, where members of his administration sorted the chips by dispensing all kinds of patronage that ranged from the merely questionable to outright fraud and manipulation. "Even as convention tactics were inaugurated," wrote Samuel Rosenman in his book, *Presidential Style,* "Harding's friends began his enmeshment. He had poor discretion in selecting his personal friends, whom he trusted without question; most of them would plague his Presidential years."

Harding was not aware of the depth of his involvement because he skirted issues and avoided getting into battles, either with Congress or with his cabinet. When he did attempt to zero in on serious official duties, he was more than likely to end up being confounded, if not depressed, by the enormity of the assignment. Once when Nicholas Murray Butler visited Harding and found him wrestling with an enormous pile of letters, he stated bluntly that it was ridiculous for the President to bother with a chore that should have been handled by a secretary.

"I suppose so," replied Harding dejectedly, "but I am not fit for this office and should never have been here."

As the pressures of his overpowering office began to grip Harding, even his hypersexuality began to self-destruct. He was no longer vigorous enough to engage in sex. It was a tough cure for satyriasis, and in effect no cure at all. He was simply being engulfed by other disabilities of a more severe and debilitating nature. Late in 1922, he suffered a series of setbacks that shocked him to the core. Hearing about irregularities in the Veterans' Bureau—the sale of war surplus materials to privileged individuals at prices far below their value—he was forced to fire his longtime friend and head of the bureau, Charles R. Forbes. This act was followed by the suicide of Charles F. Cramer, attorney for the bureau, in March 1923. Then, on May 29, another close friend, Jesse Smith, shot himself to death in Daugherty's apartment after begin ordered by the President to leave Washington.

With these and other scandals boiling over, Harding made a characteristic move. He decided that he would try to get off the hot seat in Washington by embarking on a goodwill trip to the coolest region in America, the Territory of Alaska. He left the capital by train on June 30, 1923. But he was already physically and emotionally shattered. He was eroded by a combination of forces, including his sexual excesses, the heavy consumption of rich food and fine liquor, stresses that he had never conditioned himself to parry, and heart disease.

Ironically, when he arrived at the northernmost point on his trip, Fairbanks, Alaska, the temperature had reached a record-breaking 96 degrees. Utterly fatigued, the President was ordered by his personal physician, Brigadier General Charles E. Sawyer, to take a two-day rest. As the presidential party headed south aboard the naval transport, U.S.S. *Henderson,* from Alaska to British Columbia and the West Coast of the United States, the President stopped off to make his planned series of speeches. Several had to be canceled when the President became seriously indisposed, reportedly from having consumed a platter of crab's legs.

Then, while the *Henderson* was steaming southward, she was overtaken by a naval seaplane bearing a long, coded message for the President. Those around him noted that he was visibly shaken by the news it contained and suffered a semicollapse. Although he was overheard muttering to himself something about "false friends," the actual contents of the message were never revealed. It is assumed that the text informed him about another mind-shocking scandal in Washington, which he would have to answer for upon his return. There was no escape.

An incident several days later revealed the depth of Harding's mental and physical slump. While cruising through Puget Sound, the *Henderson* crashed into a destroyer in thick fog. When a member of his party went below to guide the President to the deck, he found him lying on the bed, his face cupped in his hands. When informed that there had been a collision, Harding reportedly commented. "That's too bad, but I hope the ship sinks."

The vessel, little damaged, was able to dock on schedule at Seattle, where the President managed through sheer nerve and a need for adulation to read two speeches in a strangely listless manner. Remaining speeches were canceled and he was placed aboard a train and rushed to San Francisco as a precautionary measure. Arriving early in the morning of July 30, he was taken to a suite on the eighth floor of the Palace Hotel, where he was placed in the care of General Sawyer J. T. Boone, a naval surgeon who had been attached to the White House, and Dr. Hubert Work, a former president of the American Medical Association. Concerned that their chief was suffering from far more than the case of food poisoning reported earlier, they called in Dr. Ray

Lyman Wilbur, of the Stanford University Medical School, and Dr. Charles M. Cooper, a highly regarded heart specialist.

X-rays and laboratory tests showed that Harding was suffering from bronchopneumonia. The bulletins that were issued two or three times each day concerned themselves largely with respiration, pulse, temperature, lung congestion, nourishment, elimination, and routine bodily functions. Laymen were able to interpret little beyond the fact that the President was fatigued, had overstretched himself, and was generally fairly comfortable. By early morning on August 2, the pesky lung condition was showing "definite improvement." By 4:30 P.M., the President had enjoyed "the most satisfactory day since his illness began." The patient and his doctors were optimistic and cheerful.

By 7:35 that evening, he was dead.

Except for the expected case of national shock and endless quotes from grief-stricken individuals who simply could not realize that their leader was gone, the story of Warren Harding would have ended in a fairly clean-cut fashion with the swearing in of Vice-President Calvin Coolidge, and some sagacious remarks about the death being a blessing in disguise—what with "Teapot Dome" and other unbelievable scandals about to burst. But there was a mystery—one that kept dragging back from the grave the unfortunate man who never wanted to be president anyway. In the first place, no one seemed to be clear about the matter of just who was in the room at the time the President died. Dr. Ray Lyman Wilbur, writing a sickly sweet eulogy under the title, "The Last Illness of a Calm Man," in the *Saturday Evening Post*, reported: "His wonderful wife was reading to him, his beloved friend and physician, General Sawyer, was holding his hand, and his nurse was recording his record showing improvement when a blood vessel burst in the vital centers of the brain, his body gave a convulsive twitch, and he was dead."

Another account has it that the nurse was in another room making her records and that Dr. Sawyer (along with Dr. Boone) had temporarily left the bedside of their patient. A third account places Mrs. Harding in her room "across the corridor," and the nurse in the bathroom where she had gone to fetch a glass of water. Why the confusion when all of the individuals close to the President must have been impressed enough by this history-shaking event, if not their own personal concern, to have their whereabouts and the general scene permanently etched in memory?

Warren Harding faced his unwanted bondage and the agonies he endured as president with an admirable degree of physical, if not intellectual, courage. He lived with the rumors because for the most part they were true, and the fears of discovery because he had to. But, as the president who wanted to go down in history as being liked, he might never have had the courage to run had he suspected the manner in which his name would be dragged through a morass of rumors after his passing. Certain inconsistencies in the accounts of his death, such as the positions of doctor, wife, and nurse at the tragic moment, played into the hands of some of the more lurid practitioners of journalism. The fact that Mrs. Harding refused to permit an autopsy on her husband was also cause for juicy speculation. The "untold story" all came into focus seven years later with the publication of a book, *The Strange Death of President Harding.* The book quickly jumped to the top of the bestseller list, creating an international sensation. And well it might have, for the author, Gaston B. Means, attempted to prove, through circumstantial evidence, that Warren Harding had been deliberately murdered.

"The *pièce de résistance* was Gaston's charge that Mrs. Harding had poisoned her husband in the Palace Hotel in San Francisco," wrote Edwin P. Hoyt in a biography, *Spectacular Rogue: Gaston B. Means,* published in 1963, "in a moment when she was overcome by a desire for revenge and a fear that Harding's life was ruined anyhow, because of the scandals beginning to break around him."

Means had been employed for a while in the Department of Justice under Harry M. Daugherty when he was attorney general, and had been kicking around Washington for years. There is no doubt that he knew Harding and members of the administration and was in a position to discern many of the irregularities that were going on. According to his book, he had many long and involved conversations with the Duchess, prior to the President's departure on his last trip, during which she revealed to him, mainly by inference, what her sordid plans were. He quoted liberally, and in a florid, melodramatic style, his conversations with Nan Britton. He pointed out that Nan, along with innumerable jealous mistresses, also had sufficient cause to kill the President in a crime of passion.

The only hitch was that Gaston B. Means was a professional con man—one of the most notorious of this century. His greatest achievement was that he was able to con the unsuspecting publisher into printing an historic compendium of half truths, innuendos, and just plain lies.

It all seemed so possible—even logical. As Hoyt wrote, "It was not easy for anyone to check a statement about President Harding's personal life without going to sources where the motives might be questionable. The mystery of Harding, coupled with the notoriety of Gaston Means, made a book that appealed to a large American audience. . . . Gaston made a small fortune on this hoax."

To the credit of Warren G. Harding, and to keep the record in proper balance, it should be understood that in his last tortured weeks the President was finally making a courageous effort to *be* the Chief of State and to assume command. He himself had made arrangements for the trip west, bypassing even Harry Daugherty, who was accustomed to calling the signals. He had deliberately turned down all offers of private hospitality and the old rounds of partying, drinking, and poker playing. He had seemingly abandoned his sexual excesses and had long since sent Nan Britton packing and made genuine strides toward shaking himself free of the clutches of the self-seekers around him. Perhaps that is why the secret, coded message had shocked him into partial collapse while he was aboard the *Henderson*—just at a time when he thought that he had been effectively cleaning house.

Throughout the "Voyage of Understanding"—his tour of Alaska and the Far West—Warren Harding had noticed increasingly severe chest pain. His angina pectoris caused him more and more discomfort. He tried to hide this from his travelling companions but when, during a speech in Seattle, he was hit by an especially severe substernal pain and could barely get his breath,

Secretary of Commerce Herbert Hoover had to step in, collect the notes dropped on the floor and help the President to a chair.

Dr. Sawyer, always on hand, hustled him off to bed and gave out bulletins that his patient was suffering from Alaskan spider crab poisoning. The rest of the trip was canceled and Harding was moved to a hotel in San Francisco. The consultants called in were no more certain of the diagnosis than Dr. Sawyer and variously labeled the illness pneumonia, gastritis, and even copper poisoning.

One man was certain of the diagnosis. Three thousand miles away, in the dining room of the Massachusetts General Hospital in Boston, Dr. Samuel Levine was having lunch with his boss, Dr. Harvey Cushing. Dr. Levine was one of a new breed of cardiologist—smart, aggressive, trained in the latest techniques of diagnosis—and his conversation with Dr. Cushing went something like this:

Dr. Levine: Dr. Cushing, I've been reading the bulletins put out by the President's doctors and I'm not at all convinced he's been poisoned.

Dr. Cushing: Why not, Sam? Those men out there are pretty good doctors.

Dr. Levine: I don't think they're considering his heart—he's had typical chest pain, indigestion and collapse—he's having all the classic symptoms of a coronary occlusion.

Dr. Cushing: You may be right, Sam. It does sound a little suspicious of heart disease.

Dr. Levine: I know I'm right. The President's having a heart attack! They're missing the boat. Dr. Cushing, I think we should go right up to your office and call those doctors. This is important.

Dr. Cushing: Now, now, Sam, this is not our business. We shouldn't interfere.

And of course no phone call was made.

But Dr. Levine's diagnosis seems to have been borne out by the death of the President within a few days. His death was sudden. He was sitting in bed, asked for a drink of water, and before it could be gotten for him his head fell to one side and he was dead. A sudden change in the rhythm of his heart—ventricular fibrillation—would do this, a common, lethal complication of a heart attack.

Warren G. Harding had not been poisoned by his wife, or by his nurse, or by Alaskan crab or anything else. He had died of a massive heart attack producing sudden cardiac arrest.

"President Harding died before the American people realized his shortcomings, before historians would rate him the Presidential failure of the twentieth century," wrote Samuel Rosenman in his book, *Presidential Style.*

Yet perhaps—just perhaps—had he had more astute medical care and survived his ordeal on the West Coast, he would have returned to Washington to put his administration back in balance and end up with a record of modest, if not considerable, achievement.

10

Dignity in a Wheelchair

In November 1944, Franklin Delano Roosevelt, at sixty-two, was reelected by an overwhelming majority to remain in the White House, which he had already occupied since 1933. The election was historic for two reasons: first, as almost every single voter in the country knew, this marked the first time in history that an American president had ever been elected to a fourth term.

Second, what almost no one knew, Roosevelt was even then a dying man, with little chance of surviving the coming year, let alone a full term.

Ranking members of the Democratic party seem to have been equally unaware of the real state of the President's health and, in fact, fully expecting their most famous leader to bring World War II to its conclusion, fill out his term, and then retire with honor and acclaim for a job well done.

History was not to be so cooperative, or so kind.

During the month of October 1944, the President was unusually active as he indulged himself heartily in campaigning and speech-making, which he thoroughly enjoyed. Although he rose magnificently to each occasion, whether in large cities or travelling through the hinterlands, he sacrificed his usual regimen, which included specific periods of rest and relaxation, and to some extent his normal diet. By mid-November, with the election behind him and facing many wartime demands at home and abroad, he looked tired—as though he had been temporarily buoyed by a refreshing game that was now over. His appetite was poor. His weight was somewhat down. At the end of the month, he left Washington and journeyed by train to his retreat in Warm Springs, Georgia, for a three-week period of rest and recuperation. Visitors were forbidden, with a few exceptions, so that he could spend his time reading, motoring around the nearby countryside, and later bathing in the pool. Although he had plenty of chance to rest and exercise, he complained that he had no appetite and that food seemed to have no taste.

One of the reasons for this sojourn to build up his health and his strength was to prepare him for an international event that would not only affect world affairs during the 1940s but would leave its mark on generations to come. This was the Yalta Conference, a long-planned summit meeting between Roosevelt, Prime Minister Winston Churchill of Great Britain, and Joseph Stalin, dictator of Russia. The President was determined, among other things, to win Russia's good will and secure early participation by the Soviets in the war against Japan. He knew that he would need every ounce of his personal persuasiveness and a great show of strength to convince Stalin to intervene. He needed also to enlist the aid of Churchill, whose efforts were likely to be concentrated on plans for postwar settlements and on selling the idea of giving France more authority in the occupation and control of Germany as soon as Hitler could be brought to his knees.

On January 23, 1945, Roosevelt arrived by train in Norfolk, Virginia, and immediately went on board the heavy cruiser, *Quincy*, which had been selected to transport him to Malta. Although the sea was rough for a good part of the voyage, this exhilarated Roosevelt rather than distressing him, for he was an experienced sailor, at one time a skilled yachtsman, and a great lover of sea voyages as well. Before the President landed, however, he received disconcerting reports from Prime Minister Churchill. It appeared that Yalta, a town in the Crimea or the north shore of the Black Sea, was extremely unhealthy. "If we had spent ten years on research," said Churchill, "we could not have found a worse place in the world than Yalta. . . . It is good for typhus and deadly lice, which thrive in those parts." It was apparent that the perceptive Churchill was greatly concerned about Roosevelt's failing health, despite assurances that the President had completely recovered from his recent bronchitis and exhaustion.

The presidential party was to fly from Malta in the central

Mediterranean to an airport at Saki, eighty miles from Yalta, and then complete the journey to Livadia Palace, near Yalta, by car. The Prime Minister relayed the bad news that the road was so narrow and winding and so rutted that the expected two-hour drive would be closer to six.

Before he contended with these travel problems, Roosevelt also had to spend an entire day after his arrival at Malta on February 2 in meetings with cabinet members, military leaders, the British Combined Chiefs of Staff, and Churchill himself. He then boarded a plane for the 1,400-mile flight to Saki in the Crimea. The plane was accompanied by fighter planes because of the nearness of areas that were still held by the Germans, a situation that seemed to bother the President far less than the noise and vibrations of the flight itself.

President Roosevelt arrived at the conference table on Sunday, February 4, looking more alert than his aides had expected, but suffering from a cough that was to last four days and nights and be especially persistent when he tried to sleep. His personal physician, Dr. Howard G. Bruenn, treated him with terpin hydrate and codeine, and with nose drops before retiring to alleviate some difficulties in breathing. One of the problems that was out of the doctor's hands was the steady flow of visitors, who not only drained most of the President's time when he was not actually at the conference table, but left him no time for his usual periods of rest. Still, he had a good appetite, complained of no gastric or other upsets, and seemed to enjoy the enforced attention.

The most important question of all, in the minds of the Americans present was this: how could any president, let alone a man who had to contend with enormous physical disabilities, continue to face challenges greater than any imposed on a chief executive since the Civil War? In short, was Roosevelt really up to the task he was facing in the negotiations with Russia and Great Britain?

Roosevelt would not have hesitated two seconds then—or at any time during his terms in office—if asked whether he was equal to the greatest challenges the presidency could demand. He had been tempered for the job with a trial by fire that began in the middle of August 1921.

During the period between 1913 and 1921, Roosevelt served as assistant secretary of the Navy. In July 1918, he came down with a severe attack of influenza while on the steamer *Leviathan*, returning from an inspection of American naval forces in Europe. At the time, the ship's physician commented to his patient that no matter how miserable he may have felt, it was better by far than being exposed to the epidemic of infantile paralysis (polio) that was then striking thousands of victims along the East Coast of the United States.

"Well," replied Roosevelt, "it's getting pretty late in life to catch a thing like that."

At the age of thirty-six, he was reflecting one of the common misconceptions that only the young were susceptible to this virulent disease. His comment was particularly ironic. Three years later, on August 9, 1921, when vacationing at the family's summer home on Campobello Island in New Brunswick, Canada, he spent the day with his sons sailing, fishing, and later working themselves into a sweat fighting a small forest fire. Following these exertions, he plunged into the cold waters of the Bay of Fundy, jogged back to the house, and plunked himself down on the porch to read, still in his wet bathing suit. Suddenly he had a violent chill that made his teeth chatter uncontrollably. His wife forced him to get into bed, under blankets and with a hot water bottle to counteract the chill.

The next day, in addition to what seemed to be a common cold, he complained of a "peculiar sensation" in his legs. He noticed that the muscles of his right knee appeared weak when he attempted to stand up and that, later, he was unable to support his own weight on that leg. By the end of the second day, he was unable to move either of his legs and the family called in Dr. W. W. Keen, of Philadelphia, who was vacationing not far to the south, at Bar Harbor, Maine. The famous surgeon, who had been one of the principals in the operation on Grover Cleveland's cancerous jaw twenty-eight years earlier, recognized that there was some form of paralysis, attributable in part, he thought, to Roosevelt's indiscretion in plunging into icy waters after becoming overheated. He diagnosed a clot on the spinal cord, hedged a bit on his prognosis, but did advise a procedure that was extremely painful, and undoubtedly more harmful than beneficial: deep massage of the paralyzed muscles.

The outcome might have been fatal had not Roosevelt's uncle, Frederic Delano, summoned Dr. Robert S. Lovett, of Boston, to Campobello. Lovett correctly diagnosed the disease as anterior poliomyelitis, or infantile paralysis. He forbade further massage, pointing out that the muscles from the hips down were so sensitive to pressure and touch that even sheets and blankets had to be raised above the bed so that they did not rest on the lower part of the body. As Roosevelt wrote in a personal report on his case for the benefit of a doctor friend some three years later, all of his muscles from the chest down were involved, but nothing above except for his thumb muscles. That made it impossible for him to write with pen or pencil. For two weeks he could not urinate and had to be catheterized. He experienced also a slight difficulty in controlling his bowels.

"As to treatment—," he wrote, "the mistake was made for the first 10 days of giving my feet and legs rather heavy massage. This was stopped by Dr. Lovett of Boston who was, without doubt, the greatest specialist on infantile paralysis."

Three weeks after the initial attack, Roosevelt was moved to a New York hospital, but not permitted to go home until November, by which time he was able to sit up in a wheel chair. Although Dr. Lovett believed there was hope for an almost complete recovery, his viewpoint and that of other specialists became more pessimistic as the months passed and the patient showed excruciatingly slow progress. Some of the muscles and nerves evidenced partial recovery, but others seemed damaged beyond hope. Still, by February 1922, he was fitted with thirty-pound steel braces on both legs and had made agonized, but successful, attempts to stand up. Roosevelt himself was the most persistent advocate of exercises, stubbornly attempting to develop atrophied muscles—one at a time. Characteristic was his comment, when asked one time why he seemed to be focusing all of his attention intently on one foot, "No one knows how much fun it would be to wiggle just one little toe."

In September 1924, he journeyed to Warm Springs, Georgia,

to put himself under the care of Dr. William MacDonald, a neurologist who had been at the Yale Medical School. Mac-Donald was right out of Roosevelt's mold, a pioneer who was all but ostracized by his profession because he damned bed rest and casts and other immobilizing treatment and insisted that, after the acute inflammation had subsided, movement and constant exercise were the only procedures for overcoming total and enduring paralysis. He was described by a colleague—though affectionately—as a "martinet," who offered his patients no helping hands but insisted that they crawl along the floor and up stairs to the exercise room. "Painful at times and frustrating," wrote Dr. Raymond H. Baxter in a local newspaper account, "each [patient] had to flex and extend; lift and slowly lower, and move those toes; flex and extend; and heel to kneecap, until the sweat started and sometimes the tears."

This brief phase in the life of Franklin Delano Roosevelt, marked by the sheer courage he had to generate to accomplish even the smallest movements of his legs, may have in the end been more significant to American history than some of the world-shaking events in which he was later to be involved. As Baxter commented, "All the books which have been written about Franklin and Eleanor have missed the point that Marion [Warm Springs] played in the lives of these two people. Actually, no one has ever tried to record the tremendous impact which the salvage of this dynamic man here on the shores of Marion Harbor had on the nation and on the world."

Another fact that was little known, then or now, was that Roosevelt had a distinct tendency toward depression, which was discernible to very few people because of his ingrained ability to hide it through his words and actions. Sometimes when he was most voluble, he was also most depressed. Periods of dejection and despair occurred quite naturally during the time that he was trying to fight his way back from the ravages of polio. But they also continued, perhaps in more exaggerated form, during those periods in office when he was under intense pressures. "Roosevelt had an unusual ability to pull himself together," reported one journal on psychiatry and neurology eight years after his death, "and cover his depressions along the lines of the 'keep-smiling' code of our culture. Helpful also were stamp-collecting, enthusiasm for the sea, love of fishing and cruising, interest in the Navy; these hobbies provided outlets and took his mind off whatever depressions did befall him."

An interesting parallel was suggested, though it could never be proven, that Roosevelt's determination and success in overcoming his personal depressions later were to play a vital role in his many successful efforts to bring the nation back on an even keel when it was thrown off balance by devastating events such as the Depression, international crises, labor problems, and violent setbacks during World War II. It is certain, though, that his character, outlook, and capacity to persevere against heavy odds were tempered and molded by the seven years he spent between 1921 and 1928 trying to rebuild his leg muscles so that he could walk again. He succeeded as much as any human being possibly could. Many of the muscles were beyond repair and the best he could do was to strengthen his already powerful shoulders, his hips, and some of the lesser, auxiliary muscles in his thighs and legs so that he could move about.

His legs, with heavy braces that locked at the knee joints, were no more mobile than wooden poles. So he perfected a wooden soldier movement that consisted of keeping his body erect and alternately lifting and swinging his legs from the hips. To accomplish even this crude motion required the use of crutches (later canes) for support for his muscular upper torso.

Contending with the law of gravity was only one of his major problems. He also had to overcome the entreaties—sometimes demands—of his domineering mother, his wife, and a formidable array of other relatives and friends who urged him to give up the battle, which obviously was doomed to failure anyway. His mother, Sara Delano Roosevelt, reminded him constantly that he was of the manor born and could easily afford to emulate his patrician father and lead the life of a country landowner at the spacious family estate at Hyde Park, New York, in the historic Hudson River Valley. Such a life was, she insisted, more dignified than the cutthroat political career that he seemed eager to embrace. His wife and some of his intimate friends, who at first were afraid that his obstinacy would eventually debilitate, if not kill him, eventually came around to his way of thinking. It grew more and more obvious that his most menacing enemies were leisure and boredom. They came to believe that he should not let his disability block his almost obsessive determination to become a political leader.

As early as 1924, he was back in the political arena in a small way, acting as floor leader at the Democratic National Convention held in New York City's Madison Square Garden. On that occasion, he steeled himself to walk with braces and crutches a few feet to the lectern and stand there for more than half an hour. There, he nominated his good friend, Al Smith, as Democratic candidate for president. When he repeated this formidable act in 1928, much stronger in body and to ringing applause, it was with the understanding that he would run for the governorship of New York. He was elected then, and again in 1930, by an overwhelming majority. Since Al Smith's two bids for the presidency had ended in failure, it seemed evident that Franklin Delano Roosevelt would himself be the candidate for the highest office in the land when the Democrats met in the summer of 1932.

It was characteristic of the man that he had turned an enormous physical deficit into a major political asset. He had, in fact, undergone a unique, almost inspired, metamorphosis. Frances Perkins, whom he appointed Secretary of Labor in 1933, and the nation's first female cabinet officer, described it this way:

"Franklin Roosevelt underwent a spiritual transformation during the years of his illness. . . . The years of pain and suffering had purged the slightly arrogant attitude Roosevelt had displayed upon occasion before he was stricken. The man emerged completely warmhearted with humility of spirit and a deeper philosophy. Having been in the depths of trouble, he understood the problems of people in trouble."

He never showed any bitterness about his personal misfortune, believing rather that he was fortunate to be alive and active and that some Divine Providence had saved him from total paralysis and perhaps death. Samuel Rosenman, who authored *Presidential Style,* and who knew Roosevelt well from the mid-1920s until the time of his death, expressed astonishment that the man had a seemingly endless reservoir of energy, more than enough to compensate for the sheer physical effort he had to make to move from place to place. Speaking of the 1928 gubernatorial campaign, he wrote, "I was with him during the whole of this campaign trip and can testify to the back-breaking pace, which seemed to tire all the young reporters—and me also, then only thirty-two years of age—much more than it did him. I saw the *extra* physical effort he had to make doing all the routine things the normal person so easily does: getting downstairs each morning in his hotel, walking to his car, getting into his car by a kind of strenuous gymnastic use of his arms and shoulders, pulling himself up to his feet to speak to a street crowd in a village from his car, getting out of his car by the same strenuous tactic when he was to attend a political luncheon. . . . And then the whole process would begin all over again as he left for the meeting hall that evening and returned to the hotel. This long, tiring grind was repeated day after day."

"Did F.D.R.'s private battle teach him to identify with those who suffer?" asked author Bernard Asbell in a biography of the President, *The F.D.R. Memoirs.* "Unquestionably. Moreover it taught him the uses of patience (never a strong suit with crusaders who relied upon him, upon whom he relied, yet who continually harassed him). It heightened his sense of time and timing. 'It made him realize'—an observation of Egbert Curtis, a Warm Springs companion—'that he was not infallible, that everything wasn't always going to go his way.' More than anything, it forced him to study the uses of handicap, paradoxically giving him a leg up in a profession of able-bodied crippled men."

John Gunther described the man's dogged determination by pointing out that he refused help in getting up the stairs of his home, and would use his hands, arms, and powerful shoulders to pull himself from one step to the next. "The sweat would pour off his face, and he would tremble with exhaustion," wrote this noted author. "Moreover he insisted on doing this with members of the family or friends watching him, and he would talk all the time as he inched himself up little by little, talk, talk, and make people talk back. It was a kind of enormous spiritual catharsis—as if he had to do it to prove his independence, and had to have the feat witnessed, to prove that it was nothing."

Press secretary Steve Early, who had campaigned with Roosevelt as far back as 1920, when he was a candidate for vice-president, used to assert that he would never have become president of the United States had he not contracted polio, or some other virulent and crippling disease. He recalled that Roosevelt was "just a playboy" in those early years who spent a great deal of time playing cards, even to the point of postponing the preparation of speeches until he was almost on his way to the podium. During his interminable period of convalescence, however, he acquired the habit of reading extensively and studying the major issues of the day.

Frances Perkins made an interesting observation, pointing out that his immobility made him much more of a target than most high officials for people who had an axe to grind. As a result, he listened to some pretty tiresome complaints and quickly learned how to offset them by making positive, often productive, suggestions. "I remembered, in contrast," she said, "how he had walked away from bores a few years earlier when he was in the State Senate. Now he could not walk away when he was bored. He listened, and out of it he learned. . . ." One thing he learned was what he expressed years later in a speech when he said that "everybody wants to have the sense of belonging, of being on the inside," and that "no one wants to be left out." Through adversity, he had become more tolerant, more considerate of the human frailties of others, and less harsh on people whom he might earlier have described as "stupid" or "weak."

The very fact that he made himself accessible and that he responded to the plight of "the common man" is all the more remarkable in light of his patrician and cloistered upbringing. He did not emerge from poverty or poor schooling to assert his leadership. Rather, he had been sheltered largely within the confines of the Hyde Park estate, the compound at Campobello Island, the classrooms of Groton School, and the "Gold Coast" of Harvard University, where he enjoyed an ample allowance and the companionship of socially inclined young men from other wealthy families. It required something like the physical and mental shock of polio to jolt him out of this protective cocoon.

Still, the question remained in many minds as Roosevelt took the oath of office in 1932 at a time when the nation faced an economic crisis of historic proportions: did this hopelessly crippled man have the strength, let alone the guts, to guide the nation through the countless shoals that lay ahead?

Eleanor Roosevelt several times expressed her own belief that her husband reached the peak of his physical recovery from polio by 1928, and those who knew him personally have later reflected that they really saw no great change after that time—other than his own capabilities for using braces and canes. Roosevelt never referred to his paralysis in public (except for very rare instances), but on occasion he displayed irritation at the way others made references to it. Characteristic was the occasion on which he was shown a copy of the manuscript for a profile on him that was to appear in the old *Liberty* magazine. "There is only one statement in this article that I want corrected," said the President. "The author says in this line here that I have 'never entirely recovered from infantile paralysis.' Never recovered *what?* I have never recovered the full use of my knees. Will you fix that?"

Members of his family, and particularly Eleanor, were on occasion subjected to questioning about the President's health and his capacity to continue in office. A particularly blunt inquiry was one tossed at Mrs. Roosevelt when she was giving a talk in Akron, Ohio.

"Do you think your husband's illness has affected his mentality?" she was asked.

"I am glad that question was asked," she responded with only a momentary hesitation, "The answer is 'Yes.' Any person who has gone through great suffering is bound to have a greater sympathy and understanding of the problems of mankind."

It was not surprising that she received a standing ovation for her reply. The public was extremely protective of Roosevelt—what few Americans, that is, who even realized how severely he had been afflicted. As for the press, what has several times been referred to in biographies as a "strange conspiracy" developed. There seemed to be an unwritten, unspoken agreement among journalists, broadcasters, film producers, and other members of the media that Roosevelt's paralysis was "off limits" as a topic for discussion. This kind of code, which is almost beyond belief in today's climate of communications, was akin to that enjoyed by the Royal Family in the British press. It was debasing to the country, and to the citizens themselves, to speak about a head of state in terms of intimate necessities, bodily functions, and personal distress. So effective was this "conspiracy," recalled John Gunther, that "hardboiled newspapermen, who knew that he could not walk as well as they knew their own names, could never quite get over being startled when F.D.R. was suddenly brought into a room. The shock was greater when he wheeled himself and, of course, was greatest when he was carried. . . . During the 1930s when I lived in Europe I repeatedly met men in important positions of state who had no idea that the President was disabled."

The fact that he had to be actually *lifted* into and out of his car was never mentioned in print and certainly never filmed by news cameramen. A glance through published pictures during his era is enough to reveal that camera lenses were invariably focused on the upper torso or at angles so that the condition of his legs was not evident. Even his enemies—and they were numerous—refrained from breaking the code. Several of them had learned that to do so was far more injurious to their own cause than to Roosevelt's.

The President's own poise, personal style, and his flair for the dramatic served as highly effective camouflage. The *Journal of Social Psychology,* in a study of the public's emotional reaction following the death of Roosevelt, described his style this way: "On the screen, he was never silent or at the sidelines of a scene. His voice came over the radio in constant oratorical guise, unbroken by the natural, modulated effects of two-way conversation. His public words were formal, weighty or, at times, witty, but never the banal little trivia that all men speak in unposed moments. We do not see our leaders in underwear or without teeth (as family intimates are occasionally pictured to each other). In short, the man was there but the flesh was gone, and hence the image emerged un-mortal."

The President fully realized that on many occasions he was

placed in the highly disadvantageous position of having to be seated and *looking up* at others with whom he was carrying on a serious discussion—or, worse yet, having a confrontation. With his inborn sense of staging, he used his prominent chin to execute an upthrusting impression that in effect carried him to a higher level. It was positive, optimistic, a gesture of great confidence and so much a symbol that caricatures of the man could capture his whole being and outlook with a few clever lines. What has sometimes been referred to as an affectation—his long ivory cigarette holder—was simply an extension of the upthrusting jaw, a kind of subtle stage prop. It was claimed that those close to the President could determine his general mood or the way he was reacting to a proposal simply by observing whether the holder was pointing straight ahead, upward, or to the side.

Roosevelt always dressed in such a way that attention was focused on him from the waist up. Thus, for example, he took to wearing a U.S. Navy cape when the air was chill, complete with gold braid and a velvet collar. He had several favorite hats, too, which were deliberately selected to establish the intended impression—including a much-mashed Fedora, which he wore in all its rumpled glory with the brim turned up, fore and aft, when he was on an inspection trip afield. Such accouterments were deliberate ploys to dilute any impressions that his disability was —or could be—a problem.

No matter how cleverly and successfully Franklin Delano Roosevelt disguised his true physical condition, he and his family had to face quite bluntly the fact that he was still a patient when he was elected president and that he brought with him to this high office as serious a disability as any man who had preceded him into the White House. It would therefore seem logical that he would also bring the finest medical advisors and specialists as consultants and members of the staff. In this respect, history was not much help. In the early years, from Washington to Jackson, presidents usually sought the advice of their own family physicians and, when necessary, visited or summoned specialists for treatment out of the ordinary. Following the Jacksonian era, and especially after the Civil War, many presidents selected their physicians from the ranks of the military. This procedure stemmed from two quite natural reasons: first, the presidents themselves had been military officers and had become acquainted with doctors in the services who were brave and loyal, and who had sometimes shown considerable heroism on fields of battle; second, since they were already commissioned and receiving pay from the Army or Navy, their services were free—a not inconsequential consideration in the days when the White House staff budget was skimpy and congressional foes were constantly holding the President accountable for expenses they deemed unnecessary.

Needless to say, some of these military doctors were second-rate, long out of practice and serving mainly as figure heads or administrators rather than as practitioners.

Roosevelt and the president he most admired, Woodrow Wilson, picked their medical advisors in a most illogical way. Although both had received the best of medical care as private citizens, mainly through their own family physicians, they deliberately selected White House physicians whom they considered to be "nice fellows," even though the quality of their skill was questionable. Thus it was that Woodrow Wilson had appointed a young naval surgeon who proved little during the next eight years except the fact that he knew almost nothing about the care of hypertensive cardiovascular disease, cerebral arteriosclerosis, and stroke. Roosevelt fared little better. Years earlier, he had been aboard a naval cruiser and had enjoyed several chats with a young Navy commander, Ross T. McIntire. When he assumed the presidency, he recalled the cordial conversations and summoned McIntire to White House duty.

McIntire did provide conversation, as well as a kind of nonpolitical companionship that most presidents need to balance off the constant demands of affairs of state. Furthermore, the doctor had been educated as an otolaryngologist and an ophthalmologist, the former being particularly appropriate in light of Roosevelt's susceptibility to illnesses of the upper respiratory tract and to sinus trouble—particularly in humid Washington.

McIntire was soon promoted to vice-admiral and appointed surgeon general of the United States Navy, evidence that the

President was well satisfied. Yet the doctor was criticized by some in his profession, and on one occasion by the American Medical Association. He allowed his patient to lose an excessive amount of blood through bleeding hemorrhoids, either because of lack of attention or—as one doctor commented—"a real goof." Over a period of weeks, the President's loss of blood drained him of two-thirds of his circulating hemoglobin, a drop from a normal fifteen grams to an alarming four and a half grams. The loss was more than enough to have interfered seriously with brain, kidney, and heart functions. Dr. McIntire seemed to be under the illusion that his patient was strong enough to withstand almost anything.

Roosevelt was given very little treatment for congestive heart failure for two years prior to the spring of 1944, when a specialist was called in at the insistence of his wife and other members of the family. Was McIntire poorly qualified for his prestigious assignment? Was he less than thorough in his routine examinations? Or was he simply deceived—as so many were—by Roosevelt's hearty manner, exuberant personality, and seemingly total lack of concern about his health? Unlike many of America's presidents and other top leaders, he seemed magnificently equipped to roll with the punches and let the strains and demands of the job roll off his back. His disposition was usually buoyant, his sense of humor keen, and his eagerness to talk to people always in evidence. He was certainly one of the nation's most charismatic presidents, gifted with a personal magnetism that even his enemies found beguiling.

From the time he took office in 1933 through the end of the thirties, the President suffered numerous head colds and recurrent attacks of bronchitis and sinusitis. He also battled upper respiratory influenzal infections and several severe attacks of intestinal flu. While no single illness was cause for great concern, the cumulative impact was serious and made him a sitting duck for the diseases that were to attack him in the early forties. In the later summer of 1938, while visiting one of his sons in Rochester, Minnesota, the President suffered a spell of dizziness and showed other symptoms that were later diagnosed as the first of a series of "little strokes." But no conclusion was ever agreed upon since, clinically, there was no evidence of the kind of brain damage, such as loss of memory or changes of behavior, that follow these strokes.

Physicians who examined or treated the President for illnesses other than his polio almost invariably expressed surprise at their patient's lack of interest in what was being done medically. He followed the doctors' orders, took his prescriptions methodically, and always found time for examinations—whether routine or special—that were requested. He never commented on the frequency or nature of visits by attending physicians, and showed no curiosity about electrocardiograms and other laboratory tests that were performed. He never asked about the composition of a prescription or what it was supposed to accomplish.

The answer to this enigma lies in his mental attitude. Robert E. Sherwood said it best in his book, *Roosevelt and Hopkins:* "Although crippled physically and prey to various infections, he was spiritually the healthiest man I have ever known. He was gloriously and happily free of the various forms of psychic maladjustment which are called by such names as inhibition, complex, phobia. His mind, if not always orderly, bore no trace of paralysis and neither did his emotional constitution; and his heart was certainly in the right place."

Eleanor Roosevelt expressed this outlook from a different viewpoint, writing after his death, "I have never heard him say there was a problem that he thought it was impossible for human beings to solve. He recognized the difficulties, and often said that while he did not know the answer he was completely confident that there was an answer. . . . He never talked about his doubts. . . . I never knew him to face life, or any problem that came up, with fear."

Roosevelt's optimism was put to a real test of fire in 1942, when he had to inform Americans that they must face up to crucial defeats by the Germans in the west and the Japanese in the Pacific. He had faced moments of the greatest despair in the mid-1930s while trying to extricate the nation from the slough of the Great Depression. Yet those crises were nothing when compared with the fearful truths about the fall of Manila, the "Death March" of American and Filipino prisoners after the surrender at Bataan, and Nazi atrocities in Europe.

The President faced the greatest defeats with incredible self-assurance, often giving evidence that he had to buoy the spirits of his own chiefs of staff of the Army, Navy, and Air Force. Yet the pressures took their toll, steadily and relentlessly, despite all that has been said about the President's unique resistance to stress. During 1943, he began to show distinct signs of fatigue, culminating with an attack of influenza shortly after returning from a grueling conference in Teheran in December. He displayed the common symptoms of fever, cough, and general malaise. Although this was nothing new in his medical history, what was alarming was that for the first time he did not seem able to regain his usual vigor and buoyancy. He complained of fatigue (something he had seldom admitted to previously) and abdominal distress and distension. He was also bothered by undue perspiration, even at times when he was not physically very active. He lost between eight and ten pounds during a two-week period.

From time to time, the question has arisen: Did President Roosevelt have cancer? His weight loss might have been one sign. Also, he had apparently undergone minor surgery to have at least one mole removed, a mole that might have been a form of skin cancer known as a malignant melanoma. When questioned, Dr. Bruenn doubted that this was so. Yet the possibility is there and the answer will probably never be known.

By March 1944, the President's condition had so alarmed his wife and his daughter, Anna, that they urged Admiral McIntire to examine the President much more closely than he had been doing. When he reported back with such catch-all diagnoses as flu, bronchitis, and "overwork," they insisted on having another opinion. The President was transported to the U.S. Naval Hospital in Bethesda, Maryland, where he was examined by a young Navy cardiologist, Dr. Howard G. Bruenn. In a later clinical report, Bruenn noted that "He appeared to be very tired and his face was very gray. Moving caused him considerable breathlessness."

After thorough examination and tests, Bruenn diagnosed the trouble as hypertension, hypertensive heart disease, cardiac failure, and acute bronchitis—findings that he reported as "completely unsuspected up to this time." He recommended that the patient be put to bed for one to two weeks with nursing care, that he be placed on a restricted diet, and that he be given a prescription of digitalis and sedated at night to ensure a refreshing sleep. Incredible though it may seem, the recommendations were "rejected because of the exigencies and demands on the President." Instead, Roosevelt was placed on modified bed rest and dosed with cough syrup!

For a time, the situation resembled that of Woodrow Wilson all over again. The President had to sleep partially upright, propped with pillows, to prevent difficulty with breathing. (There is evidence that he was suffering from chronic obstructive lung disease, then known as emphysema.) During the day, he occasionally lapsed into a slack-jaw appearance, at which times he would also lose the thread of conversations and forget his train of thought.

Another disturbing fact was that the President's medical records were incomplete, or certainly not made available to Bruenn when needed. Later, they mysteriously disappeared altogether, including the original hospital chart with progress notes and the results of various laboratory tests. Since these had been kept in the safe at the U.S. Naval Hospital in Bethesda, it can only be surmised that they were deliberately removed, and possibly destroyed.

When Dr. Bruenn was interviewed for this book in May 1979, he was more generous than many of his colleagues in his assessment of Admiral McIntire. He refuted the claim of at least one biographer that he was "completely under the thumb" of McIntire and expressed gratitude that the admiral had permitted him to take over the President's care. He did not deny that McIntire had missed the boat during these two critical years and seemed totally ignorant of the President's real condition or the results of tests that had been made during that time. Dr. Bruenn treated the President with the standard medications of the day: digitalis to strengthen the heart, mercury and aminophylline to get rid of retained fluid and phenobarbital to lower the alarmingly high blood pressure. He also insisted on a strict routine of rest during the day, elimination of excess salt from the diet, and an early bed-time.

Only after the President's dramatic response to these measures did McIntire admit that Bruenn should continue his course of therapy. Even McIntire's group of friendly consultants, Dr. Frank Lahey, Dr. Ray Lyman Wilbur, and others, had to admit that the loss of ten pounds of edema fluid and the clearing of congested lungs left the President in much better condition.

Dr. Bruenn's persistence in praising Dr. McIntire for stepping aside is touching and in the tradition of medical ethics of the 1940s. The record, however, shows without doubt that Roosevelt had been so badly mishandled medically over a period of years that it was a remarkable feat to get his system back into good running order. At least two years of untreated hypertension and congestive heart failure had taken its toll. Anoxia (lack of oxygen) of various organs, the brain, and kidneys is not something that even a patient at rest can withstand for very long. Add to this a strenuous physical and emotional life and it is no wonder that the patient became almost euphoric when Bruenn's initial therapy produced such a dramatic improvement.

Bruenn was also critical of the part played by Eleanor Roosevelt as her husband became increasingly ill. Although on the one hand she voiced concern that he was not receiving enough medical care, on the other hand she badgered him endlessly about projects and causes in which she was interested, insisting that he take action on their behalf. On one typical occasion, while he was in Warm Springs regaining his strength after a bout of illness, she phoned late in the evening while Dr. Bruenn was in the room getting his patient comfortable for the night. Part of the ritual was an informal chat about subjects of passing consequence and mutual interest, to put the President in a relaxed frame of mind and help him forget the pressures and get to sleep quickly and easily. Eleanor had just returned from a meeting with a Yugoslavian youth organization. She was aroused over the plight of the country and insisted that her husband should send immediate assistance. Roosevelt tried, patiently, to explain that such a move would require an invasion by paratroops, and would probably fail because, among other things, such an action would require approval and coordination that would not be forthcoming from America's Allies. For forty-five minutes Mrs. Roosevelt persisted in trying to goad her husband into an undertaking that he knew was out of the question. Bruenn said that he could sense the President's blood pressure rising and see his whole body tensing. It was little wonder that incidents like this gave him the impression that Eleanor was cold and thoughtless.

Shortly after their last child, John, was born in 1916, Eleanor came upon letters written by Lucy Mercer Rutherfurd to Roosevelt and brought into the open this clandestine relationship of many years. After explosive threats of divorce, a compromise was reached: Franklin would give up Lucy and Eleanor would no longer have to fulfill her wifely duties. Eleanor held to her part of the bargain, but Franklin did not. The intimacies of their first ten years of marriage evaporated and their relationship became a working partnership, with all evidence of love relegated to the past.

By 1944, Eleanor had developed a life and world of her own and at times was even able to exclude her husband from her activities, much to his dismay. Eleanor turned away and relinquished her wifely responsibilities to other women around FDR. Her duties as hostess at Hyde Park, the family estate on the Hudson River, fell more upon FDR's mother, and her social and intellectual talents were turned more and more toward her two good friends and roommates, Nancy Cook and Marion Dickerman. Her emotional needs were met in part by association with these two domineering women, as well as with her journalist friend, confidante, and traveling companion, Lorena Hickok. Given the previous emotional stresses to which Eleanor Roosevelt was subjected and her strict Victorian upbringing, it does not seem unusual that she should turn to female companions for affection, rather than seek a male substitute for her husband.

At one point, Bruenn gathered the family together to report on the President's health. It gave him a natural opportunity to suggest that each member go a little easier on the man and avoid confrontations that would have an adverse effect. He particularly pointed to the dinner hour and evenings as periods when the atmosphere should be convivial and free from stress. "But Mrs. Roosevelt could never seem to understand this and was constantly needling F.D.R. at the worst times," he recalled.

Roosevelt's steadily failing health and increasing medical attention seem to have made very little impression on either the politicians or the voters. The public had been greatly uplifted by the progress of the war in Europe, particularly after the D-Day invasion of France by the British and Americans in June, during the greatest seaborne operation in history. In mid-July, three months after Bruenn's treatments had begun, Roosevelt crossed the country by train, stopping briefly in Chicago, where the Democratic Convention was being held. He spoke often en route over a national radio hook-up and seemed to be in excellent health and exuberant spirits. It was no surprise when he was nominated for an unprecedented fourth term.

Was the American public completely unaware of the state of the President's health? Walter Lippman, the noted columnist, wrote that the Democrats attending the convention were certain that they were nominating a candidate who would die in office and that they therefore selected Harry S. Truman as a strong, if then little known, running mate. An editorial in the *Saturday Evening Post* shortly after the President's death was headlined "Everybody Knew It But the People."

> Actually, the state of Mr. Roosevelt's health was a secret from millions of Americans who voted for the President on the theory that he could reasonably be expected to live out his term of office, where he was indispensable if America was to achieve a strong and lasting peace. To be sure, some voters thought they detected signs of unfamiliar weakness in Mr. Roosevelt's radio voice. Others thought the pictures of the President revealed signs of serious illness, but doubters were continually assured by Admiral Ross McIntire, the President's medical adviser, that his patient was "in better physical condition than the average man of his age," that his health was "good, very good," that he was "in splendid shape."

The *Post* decried the fact that some journalists and politicians who dared to hint that the President was not a well man were rebuked as "little better than fifth columnists" by Roosevelt supporters. Robert Hannegan, chairman of the Democratic National Committee, asserted that questions about health were part of a whispering campaign conducted by the Republicans. Thomas E. Dewey, the Republican candidate, carefully avoided any inferences about the President's condition. However, he was boosted as being youthful, a man of energy, and at the peak of his career, and he did level his attack on "the tired old men" who were running the government.

The point of the *Post* article was this:

> It is impossible to plan a precise course which will prevent a courageous President in failing health from daring fate once more, or discourage politicians dependent on the prestige of a popular leader from pushing an ailing man into a campaign. But at least we can make it plain that those who ask questions shall receive answers, and not be brushed off as malicious obstructionists. . . .

As for Roosevelt himself, he never gave an inch, never acknowledged the possibility that he could be too infirm to run for reelection. His courage almost approached the foolhardy, possibly because the only real fear he ever had was that he would be forced into retirement and inaction. In November 1944, an incredible event took place that reveals the totality of his commitment. Aware that there had been persistent rumors about his health, New Dealers suggested that the President make a key public appearance in New York City to show that he was as fit as ever. When the appointed day arrived, the weather was as ominous as it could possibly have been, with gusty winds, sleet, and a driving, freezing rain. It was so miserable that even the Republicans would not have been able to raise a critical voice if the appearance had been postponed. But Roosevelt insisted on going ahead with the plans. During the entire day, he rode through the streets of New York City in an open car—smiling, waving, and giving every sign that he was fully enjoying the experience. This exhausted everyone in the party, as well as members of the press, and left them all soaking wet—including the President. Roosevelt went back to his hotel, bathed and changed, and appeared before the Foreign Policy Association that evening to deliver a major political address.

With the election over and Dewey roundly defeated, the President focused his attention on the operations that were underway to bring World War II to a successful conclusion and particularly on his involvement in the conference at Yalta.

The formal meetings of the Crimean Conferences, which were usually convened at 4:00 P.M. at the Livadia Palace, were not lengthy—three to four hours. But the pressures were strong and great concentration was required to review and assess all of the issues at hand. Furthermore, the meetings were preceded by lengthy discussions with aides, military experts, and other specialists on whom the President had to rely for information and advice. Samuel Rosenman captured the impact of it all when he wrote, in *Presidential Style,* "Ask any experienced lawyer about his nervous tension before and during a trial in which the life or death of one client is involved. How must Roosevelt's nerves have felt about the trial of wits, and armed power, and horse trading, and grand global politics before and during Yalta where, he was convinced, the fate of the entire future world was involved?"

The President was described as having an air of apparent nonchalance at the conference table as he negotiated and bargained, making what he hoped were major gains and yielding on minor ones. "But," wrote Rosenman, "it was a trial which left its effects. I know because I came home with him on his ship and saw him each day. . . . The buoyancy of the recent campaign, the excitement of preparing to go to Yalta had disappeared. In their place was gray fatigue—sheer physical and mental exhaustion. To add to it all, his great friend and secretary, General Edwin Watson, died on the cruiser on the way home."

Roosevelt and Churchill knew each other's styles, knew how to bargain, and how to assess the fact that they eventually had to answer to their own countrymen. But Stalin was an enigma, a man who dictated and was not accountable to voters or legislators. Elements of hostility and distrust fueled the tensions at Yalta, no matter how Roosevelt strove to maintain an air of congeniality and mutual understanding. Photographs taken of the three men show a president who looked haggard, with the usual circles under his eyes having a haunting and ominous look. All three leaders were said to be sick, but Roosevelt seemed the sickest of all.

By the fourth day of the conferences, the President was in serious trouble. Dr. Howard Bruenn reported the situation in his notes:

> On February 8, after an especially arduous day and an emotionally disturbing conference (he was worried and upset about the trend of the discussions that day at the Conference, namely Poland) he was obviously greatly fatigued. His color was very poor (gray), but examination showed that his lungs were clear and the heart sounds were of good quality—regular in rhythm and rate (84/min). The blood pressure, however, for the first time showed pulsus alternans. A change in his routine was enforced. His hours of activity were rigidly controlled so that he could obtain adequate rest. No visitors were allowed until noon, and at least an hour of rest was enforced in the afternoon before the Conferences.

Lord Moran, Winston Churchill's physician, wrote in his diary, "To a doctor's eye, the President appears a very sick man. He has all the symptoms of hardening of the arteries of the brain in an advanced stage, so that I give him only a few months to live." Moran refers to Roosevelt's uncharacteristic tendency to be irascible at times, touchy, and irritable if forced to concentrate on a subject for very long. He was surprised by Roosevelt's lack of drive and by the fact that even Churchill did not seem able to make him understand that Stalin was deliberately playing them against each other, attempting to split them in order to achieve his own ends. Again and again, the President seems to have fallen into traps set by Stalin—and to some extent even by Churchill —losing points that he would never have conceded had he been in good health and with his earlier ability to control situations.

With Yalta behind him, for better or worse, the President should have been able to relax. Instead, he plunged into a busy schedule immediately following the adjournment of the Crimean Conference on Sunday, February 11. He journeyed to Egypt for meetings with King Farouk, Haile Selassie I of Ethiopia, and King Ibn Saud of Saudi Arabia. He stopped at Alexandria for a three-and-a-half-hour conference with Prime Minister Churchill and for discussions with Secretary of State Edward Stettinius, who had gone to Moscow to meet with Foreign Commissar Vyacheslav M. Molotov. He made a final stopover at Algiers, with the expectation of meeting with General Charles De Gaulle, Provisional President of France, but the latter declined the invitation and the President then put to sea aboard the *Quincy* for the voyage home.

Arriving back in the States after the few days of enforced leisure at sea, he completely ignored the doctor's orders to include rest in his regimen and filled his calendar with appointments and meetings. The end of the day saw no relaxation, as he continued working into the evening, countering the doctor's protest with his own protest that he was behind in his schedule and would sleep much better if he could just get a couple of additional matters out of the way. What disturbed Bruenn most was that he was losing weight and had such a poor appetite that he was approaching a condition of malnutrition. Suspecting that his regular intake of digitalis might be the cause, Bruenn temporarily suspended the prescription for a few days, but with no improvement and the continuing complaint that the President had no taste for food.

By the end of March, his appearance was so shocking and his fatigue so great that he was all but ordered to take a period of total rest. His blood pressure remained worrisome. He had reverted to the same slack-jawed look that had concerned his aides earlier. He was unable to concentrate or maintain a clear thread of thought. He displayed irritation and unexpected changes of mood. He began experiencing chest pains—warnings of angina pectoris—that stopped him in the midst of whatever he was doing and made him break out in a cold sweat.

Even as Roosevelt left for Warm Springs, Georgia, on March 29, rumors were spreading across the country that the President was a very sick man. The first indication—whether valid or not —had come around March 1, when the presidential bodyguards were ordered to mount a round-the-clock watch on Vice-President Harry S. Truman. At that time, the word leaked out that the order was based on the possibility that "the President may go at any time." In early April, former war production director Donald Nelson is said to have told a friend in confidence, "It'll be the greatest miracle in the world if the President lives two months."

A few days after arriving in Warm Springs, where the weather was most enjoyable, Roosevelt appeared to be rebounding as he had done so often in the past. His appetite returned, and with it his buoyancy and spirits. His color improved. He was so rested that he insisted on taking short drives into the countryside and began making plans for weekend entertainment, including a minstrel show and barbecue.

On the morning of April 12, 1945, the President could not resist the urge to phone the White House and find out what was going on. At that time, he informed his secretary, Jonathan Daniels, that he was even then in the midst of drafting a speech that he would deliver over the air from "The Little White House" two days later. Dr. Bruenn had seen the President at 9:20, a few minutes after he had awakened and noted nothing unusual except for a slight headache and some stiffness of the neck, both of which disappeared after slight massage.

"He had a very good morning," recalled Bruenn, "and his guests commented on how well he looked." At about one o'clock, he was sitting in his favorite leather chair, reading his papers and occasionally bantering with his cousin, Margaret Suckley, who was keeping him company and crocheting, and with Elizabeth Shoumatoff, a noted artist who was making preliminary sketches for a new portrait. Lucy Mercer was sitting nearby.

All at once, he clapped one hand to his head and gasped, "I have a terrific headache."

The President slumped down, unconscious. Within minutes, he was carried to his bed by his valet, Arthur Prettyman, and his clothing loosened. Bruenn was summoned and arrived at 1:30, about fifteen minutes after the attack. It was almost immediately apparent to him that the President had suffered a massive cerebral hemorrhage. After applying hot-water bottles and administering medication intravenously, he phoned Admiral McIntire, then in Washington, who in turn contacted Dr. James E. Paullin of Atlanta, a specialist in internal medicine.

Dr. Bruenn's log describes the rest:

> 3:15 PM: Blood pressure was 210/110 mm Hg; heart rate 96/min; right pupil still widely dilated. . . . Occasional spasm of rigidity with marked slowing of respiration was noted. During latter phases, he had become cyanotic.
>
> 3:30 PM: Pupils were approximately equal. Breathing had become irregular but of good amplitude.
>
> 3:31 PM: Breathing suddenly stopped and was replaced by occasional gasps. Heart sounds were not audible. Artificial respiration was begun and caffeine sodium benzoate given intramuscularly. At this moment Dr. Paullin arrived from Atlanta. Adrenalin was administered into the heart muscle.
>
> 3:35 PM: I pronounced him dead.

The shock of the President's death was so great and so extensive that interviews were made and full-scale surveys completed to determine the psychological impact on America. "The death of Roosevelt came as a complete surprise to the public," reported the *Journal of Social Psychology* in one such study. "The result was a mass traumatic episode of several days' duration." Many people refused to believe—could not believe—the news. Public figures described him as "the greatest American in history" or "a colossal figure" or "the most important man in the world." Many people fainted. Some had heart attacks. In Los Angeles, a mechanic turned to a fellow worker and said, "I hurt all over—I can't stand the news," and dropped dead. Close associates of the President sobbed openly. Archibald MacLeish, the noted poet and then assistant secretary of state, went completely to pieces while in the midst of a radio tribute the next day and was unable to continue.

Eventually, of course, the nation returned to its normal state. Harry Truman took over the presidency and proved to be—to the astonishment and delight of Americans all over—a man of decision, honesty, and uncommon bluntness.

It remained only for the man who was closest to the scene during the President's last year to ponder a question that is unanswerable, yet eternally provocative. As Dr. Howard G. Bruenn concluded his notes in the *Annals of Internal Medicine* fifteen years after he had pronounced Franklin Delano Roosevelt dead at Warm Springs, Georgia, "As a result of this unforgettable experience, and as a practicing physician, I have often wondered what turn the subsequent course of history might have taken if the modern methods for the control of hypertension had been available."

11

A Profile in Courage

In just about every way possible, Harry S. Truman was the antithesis of Franklin Delano Roosevelt. The son of a muletrader, he was a small-town Missouri boy without a college education who had to work to help support the family while he was still in his teens. Physically, he was hardy and relatively free from illness most of his life—certainly one of the healthiest presidents and a man who liked to walk at a brisk pace. Just sixty when he was sworn in on April 12, 1945, he was a man of great energy who worked harder and longer than any man who ever occupied the White House, and with absolutely no evidence of stress or overwork. He rose at 5:30 each morning, as he had been accustomed to doing since his early days as a farmer, and usually fitted in a swim and a walk of a mile or two before breakfast.

Truman was subjected to pressures as punishing as those that Roosevelt had to face, including the decision to drop atomic bombs on Hiroshima and Nagasaki and the intricate negotiations with Churchill and Stalin at the Potsdam Conference in Germany, which lasted from mid-July until early August 1945. Like his predecessor in one respect at least, he had an uncanny knack for bouncing back from seeming adversity. As he geared himself for the reelection campaign in the early summer of 1948, adding a cross-country speaking tour to his already crammed calendar, he was faced with one of the major international crises of the postwar era. The Russians were cutting off all ground transportation to Berlin, with the intention of pushing American forces out of the area and winning a strong advantage in the peacetime battle for control. Truman immediately broke the blockade by ordering the Air Force to make round-the-clock flights to supply the city. He maintained this "Berlin Airlift" for eleven months, until the Russians backed down.

Truman was known, too, for his guts in recovering from a political setback when the Republican candidate for the presidency, again Governor Thomas E. Dewey, showed such great strength that he was the almost-unanimous choice of the public-opinion polls. The press, too, predicted Truman's overwhelming defeat. True to character, Truman embarked on a back-breaking campaign trip that lasted from Labor Day to Election Day with such vigor and down-to-earth common sense that he picked up hundreds of potential votes at every stop and with every speech. With the experts and political analysts still echoing their conviction that Truman was bound to lose, the Man from Missouri achieved an astonishing upset. His greatest moment of satisfaction came when he arrived in Washington from his home in Independence waving an issue of the *Chicago Tribune* with the premature headline, "Dewey Defeats Truman."

When he left office in March 1953, he expressed his healthy outlook toward this most demanding of jobs by remarking "I wasn't one of the great Presidents, but I had a good time trying to be one, I can tell you that."

Not until many years after returning to Independence, Missouri, did he show signs of any serious, continuing illness when he was diagnosed as having colitis. Yet he lived in relative good health during most of his years in retirement, dying on the day after Christmas 1972, at the age of eighty-eight. Several other presidents have been as free of disease. Martin Van Buren, James Buchanan, William McKinley and Theodore Roosevelt were all extremely healthy during their terms of office. Herbert Hoover hardly missed a day, while Calvin Coolidge calmly lay down and took a nap every afternoon to keep himself in good health.

Truman's successor in office, Dwight D. Eisenhower, was not so fortunate from a medical standpoint, despite his arrival in the White House as a man of great vigor and with an impressive record of accomplishment in the field. When he became President in 1953, at the age of sixty-two, he had already enjoyed several distinguished careers, including positions as the Supreme Commander of Allied Expeditionary Forces in Europe, president of Columbia University, and Supreme Commander of NATO forces in Europe. His medical problems surfaced on September 23, 1955, when he suffered what was described in the newspapers as a "digestive upset" while vacationing in Denver. The next day, Vice-President Richard M. Nixon received a call from White House Press Secretary James Hagerty informing him that the upset was in actuality a coronary thrombosis and that the leadership was now at least temporarily in his hands.

While the news of the heart attack was unexpected, and while it caused the stock market to plummet by some $12 billion, it did not panic Nixon. He and Eisenhower had long since discussed what should be done in the event of presidential disability, referring back to the insoluble problems caused during the Wilson administration by the President's secrecy and lack of communication before his illness struck. Thus Nixon held a cabinet meeting almost immediately, at which time he was able to report on the status of all major White House affairs and chart an orderly course of action during the President's hospitalization.

Over a period of some 130 years since John Tyler had asserted his right to the highest office at the death of Harrison, a number of amendments had been added and the Constitution clarified to cover situations likely to present problems relating to presidential disability and succession. Unfortunately, it was still not clear *who* can decide whether the chief executive should be replaced or how to classify "disability" if the man in office is conscious and still functioning to some extent. Eisenhower and Nixon thought that they had resolved the dilemma with their "letters of intent," but the precedent has not been followed by their successors.

Looking back, it is easy to see why Eisenhower had brought up the subject of presidential succession in the first place. During the summer, he had noticed some symptoms that were disturbing, yet difficult to define: a tightness in the chest, which did not loosen right away, a shortness of breath and undue perspiration when walking up a long flight of stairs or playing golf, attacks of indigestion, and palpitations of the heart. He was also concerned about the fact that, while he usually felt fit and relaxed in the morning and able to tackle the toughest challenges, by mid-afternoon he was lagging. His legs would begin to tire, his hands would feel shaky, his speech would occasionally slur a bit, and he several times caught himself stumbling or misjudging the position of an object he was about to pick up.

His old friend and personal physician, Major General Howard McCrum Snyder, had given him a series of thorough checkups that revealed little. The doctor ultimately diagnosed the problem as a mild form of angina pectoris and prescribed nitroglycerine tablets. The diagnosis seemed correct, since the pills did indeed bring relief whenever he felt an acceleration of his pulse or pressure under his breastbone. Nevertheless, with his military background and his soldier's training to anticipate every contingency, he made it a policy to inform the Vice-President on all matters of importance in the executive branch.

Eisenhower was, if anything, a little too communicative, in that he somewhat naively revealed his viewpoint to those outside the White House circle. During that summer, for example, he had informed leaders of the Republican party that they should be wary of considering anyone—even the President—as being "indispensable." The press immediately suspected that something was wrong, especially when the President commented, "Human beings are frail, and they are mortal. Never nail your flag so tightly to the mast so that if the ship sinks you cannot rip it off and nail it to another."

By late October, the President was out of his bed and walking and by November 11 he had been discharged from the hospital for a period of convalescence in Georgia and Florida. He finally returned to the White House in early January of 1956.

During this period a phenomenon was taking place in regard to the subject of a sick president. It had not occurred during the many illnesses of Franklin Delano Roosevelt; nor during the year and a half that Woodrow Wilson lay incapacited in the hidden confines of the White House; nor during any other presidential illnesses in the country's history. The phenomenon manifested itself in clinical reports and daily (sometimes hourly) bulletins. Through newspapers, radio broadcasts, and television screens, the reading, listening, and watching publics were brought realistically, and sometimes not too pleasantly, on the scene. It was revealed at one time that the President had to urinate into a milk bottle when no bed pan was handy, and at another time that his pajamas were changed because he had soiled the first pair. Americans learned that presidents were, after all, mere human beings when it was graphically recounted that he vomited on the carpet. Or that a nurse had inserted a thermometer in his rectum to get a more accurate temperature reading. Or that he had been constipated for three days. And so on, ad nauseum.

Within hours of the announcement that Eisenhower had suffered a coronary, an army of media people, made up of journalists, news analysts, columnists, television camera crews, radio broadcasters, and others, was descending on Denver. Just to take care of the overflow, special housing arrangements had to be made at nearby Lowry Air Force Base. In addition, special medical teams were flown in, which included such specialists as Dr. Paul Dudley White, the noted cardiologist from Boston, Dr. James Watts, head of the National Heart Institute, and Dr. Thomas Mattingly of Washington's Walter Reed Army Medical Center, also a top-ranking cardiologist.

For many Americans, the President's continuing battle against disease was a kind of real-life soap opera. They quickly became acquainted with medical terminology, and the nature of coronary arteriosclerosis and coronary occlusion. They could easily have passed a test on the relationships between stress, obesity, diet, and genetic tendencies in the prevention and control of the President's disease. The whole powerful drama included its share of goofs and shortcomings and even villains. Reporters, in their race to ferret out new findings, were sometimes able to ask searching questions that titillated the public. Why, for example, had Dr. Snyder shown such poor medical judgment as to permit the President to *walk* to a waiting car after he had just diagnosed the illness as a coronary occlusion?

Digging through history in his search for something that would provide a different angle, another journalist was able to make the comparison that Dr. Charles E. Sawyer, President Harding's physician, had been guilty of the same error thirty-two years earlier—and Harding had failed to survive.

It hardly seems rational that such a change in the nation's mores could have taken place in the space of just two administrations, ranging from the "conspiracy of silence" during Roosevelt's era to this anatomical fixation during Eisenhower's.

The only fortunate aspect of the President's disability was that he was hospitalized at a time when there was no national or international crisis. "I can be grateful for many things," wrote Eisenhower in his biography several years later, "not the least of which was the fact that I could not have selected a better time, so to speak, to have a heart attack. . . . The economy was booming, Congress was not in session. I had been able to handle with Foster [John Foster Dulles] the major foreign policy problems and at that moment there was no new crisis pending in the world."

However, he went on to say that certainly if there had been any crisis, particularly one requiring the dispatch of armed forces, he would have been able to assess the situation and make a rapid decision after the first forty-eight hours of his heart attack. This was an unusually optimistic—if not unrealistic—statement by a man who was sick enough to have to remain out of action for more than three months!

Six months after his return to Washington, on June 8, 1956, the President was again stricken with a serious illness, this time ileitis, which required him to undergo an operation at Walter Reed Hospital and spend six weeks recuperating. Once again, Snyder misdiagnosed. Once again, excellent consultants saved the day. Once again, an army of communicators went to work to make sure that the public was informed on his progress several times a day. Americans quickly learned that ileitis was an inflammation of the ileum, the lower section of the small intestine, and that there were many unpleasant, painful, and messy aspects of the disorder. Furthermore, the President was having great difficulty with an obstruction in the intestine, which led to speculation (fortunately unfounded) that it might be cancer.

Eisenhower remained in good health after recuperating from ileitis for almost a year and a half. On November 11, 1957, he was pronounced in "excellent health" following a two-day annual physical examination at Walter Reed. Exactly two weeks later, he suffered a stroke while dictating a letter to his secretary and was unable to speak properly. This time, when word got out, there was panic. The stock market dropped by nearly $4.5 billion in the space of less than half an hour. The nation was prepared for the worst.

In the midst of a hurried conference called by Vice-President Nixon at the White House, cabinet members and aides were astonished to see the President suddenly shuffle into the room, having gotten out of bed expressly against the doctor's orders. He kept insisting he was all right, but evidenced considerably difficulty in expressing himself. Then he about-faced and headed back for his bedroom, with the parting remark, "If I cannot attend to my duties, I am simply going to give up this job!"

Somewhat in shock, the President's assistant, Sherman Adams, turned to Nixon a few minutes later and gapsed, "This is terrible, a terribly difficult thing to handle. You may be President in the next 24 hours!"

What Eisenhower had experienced on this occasion was a vascular spasm of a small cerebral blood vessel, later described as a "small stroke."

Now thoroughly accustomed to taking over as "acting president," Nixon accepted his increased responsibilities, not knowing how long he might have to hold them or whether, in fact, the fears of Adams might indeed come true. This time, however, the disability was of short duration and Eisenhower was able to return to work by December 3. He suffered no further attacks while in office.

Eisenhower remained in relatively good health until April 1968, when he was again stricken. This time, it was the beginning of the end. Through the spring and summer of that year, he had three more heart attacks. Using the latest methods, medications, and equipment, medical teams managed to bring him around each time, even though on several occasions his blood pressure dropped to zero and he lost consciousness. "It is scarcely an exaggeration," said one report, "that he 'died' 14 times." Yet each time he recovered, sometimes through the use of experimental drugs and often by the use of electric shock treatments to correct otherwise uncontrollable changes in the rhythm of the heart. Six months later, evidencing only minor damage to his memory and intellectual functions, Eisenhower was strong enough to withstand surgery for treatment of an intestinal obstruction from his earlier ileitis. Within a month, though, even the latest drugs and equipment were not equal to the task of keeping the old general alive. He died of what is called "pump failure" on the 28th of March, 1969, at the age of seventy-eight. His arteriosclerotic coronary arteries were no longer able to supply the heart muscle and keep it functioning.

Because of the three major "scares" during the Eisenhower administration, a great many discussions and hearings took place on the controversial issue of presidential succession. This was also the subject of a much-read book by Senator Birch Bayh, *One Heartbeat Away: Presidential Disability and Succession,* published in 1968. The problem was not so much the death of the president in office, which had occurred numerous times during the country's history, but the matter of *disability* and the assurance that the vice-president was at all times capable in every way of taking over. Eisenhower himself was outspoken on the subject. "I have a personal approach to this whole problem," he said, "because three times, while in the Presidency, unforeseen circumstances reminded me that I might be one of those people found with a disability to carry out my duties."

Despite all the discussions, and the general belief that the vice-president was really the one who would have to make the decision about the president's competency in the final analysis, the question was never fully resolved.

It is not surprising that in early July 1960, as the Democratic convention was opened in Los Angeles, the subject of health was uppermost in the minds of the delegates who were about to select their presidential candidate. They had a frontrunner in the person of John Fitzgerald Kennedy, forty-three, senator from Massachusetts for eight years, former congressman, war hero, and author of a best-selling, Pulitzer-Prize-winning book. The problem was not the candidate's abilities as a leader or his talents as a vote-getter—already long proven—but the whispering campaign about his physical condition. He was known to have a severe and excruciating back problem that had totally incapacitated him on many occasions in the past. He admitted to having a "partial adrenal insufficiency," a disorder of the adrenal glands, situated on the kidneys and the source of vital hormones (adrenalin and cortisone). Most disturbing of all, he was said to have been suffering for a number of years with Addison's disease, a rare ailment characterized by weakness, low blood pressure, and changes in the skin—all caused by malfunction of the suprarenal (or adrenal) glands.

Kennedy, members of his family, and close associates had long denied that he had Addison's disease. The rumor had started, they said, because of the injuries and illnesses suffered by the future President during his heroic efforts in the Pacific during World War II, at which time his PT boat had been sliced in half by a Japanese destroyer. Kennedy and ten other survivors clung to the wreckage for some fifteen hours, before drifting to an island and eventually being rescued by Navy searchers. As a result of that harrowing experience, he had aggravated his already crippled back and contracted malaria. Later, it was claimed that the long exposure and the effort to survive had caused lasting damage to his adrenal glands.

It was this combination of disabilities, stress, and malaria that had led to the erroneous conclusion about Addison's disease —so said the Kennedys.

Investigative journalists and others with special reasons for such curiosity began to take a closer look at John F. Kennedy's medical records as the time approached for the selection of presidential candidates during that early summer of 1960. They started with the back problem, which had never been denied and which would have been impossible to cover up. Kennedy had undergone surgery for his back in 1945 and again in October 1954. In February 1955, he had a further operation—the previous one not having been entirely successful—at which time a metal plate was removed. According to accounts by those who knew him well, he suffered intense pain, complicated by local infection and a resulting abscess that required draining and continuing treatment.

It was learned that the *Journal of the American Medical Association* had published in 1955 an article on the case of a man who had undergone lumbosacral and sacroiliac fusions, which in themselves involved a "severe degree of trauma." The subject was even more justified for inclusion in a medical journal because the patient was suffering from Addison's disease, a fact that enormously increased the risk of death and lessened the chances of success. Adhering to the AMA's policy, no names were mentioned. However, putting two and two together, an increasing number of people deduced that the case could have referred to no one but John F. Kennedy. Why? The patient was thirty-seven years old—so was Kennedy at the time of his operation. The date was October 21, 1954—the same as the date of Kennedy's hospitalization. And many of the other details presented in the clinical paper jibed with the circumstances and nature of the Kennedy operation.

The *JAMA* article stated flatly that the patient in question had been suffering from Addison's disease for seven years. It also mentioned that he had been taking medication for several years, including 25 mg. of cortisone daily. Cortisone can induce a state of euphoria and can dramatically increase energy and endurance, though the stimulus is artificial. It can also trigger sexual desire.

If the *JAMA* article really was documenting this case, and if the patient really did have Addison's disease and was relying heavily on a drug that altered mind and body, was Kennedy a fit candidate for the presidency?

Cortisone, a complex drug, is a steroid hormone with many primary and side effects. Its early use, after having proven to be effective against disabling arthritis, was associated with expansive euphoria. There were cases of patients jumping out windows because they had the impression they could fly. Its early use also activated dormant pulmonary tuberculosis. Some patients, who found that their arthritic joints no longer incapacitated them, remained invalids because now they had to return to bed to be treated for tuberculosis. It was this same terrifying sequence of events which, in 1962, killed Eleanor Roosevelt. After weeks of cortisone therapy for an obscure type of anemia, she died when the treatment caused her latent tuberculosis to flare up unexpectedly.

If a list of the dangers and long-term effects of cortisone had been circulated at the Democratic convention and associated with John F. Kennedy, his chances for nomination would have dimmed. Who would vote for a candidate who was forced to take a medication that was known to have caused high blood pressure, heart failure, weakening of the bones, stomach ulcers, convulsions, increased pressure in the brain, diabetes, cataracts, and glaucoma? Who would vote for a man dependent upon a drug that would make his face fat, his skin flushed, his neck thick, and which was known to produce psychic derangements that ranged from euphoria to depression?

Other information surfaced at the time the Democratic convention was convening, and would continue to come to light, suggesting that John F. Kennedy had a number of serious medical problems. If he were to be elected, it was implied by some of his political opponents, the country would be faced with the same kinds of disability crises that had given a bad scare to Americans during the Eisenhower administration—or worse. With the Cold War escalating in Europe and Communism's tentacles reaching right across the Atlantic to Cuba, one thing America did not need was a serious confrontation with the Russians at a time when the president was out of action.

Prior to his 1954 operation, a double fusion of spinal vertebrae at the Hospital for Special Surgery in New York City, numerous tests had to be made because of potential risks that were apparent to his doctors. The operation was postponed several times. In their book, *The Search for JFK,* Joan and Clay Blair, Jr. discuss the interview they held with Elmer C. Bartels, a doctor at the Lahey Clinic in Boston, who had studied Kennedy's case. Bartels, a gland specialist, "told us flatly and unequivocally," wrote the Blairs, "that Jack had been diagnosed as having Addison's disease in England and had been sent to Boston to continue treatment. It was not a 'partial adrenal insufficiency,' but truly Addison's disease."

Bartels told the Blairs that the staff at the Lahey Clinic "firmly opposed the idea of the operation," largely because of the increased risk, even with hormones to counter the adrenal deficiency. The Lahey Clinic all but refused to perform the back operation in Boston, and it was for this reason that Kennedy went to the hospital in New York. At the time of the operation, the situation was so critical that the last rites of the Church were said and the immediate family members were described as praying in an outside room during the long hours required for the surgery. "Jack survived, though just barely," wrote the Blairs.

His wife, Jacqueline, watched in horror shortly after the operation at a time when the patient was given a blood transfusion. She saw her husband's face swell grotesquely from an adverse reaction. All of his life he had suffered allergies of various kinds, many of them never isolated, and was particularly allergic to dogs and other animals, and to ordinary house dust. One of these allergies was to cause new trouble and great pain three years after the back operation. Suddenly, in mid-September 1955, the scar on his back became reddened and very sensitive. He contracted a fever and was hospitalized again, this time so that under general anaesthesia a wide incision could be made in the abscess that had formed and it could be drained. According to Dr. Janet Travell, who became his personal doctor during the mid-1950s and who was later appointed as the White House physician after he took office, the reasons for the sudden flare-up were not known at the time. Some time later, as the result of a medical study and her increasing knowledge about Kennedy's allergies, she decided that the problem was "an allergic reaction to the suture material."

During his 1960 campaigns in the presidential primaries, he developed severe laryngitis. By the time he had covered some seven states and was in West Virginia, he could barely whisper. The situation became so bad that he had to distribute handwritten notes that read, "Sorry—I have lost my voice—but I would appreciate your vote anyway—thanks! John Kennedy." Dr. Travell attributed the laryngitis to an allergic reaction to antigens he inhaled while on the tour. After he became the presidential candidate, he used the services of a speech therapist on the campaign trail who taught him how to ease the strain on his sensitive vocal chords by projecting his voice more effectively and making better use of amplifying equipment at large gatherings of voters.

Dr. Travell played a key role in the campaign in a way she had neither expected nor anticipated. By this time, she had become the leading expert on the state of Kennedy's health and his medical history. "Speculation concerning Senator John F.

Kennedy's 'Addison's disease' did not come up as a hot political issue until July 1960, in the second week before the Democratic National Convention in Los Angeles," she wrote in her autobiography, *Office Hours: Day and Night.* As much as a year earlier, he had told her that the status of his health was a matter of political concern and had asked her to write up an official medical statement. As she pointed out, no one—neither he nor doctors acquainted with his history—had ever made a secret of his adrenal insufficiency, and she did not bypass this in her own report. She stated that he had suffered a back injury in 1939 that had been reinjured during World War II and that he had undergone a disc operation in 1944, the spinal fusions already referred to, and the follow-up treatments.

Dr. Travell emphasized at that time that Kennedy had tremendous physical stamina, the ability to meet demanding schedules with outstanding vigor, and enough endurance so that he could work seven days a week without evidence of physical stress and with very little time off for holidays or vacations. Surprisingly, in view of the problems he had encountered with allergies and back flare-ups, she also stated that he had above-average resistance to infections.

Dr. Travell said—and continues to assert—that John F. Kennedy did *not* have Addison's disease. But she did point out that even in the medical profession itself there was some confusion about the disease because of a continuing change in the outlook and the fact that "medical miracles," in the form of oral preparations particularly, had taken Addison's off the list of maladies that were usually fatal. With medication that had not been available prior to the 1950s, it had become possible to correct the deficiency and assure most victims of a near-normal life span.

On one occasion when Kennedy was still senator she proposed a plan of action that she felt would inform the public, as well as provide general practitioners with a better understanding.

"Senator," she said one day when he was in her office, "I think a series of reviews in the medical journals and popular magazines should be written right away. People don't realize how the outlook has changed in Addison's disease."

"But I don't have it," replied Kennedy.

"That's right, Senator. You don't have classical Addison's disease. But the language is changing, too, and doctors disagree, maybe because they aren't talking about the same thing."

"Doctor, you'll never educate all those Republicans," he answered tartly.

"I dropped the subject," she said resignedly, "but not my desire to clarify a remarkable course of events in medical history."

She had sound reason to wish that the proposed series of, articles had seen their way into print when, some eight months later in early July, she received a long-distance phone call from his close friend and brother-in-law, Sargent Shriver. There was a political problem. Within his own party, supporters of Lyndon B. Johnson had given loud voice to the question: is Kennedy really well enough to run for office?

"It's that rumor about Addison's disease," said Shriver, "They claimed he's living on drugs—cortisone."

Kennedy's brother, Bobby, had tried, apparently with little success, to denounce the claims of disease and addiction.

"Jack hasn't taken cortisone in years," Travell assured Shriver, "Of course, he does take some relatives of cortisone, but in the way he uses them, in physiological doses, they're not *drugs*. Bobby can say that those hormones are natural constituents of the body and they're given prophylactically to make up for some deficiency of his adrenals when he's under stress. Jack feels so well that his doctors are not inclined to stop them now."

At the urging of both Bobby and Jack, Dr. Travell and another physician who had helped her draw up her earlier statement about the senator's health, Gene Cohen, permitted the use of their names in a joint release to be issued that night, the Fourth of July, 1960, to the press.

Just the fact that a release had been prepared and distributed proved to be a political bombshell. The next day, newspaper headlines and stories bore witness to the fact that the press was now alarmed about the health of presidential candidates in general, and Kennedy in particular. Fuelling the fire were some remarks by the cochairman of the Citizens for Johnson committee to the effect that "Senator Kennedy, who appears so healthy that it's almost illegal, is really not a well man." The critic, Mrs. India Edwards, said that she strenuously objected to Kennedy's "muscle-flexing about his youth as if he were in better health than any one else," and claimed that he would not even be alive if he had not relied on a regular intake of cortisone.

In *The Search for JFK*, Joan and Clay Blair, Jr., asserted: "At some point Jack began taking cortisone, probably first by injection, then orally. Our guess is about 1949, when cortisone first began to be available." They cited Dr. Elmer C. Bartels as the source for a statement that "the Kennedys maintained safe-deposit boxes around the country where they kept a supply of cortisone and DOCA—so that Jack would never run out." DOCA was a synthetic substance, desoxycorticosterone acetate, which prompted a hormone-like activity and greatly reduced the fatalities among those who had fallen victim to Addison's disease.

Most of these medical discussions and charges were over the heads of the public, but they did raise visions of specters in the Kennedy medical chest and almost sabotaged his campaign for the candidacy. As it turned out, when Senator Johnson announced his own candidacy, he pretty much buried the health issue. He admitted that he, too, had faced his share of health problems in the past, including a heart attack in 1955, but that both he and Jack were in good health and had proven their fitness during their demanding campaign tours around the country. In retrospect, Johnson was being canny and foresighted—leaving the door open so that he would be the logical running mate for Kennedy if the latter were to receive the first spot on the Democratic ticket.

After that point, the subject of health seemed to have little impact, if any, on Kennedy's campaign for the presidency. When he went to the White House, he carried with him his ever-present back problem, which was pretty much public knowledge. In fact the famous Kennedy rocking chair, which had been designed by Dr. Janet Travell when she was trying to treat his ailment in the 1950s, became a visible symbol of his administration.

From the time he took office in March 1961, until that traumatic November 22, 1963, when he was assassinated in Dallas,

Texas, John Fitzgerald Kennedy faced and dealt with many crises, both domestic and foreign. These included the crisis over Cuba in 1962 that almost precipitated World War III, deteriorating relations with the Russians, riots and continuing unrest over the problems of civil rights, and critical decisions about nuclear arms and atomic tests. The threat of disability and hospitalization from Addison's disease, or any other major illness, never surfaced again. Even his most outspoken political enemies had long since abandoned making any inferences that he was unfit for the pressures and stresses of office.

There is no doubt, however, that he on many occasions had to summon considerable courage to keep from giving in to his back problems. His mother, Rose Kennedy, wrote that her son waged a constant battle against "misfortunes of health" all of his life. His brother, Bobby, stated that "at least half of the days that he spent on this earth were days of intense physical pain." And yet, he said, "I never heard him complain. I never heard him say anything that would indicate that he felt God had dealt with him unjustly. Those who knew him well would know he was suffering only because his face was a little whiter, the lines around his eyes were a little deeper, his words a little sharper. Those who did not know him well detected nothing."

Dr. Janet Travell, appointed White House physician and concerned about the effect that the pressures might have on his spinal problems, as well as his general health, suggested shortly after the inauguration that either she or the assistant White House physician accompany the President during his trips around the country and abroad. Kennedy strongly resisted the idea. She had also suggested that a doctor ride directly behind the President whenever he drove in a motorcade with visiting heads of state. What she had in mind was that, in case of an assassination attempt, a doctor might mean the difference between life and death in the event that the President were seriously wounded. It was a prophetic thought. But, as she commented after the assassination, "As it turned out, on the motorcade in Dallas no physician could have changed the outcome."

The President overruled his personal physicians on these suggestions and others. "Doctors," he said, "have better use for their time than to follow me around."

He was right in one respect. Dr. Travell summed up his record of illness while in the White House by saying, "During his one thousand days as President, he missed one full day, June 22, 1961, from his office on account of an acute infectious illness. . . . At the time of his death, his health was at optimal efficiency for the performance of the functions of the Presidency."

12

Conclusion: A Shared
Responsibility

Personal courage in the face of illness takes many forms, not necessarily all dependent upon the seriousness of the malady or the extent of the pain. Some cultures demand stoicism, silence, and withdrawal; others encourage a vociferous and hyperactive attack on the unseen foe. Some races are taught that the victim should continue the fight until collapse; others that subjugation and the acceptance of the outcome are the proper expressions of human dignity, especially if death seems to be imminent. Asian peoples are likely to retreat into the family fold and let the disease enfold them with a hush. Middle Easterners face medical traumas with moaning, wailing, and the wringing of hands. It is mainly the Western Christian culture that seems to expect the sick or dying to carry on in the face of recognized odds, putting up a good front and not letting one's friends and relatives down while there is still strength in the lip muscles to manage a smile.

The following conversation took place between an older doctor and a patient of similar age during a house call in a New York suburb:

Doctor: There is a tumor here (examining the abdomen). The proper course is hospitalization, some testing, you know, to see what can be done.
Patient: What *can* be done? You mean surgery?
Doctor: Ah, that's a possibility.
Patient: Now, Bert, you know the growth is really too far ahead of us. Isn't it?

Doctor: Perhaps. But perhaps a consultation would turn up something we don't know, something that could be done.

Patient: I rely on your judgement. There really *isn't* anything that can be done, is there?

Doctor: That's right.

Patient: How much time do I have left, do you think?

Doctor: Well, a few months. I'd say. But this is an easy case, no pain involved. We have medication that helps. Also, there should be no interference, very little, with your mental capacities. Until the very end. Your family and friends will be a great help.

The patient made his peace, in the face of this undeniable news, and continued to live as normal a life as possible, without upsetting the members of his family more than necessary and without bemoaning his fate. He died quietly a few months later, as expected, with no emotional outbursts and no expressions of rage or feelings of having been cheated.

Most American presidents died in this manner. Their deaths were different only in that they were shared by millions of their countrymen, instead of a handful of relatives and friends. This sense of *sharing* is a vital ingredient. Every American citizen past the age of twenty has experienced the national emotion at the death of several presidents, and has been grateful that the failing patient has died in a way that could be termed "courageous."

Except for John F. Kennedy, every president has died in bed, and most of them long after leaving the presidency. So the problems, the traumatic events, the stresses of making decisions under difficult circumstances—these have all found focus in presidential *illnesses* rather than death. It is an odd phenomenon, therefore, that so few presidential campaigns have successfully made an issue of a candidate's health. The classic exception is that of Senator Thomas Eagleton, who was turned down as a running mate for Senator George McGovern in the presidential campaign of 1972. When it was reported, and admitted, that Eagleton had suffered from depressions requiring shock therapy, the Democratic party took him off the ballot.

If depression had been such a tainted term in past elections, America would never have had a Jefferson or Lincoln in the presidency. Instead of James Madison, the fourth President might have been Charles Cotesworth Pinckney, of South Carolina, for "Jemmie" Madison had a history of hysterical epileptic fits and a paranoiac fear of audiences when he arose to speak. And it goes without saying that Woodrow Wilson would probably never even have attained the governorship of New Jersey if the voting public had been worried about "nervous breakdowns," with which he was afflicted not once or twice, but periodically.

Why have voters generally been so apathetic to the issue of health that they would elect Franklin D. Roosevelt after it was revealed that he was suffering from "hypertension, hypertensive heart disease, cardiac failure, and acute bronchitis?" Or William Howard Taft, who was a heavy eater, a poor exerciser, and so obese that he was joked about for having several times become stuck in the bathtub? Or William Henry Harrison, who was old for his time (sixty-two) and had a history of being frail and susceptible to recurring fevers (and who proved his frailty by dying one month after taking office)?

Looking at the opposite side of the coin, a relatively few presidential candidates have successfully used *good* health as proof of their qualifications, if not capabilities. John F. Kennedy was a case in point, depicted hatless, with the tousled hair of an outdoorsman, and described as a man who had pursued his entire political career "vigorously." Theodore Roosevelt was the epitome of heartiness. Although he came to the presidency the first time as a result of McKinley's death, he campaigned successfully the second time as one of the most forceful and colorful political figures in generations. One of his greatest selling points—and one that certainly appealed to the average voter—was that he had attained his health and vigor through a rigorous campaign of body-building, following a sickly childhood.

"Teddy" Roosevelt was perhaps the finest example of a healthy, well-adjusted president. He was never known to be moody while in the White House, although he had plenty of pressures and excuses for shows of temperament. In fact, he seemed to encourage challenge and stress and had a knack for throwing himself into the fray and infecting others about him with the sheer joy of competition and meeting dissension head on. He enjoyed a hearty appetite, yet knew how to fuel his own insatiable energy requirements and still stay slim. He slept soundly and deeply, invariably awakening totally refreshed, and with a bounce and exuberance more characteristic of an athlete preparing for a contest than a statesman plagued with intricate and incessant demands.

He was so successful in revitalizing the healthy image of the presidency that it is a wonder that the voting public did not project his style as a kind of criterion for future presidential qualifications.

Theodore Roosevelt proved his toughness and resiliency on a number of occasions, most notably on October 22, 1904, when, at the age of forty-six, he was thrown from a bucking horse. Landing squarely on his head and face, he remained for some time in a state of shock and was so badly injured with cuts and abrasions that his face swelled up to the point where he was unrecognizable. While specialists agonized over the presidential injuries, fearful that his spine had been fractured and his brain damaged, Roosevelt made a rapid and surprising recovery and was back on his feet within several weeks.

No other president has reflected this same exuberant good health, although Truman was considered to be in top condition during his years in office and Gerald R. Ford was in fine shape when he took over after the resignation of Richard M. Nixon in August 1974. Ford, the only president to enter the White House without winning a national election, was sixty-three at the time, but looked and acted more like a man ten years younger. He still retained many of the physical characteristics and physique displayed in photographs of him that were taken when he was varsity center on the University of Michigan football team in 1935 and later assistant football coach at Yale University while studying at Yale Law School.

As for later American presidents—Johnson, Nixon, Ford, and Carter—only history will look back objectively and record the real nature and extent of their inner struggles and courage in overcoming disabilities to discharge the overwhelming demands of the job. Richard M. Nixon's emotional and psychological profiles have been written up by medical specialists and lay authors alike in articles and books, only to confuse an already perplexing image. No biographical lens has yet been focused sharply on a unique courage that he brought with him to the White House. A case in point was his determination to go through with his plans for a good-will trip to mainland China in February 1972. He made the trip and reopened the long-closed door with China, despite an acute and dangerous case of phlebitis, extremely painful inflammation of the veins in his legs.

Jimmy Carter made an an attempt, not altogether successful, to project a robust image. But he left this illusion on the cutting-room floor when he entered a long-distance foot race—preposterously with the consent of his own White House physician. Some months later, assessing Mr. Carter's chances for a second term, *The New York Times* described his physical collapse during the race as one of several events "that tend to damage his Presidential image."

Lyndon B. Johnson has been profiled with considerable sympathy by authors who have forgiven his shortcomings on the grounds that he was a professional politician and that most of his questionable practices and decisions while in office were matters of recognized political wheeling and dealing. He also had won the understanding of the public during his much-publicized heart attacks, starting with one that almost killed him when he was majority leader of the Senate in July 1955. "It was as bad an attack as a man could have and still live," he said later during his six months of convalescence. To his credit, and in line with the style of most American presidents who have been seriously or critically ill during their administrations, he continued to work hard during both his terms, pushing himself to the limit.

Yet even presidents have to give in somewhere along the line and admit that courage and determination are not always enough to overcome the disabilities, handicaps, and constant pressures. Lyndon B. Johnson summed it all up simply and understandably when, after deciding that he could not—should not—run for office again, he said that he wanted to be "like an animal in the forest, to go to sleep under a tree, eat when I feel like it, read a bit, and after awhile do whatever I want to."

That decision also took a special kind of presidential courage.

Bibliography

The following books are suggested for readers who might be interested in knowing more about some of the presidents covered in the preceding chapters. They were useful to the authors in compiling background information and exploring the significance of national and international events with which the presidents were concerned. Only a handful, however, contain much information about disabilities and health. For such references, the authors had to turn to hundreds of medical journals, professional papers, clinical reports, diaries, and other obscure sources that would be difficult for most readers to locate.

Physicians, scholars, and others interested in specialized sources should write to John Moses, M.D., Council to Study the Fitness of Leaders (CSFL), 45 Popham Road, Scarsdale, New York 10583.

Asbell, Bernard. *The FDR Memoirs.* New York: Doubleday, 1973.
———. *When F.D.R. Died.* New York: Holt, Rinehart & Winston, 1961.
Bailey, Thomas A. *Presidential Greatness.* New York: Appleton Century Crofts, 1966.
Baker, Ray S. *Woodrow Wilson: Life and Letters.* New York: Doubleday, 1937.
Barber, James D. *Presidential Character.* New York: Prentice-Hall, 1972.
Barnard, Harry. *Rutherford B. Hayes and His America.* Indianapolis: Bobbs-Merrill, 1954.
Bayh, Birch. *One Heartbeat Away.* Indianapolis: Bobbs-Merrill, 1968.

Bishop, James. *FDR's Last Year.* New York: Morrow, 1974.

Blair, Joan, and Blair, Clay, Jr. *The Search for JFK.* New York: Putnam's, 1976.

Burns, James MacGregor. *John Kennedy: A Political Profile.* New York: Harcourt, Brace, 1960.

Clark, L. P. *Lincoln: A Psycho-Biography.* New York: Scribner's, 1933.

Dale, P. M. *Medical Biographies: The Ailments of Thirty-Three Famous Persons.* Norman: University of Oklahoma Press, 1952.

Daugherty, Harry M. *The Inside Story of the Harding Tragedy.* New York: Churchill, 1932.

Davis, Burke. *Old Hickory: A Life of Andrew Jackson.* New York: Dial, 1977.

Dolce, Philip C., and Skau, George H. (eds.). *Power and the Presidency.* New York: Scribner's, 1976.

Donovan, Robert J. *Eisenhower: The Inside Story.* New York: Harper & Row, 1956.

Feerick, John D. *From Failing Hands: The Story of Presidential Succession.* New York: Fordham, 1965.

Freud, Sigmund, and Bullitt, William C. *Thomas Woodrow Wilson: A Psychological Study.* Boston: Houghton Mifflin, 1967.

Gilbert, Judson Bennett. *Disease and Destiny: A Bibliography of Medical References to the Famous.* London: Dawsons of Pall Mall, 1962.

Goldhurst, Richard. *Many Are the Hearts.* New York: Reader's Digest, 1975.

Grayson, Cary T. *Woodrow Wilson: An Intimate Memoir.* New York: Holt, Rinehart & Winston, 1960.

Group for the Advancement of Psychiatry. *The VIP with Psychiatric Impairment.* New York: Scribner's, 1973.

Gunther, John. *Roosevelt in Retrospect.* New York: Harper & Row, 1950.

Hoover, Herbert. *The Ordeal of Woodrow Wilson.* New York: McGraw-Hill, 1958.

Hoover, Irwin H. *Forty-Two Years in the White House.* Boston: Houghton-Mifflin, 1934.

Hunt, Irma. *Dearest Madame: The Presidents' Mistresses.* New York: McGraw-Hill, 1979.

James, Marquis. *Andrew Jackson: Portrait of a President*. Indianapolis: Bobbs-Merrill, 1933.

Lash, Joseph P. *Eleanor and Franklin*. New York: Norton, 1971.

Leech, Margaret. *In the Days of McKinley*. New York: Harper & Row, 1959.

Lewis, William Draper. *The Life of Theodore Roosevelt*. Philadelphia: Winston, 1919.

McIntire, Ross T. *White House Physician*. New York: Putnam's, 1946.

Marx, Rudolph. *The Health of the Presidents*. New York: Putnam's, 1961.

Means, Gaston B. *The Strange Death of President Harding*. New York: Guild, 1930.

Nevins, Allan. *Grover Cleveland: A Study in Courage*. New York: Dodd, Mead, 1932.

Park, Roswell. *Selected Papers Surgical and Scientific*. Buffalo, N.Y.: privately printed, 1914.

Remini, Robert. *Andrew Jackson*. Boston: Twayne, 1966.

Roosevelt, Elliott. *An Untold Story: The Roosevelts of Hyde Park*. New York: Putnam's, 1973.

Rosenman, Samuel. *Presidential Style*. New York: Harper & Row, 1976.

Ross, Isabel. *The President's Wife: Mary Todd Lincoln*. New York: Putnam's, 1973.

Russell, Francis. *The Shadow of Blooming Grove*. New York: McGraw-Hill, 1968.

Sandburg, Carl. *Abraham Lincoln: The War Years*. New York: Harcourt, Brace, 1939.

———. *Mary Lincoln, Wife and Widow*. New York: Harcourt, Brace, 1932.

Schlesinger, Arthur. *The Age of Jackson*. Boston: Little, Brown, 1945.

Sievers, Harry J. *Benjamin Harrison: Hoosier Statesman*. New York: University Publishers, 1959.

Simon, John Y. (ed.). *The Personal Memoirs of Julia Dent Grant*. New York: Putnam's, 1975.

Taylor, Tim. *The Book of Presidents*. New York: Arno, 1972.

Thayer, William Roscoe. *Theodore Roosevelt: An Intimate Biography.* New York: Houghton Mifflin, 1919.

Travell, Janet. *Office Hours: Day and Night.* Mount View, California: World Publications, 1968.

Tumulty, Joseph P. *Woodrow Wilson As I Knew Him.* New York: Doubleday, 1924.

White, William Allen. *Masks in a Pageant.* New York: Macmillan, 1928.

Wold, Karl. *Mr. President—How Is Your Health?* St. Paul: Bruce, 1948.

Index